Treason
by the
Book

Treason
by the
Book

Jonathan D.
Spence

Viking

VIKING

Published by the Penguin Group
Penguin Putnam Inc., 375 Hudson Street,
New York, New York 10014, U.S.A.
Penguin Books Ltd, 27 Wrights Lane,
London W8 5TZ, England
Penguin Books Australia Ltd, Ringwood,
Victoria, Australia
Penguin Books Canada Ltd, 10 Alcorn Avenue,
Toronto, Ontario, Canada M4V 3B2
Penguin Books (N.Z.) Ltd, 182–190 Wairau Road,
Auckland 10, New Zealand

Penguin Books Ltd, Registered Offices:
Harmondsworth, Middlesex, England

First published in 2001 by Viking Penguin,
a member of Penguin Putnam Inc.

1   3   5   7   9   10   8   6   4   2

Excerpt from "Reflections on Espionage" by John
Hollander reprinted by permission of the author.

Map by Compass Projections

LIBRARY OF CONGRESS CATALOGING IN PUBLICATION DATA
Spence, Jonathan D.
Treason by the book / Jonathan D. Spence.
p.   cm.
ISBN 0-670-89292-0
1. Tseng, Ching, 1679–1736.   2. Revolutionaries—
China—Biography.   3. Yung-cheng, Emperor of
China, 1677–1735.   I. Title.
DS754.74.T74 S64 2001
951'.032'092—dc21
[B]   00-043805

This book is printed on acid-free paper.
⊚

Printed in the United States of America
Set in Stempel Garamond
Designed by Jaye Zimet

To
Annping

> . . . *putting the plain*
> *Sense into travelling garb is a kind of*
> *Singing.*
>
> *John Hollander,*
> *"Reflections on Espionage"*

Foreword

One of history's uses is to remind us how unlikely things can be. The strange case of the conspirator Zeng Jing, the emperor he tried to overthrow, and the text that they ended up coauthoring, seems a perfect proof of that contention. And yet, another of history's uses is to show us how pragmatically people can respond to the most unlikely circumstances. Once again, Zeng Jing and his emperor light the way.

That there is so much documentation to illuminate these particular moments from the 1720s and 1730s in imperial China is due to the astounding thoroughness of the scholar-officials of the last dynasty, who witnessed—and sometimes gave wings to—the events as they unfolded. Not only did their streams of reports to the throne encapsulate their own responses to what was happening in their various jurisdictions all across China, but also the rules of procedural propriety led them to repeat in their own reports the exact words used by the emperor in all his comments to them, and in addition to enclose for the emperor's benefit the drafts of any treasonous material that happened to fall into their hands. These documents, infinitely precious to the historian, were in turn preserved by generations of court archivists; after the Qing dynasty fell in 1912, these archives entered a precarious stage of their existence, often moving in their crates just ahead of the encroaching battle zones. But at the close of the twentieth century they ended up stored in climate-controlled sanctuaries, some in Taipei and some in Beijing, waifs of the political revolution that for so long ravaged China, yet, magically, not its victims.

The Zeng Jing case erupted in 1728, and by 1736 the court considered it officially closed. But almost from its beginning the antecedents to the case were seen to lie far back in the past, partly in the military and intellectual battles of the mid-seventeenth century, when the Ming dynasty succumbed to the conquering Qing, and partly far earlier, back in the classical age, when the earliest Chinese philosophical and historical texts began to take form, before even the time of the teacher Confucius. Similarly, the resonances of the case continued long after its declared terminal date, not only into and through the collapse of the Qing dynasty in the late nineteenth and early twentieth century, but right on down to our present day: as recently as 1999 a Chinese publishing house produced a transcription of many of the key documents from the case to answer the curiosity raised among Chinese viewers by a successful TV series on the life of Emperor Yongzheng, the ruler Zeng Jing sought to destroy.

The Zeng Jing case is not, however, just a story of an emperor and his enemies; it is also a story about words, about the manuscripts in which they first found expression, and the books in which they gained a chance at a wider readership. And it is a story about one book in particular, called *Awakening from Delusion (Dayi juemi lu)*, which thanks to an imperial command became the most widely read and recited book in China during the early 1730s. And thus my own book becomes, in part, a book about book making and distribution, about lecture tours and self-advertisement, about captive audiences and hostile critics.

This is, especially, a story of eighteenth-century Chinese struggling to be accepted as scholars, yet at the same time enmeshed in a web of tests and qualifying examinations; of people greedy for learning, forced to endure what they saw as the often arbitrarily negative decisions of those who happened to outrank them. Typecast as failures within elite literary and official circles, many of those rejected believed in their hearts that they were the intellectual equals of their judges. Zeng Jing was one such man, and so were many of those who quite accidentally got swept up in the case.

At another level, it is a book about a world most of us have lost, in which the arrival of every stranger in one's home village was an event, to be mulled over and reflected upon for years. In such a world—for instance, out in the hilly and isolated countryside of southeastern Hunan, in which much of the action initially took place—the emperor's court in Beijing was like the moon: those claiming to be harbingers of news from there were treated with breathless seriousness, fed and sheltered, and speeded on their way with gifts. And because the political arena was known to be dangerous, the world of the time was one of constant rumor, as so many of the documents show, and of rumor's varied corollaries: absolute gullibility, desperate insecurity, constant and unthinking generosity.

As I worked at this book, I also discovered how much it was becoming a book about investigative procedures, something I had not originally anticipated. The way that the investigation of the Zeng Jing case developed was in many ways possible only in the kind of society where memories were honed by lack of other distractions, and where villagers and townspeople alike were capable of painstaking, step-by-step recapitulations of long-past events. At the same time, their constant embellishments and repeated lies were fruits of the same world, in which memories split and grew, nourished in the soil of one's own imagination. Because the investigating officials were, in the main, tough and focused, and the resources and manpower available to them were so vast, such realities complicated but did not stall their onward march toward the truth. Even when they were deflected, the emperor called them back onto the track. To combat the deeply personal nature of the local memories, these investigators were forced to pursue their searches into many byways, any or all of which might yield their riches: wall posters and fliers, pamphlets, drafts of poems and essays, coded phrases, veiled allegories, dreams. Their techniques included constant pressure on reluctant witnesses, repeated cycles of questioning, demands for written confessions, torture and threats of torture, family pressures, isolation, deception, fake friendships, broken oaths, even the circulation of painted identification portraits of those believed to be on the run.

To us now, this has a somewhat modern ring, and evokes memories of later regimes in China and elsewhere. But the context and details of this particular case were closely tied in space and time, and unfolded the way they did largely because Zeng Jing and his ruler, Yongzheng, were the people they were. They never met, and yet we can say they came to know each other. Their signals to each other were sometimes veiled, but almost always decipherable. Both of them believed in their country and in themselves, and their curious quest for mutual understanding has miraculously survived, so that we in turn, so long after, if we push aside the encroaching branches and narrow our eyes against the dark, can trace at least a partial course along the avenues of their minds.

Acknowledgments

Like most historical explorations, this one could never have been completed without the aid and encouragement of many scholars, librarians, friends, and family. Crucial at an early stage was the assistance of Shi-yee Liu; her imaginative and meticulous searches through the published transcripts of both the Taipei and the Beijing Palace Museum holdings of materials from Yongzheng's reign gave this project a depth of character and incident that I had not dared to believe possible when I first began to pursue Zeng Jing. She also helped me map the structure and contents of the document entitled *Awakening from Delusion,* a task carried forward by another spirited and indefatigable helper, Zhao Yilu. Ms. Zhao also scanned for me a massive number of Chinese research articles on the three principal figures in these events: Zeng Jing, Lü Liuliang, and Emperor Yongzheng.

In many cases, the fact that I even knew of these articles' existence was

due to the wide scholarship and unfailing generosity of Tony Marr, my
friend from earlier Yale days and, while this book was being written, curator of the Gest Collection of East Asian materials at Princeton University.
Mail from Tony was always full of surprises. At Yale's own collection of
East Asian materials in Sterling Memorial Library, the erudite Chen
Hsiao-chiang was a constant guide and helper; in addition to which, her
ease and speed in making electronic searches greatly expanded the circles
of material I could draw upon—materials then hastened to me by Yale's
imperturbable interlibrary loan staff. For the elucidation of several technical Japanese materials, I owe a debt of gratitude to Yuka Hara. And at
the Library of Congress, the East Asian collection's curator, Dr. Wang
Chi, kindly answered all my queries concerning the library's own early
edition of the *Awakening from Delusion,* as well as sending me photo-
copies of key passages and the handwritten colophon, so that I could
compare them with the Yale edition of the same work.

Ch'ung-ho Chang Frankel, my former teacher, a great calligrapher,
and a longtime friend, literally gave me an early edition of one of the most
important Shanxi materials on the Zeng Jing case, and helped decipher
many examples of Emperor Yongzheng's difficult running script, correct
readings of which had often eluded me altogether. In this task of decipher-
ing, as in scanning and double-checking other key references, Qinan Tang
proved an eager and able helper. Important reference materials were also
given to me at different times by Professors Anita Andrew, Thomas Fisher
(a major pioneer in studies of both Lü Liuliang and Zeng Jing), Kandice
Hauf, Peter Perdue, Shao Dongfang, and Silas Wu. It was in an essay by
Wu Hung that I first encountered the masquerade images of Emperor
Yongzheng, one of which forms the cover of my own book. I am profoundly grateful to all these scholars and helpers.

At the Academia Sinica, in Taipei, home of so many major scholars,
where my January 1999 visit was arranged by Professor Chen Jo-shui and
made possible by the Chiang Ching-kuo Foundation, Professor Liu
Cheng-yun, for no reason other than his innate graciousness and sense of
scholarly solidarity, undertook for me a lightning computer scan of the
Academia Sinica's collection of Ming and Qing dynasty manuscripts
known as the "Ming-Ch'ing Tang-an," a rich storehouse of fragmentary
materials, mainly drawn from Grand Secretariat archives. The series of

references he found, and promptly shared with me, provided a crucial link in my knowledge of the distribution system that had allowed *Awakening from Delusion* to be spread across the country with such astonishing speed and thoroughness. In addition, Professor Liu gave me a copy of the invaluable essay by Wang Fan-sen on Zeng Jing's case as a social history source. On that same trip—thanks to Professor Wang Ayling, who arranged a visit to the Taipei Palace Museum archives, and to the two tenacious and patient archivists there, Kuo Hsiu-hsia and Lu Yu-nu—I was given the unforgettable opportunity to hold and read Zeng Jing's own handwritten letter of October 1730 thanking the emperor for his gift of one thousand ounces of silver. And finally, the opportunity to visit Zeng Jing's home county of Yongxing in southeastern Hunan, the emotional climax to my historical explorations, was facilitated by many people: Nancy Chapman and her staff at the Yale-China program; Bill Watkins, field officer of the program in China, and the most enthusiastic guide anyone could ever find; Bill's brother-in-law; along with the cadres, local scholars, and other assembled well-wishers from the Yongxing county government. Thanks to them, I was able to get to the northern reaches of Yongxing county and—in my own mind at least—to stand as close as breathing to the spot where Zeng Jing once watched by the side of the Anren road.

As so often in the past with other books, so in this one too, lectures I was invited to give at various places (as my ideas were slowly coming together), along with questions asked by the audiences there and references provided by them, helped sharpen my thoughts on what I was doing. This was true on at least four separate occasions when I lectured to student and faculty groups at Yale, as well as at several other gatherings: at the University of Utah, at Harvard University, and at the Academia Sinica in Taipei. All of these were memorable for me, though perhaps none of them can quite compare with the evening in Montana, when a group of friends sat with Jack Horner on a hillside, not far from the spot where he found his first clusters of fossilized dinosaur eggs, discussing Zeng Jing's desperate mission as the sun set and the light slowly faded from the sky.

In the early stages of work on this manuscript, I was spurred on by the enthusiasms of Andrew Wylie and Zoe Pagnamenta, and I thank them for their confidence; at a later stage, I gained greatly from the thoughtful comments of my two editors, Carolyn Carlson at Viking Penguin in New

York and Stuart Proffitt at Penguin U.K. in London. John Hollander, whose long poem "Reflections on Espionage" enchanted and moved me when first I read it years ago, as it enchants and moves me still, kindly allowed me to draw some words from his poem as the epigraph for this book. (It has, indeed, not always been easy to repress the thought that Lyrebird was somehow monitoring all these transmissions.)

Above all, my thanks to Annping Chin. She has watched all this grow and come together, answered my endless queries, read it all, thought about it all, and—with Maddux as a constant and ever-thoughtful shadow—helped again and again to assuage my desperation and perpetual bewilderment at the arcane mysteries of today's technology. To her, this book is dedicated.

J.D.S.
August 24, 2000
West Haven

Contents

—

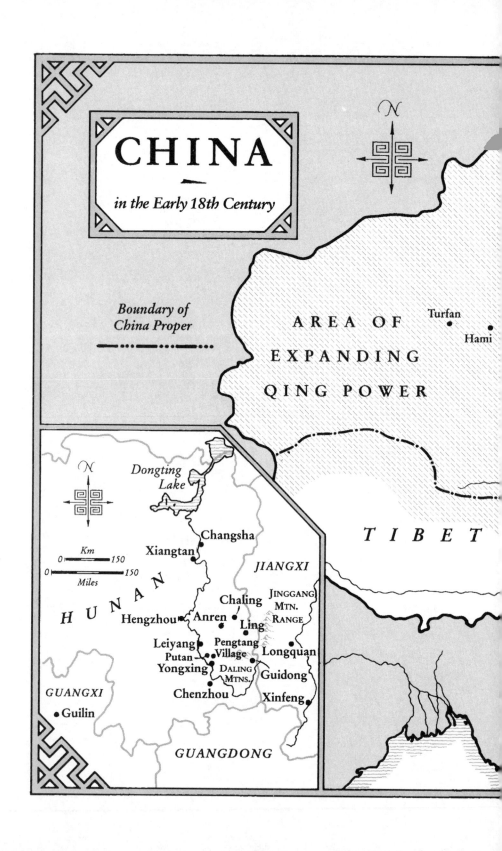

CHINA
in the Early 18th Century

Boundary of
China Proper

AREA OF
EXPANDING
QING POWER

Turfan

Hami

TIBET

Dongting
Lake

Km
0   150
0   150
Miles

Changsha

Xiangtan

JIANGXI

H U N A N

Chaling

JINGGANG
MTN.
RANGE

Hengzhou   Anren   Ling

Leiyang   Pengtang
Putan   Village
Yongxing   DALING
           MTNS.

Longquan

Guidong

GUANGXI

Chenzhou

Xinfeng

Guilin

GUANGDONG

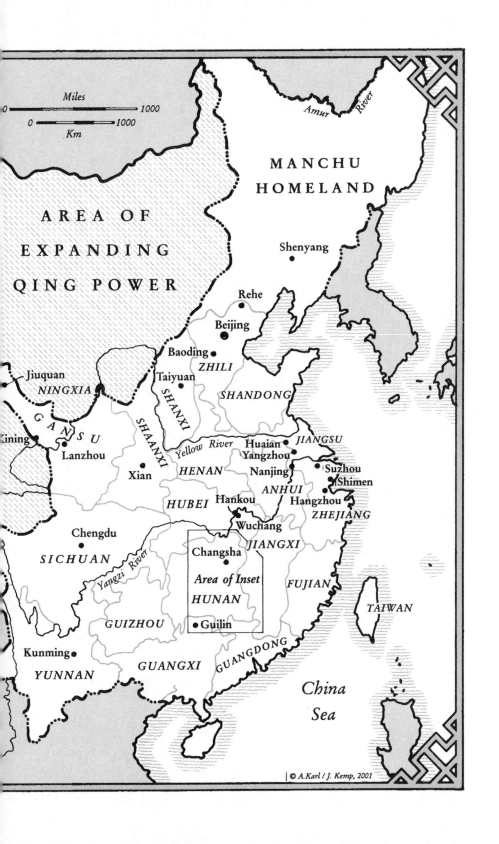

MANCHU HOMELAND

Amur River

Shenyang

AREA OF
EXPANDING
QING POWER

Rehe

Beijing

Baoding
ZHILI

Jiuquan
NINGXIA

Taiyuan
SHANXI

SHANDONG

Xining
GANSU

Lanzhou

Yellow River
Huaian
Yangzhou
JIANGSU

SHAANXI

Xian
HENAN

Nanjing
Suzhou
Shimen

Chengdu

HUBEI
Hankou
ANHUI
Hangzhou
ZHEJIANG

Wuchang

SICHUAN

Yangzi River

Changsha
JIANGXI

Area of Inset

HUNAN

FUJIAN

TAIWAN

GUIZHOU

● Guilin

Kunming
YUNNAN

GUANGXI
GUANGDONG

China
Sea

Miles
0   1000
0   1000
Km

| © A.Karl / J. Kemp, 2001

Prologue

*The
Letter*

The man holding the letter stands by the side of the road, at the foot of the Drum Tower, gazing down the long avenue that stretches straight through the city of Xi'an to the closely guarded West Gate, a mile away. To his left, the view is blocked by lofty walls, those of the spacious compound that serves as office and residence to the governor-general of the western provinces. That is why the man has chosen this spot to wait: he knows that Yue Zhongqi, the current governor-general of the region, is attending an official reception at one of the pavilions out in the suburbs beyond West Gate, and will be returning down this road to his compound as soon as the morning ceremony is over. That will be the time to act.

The waiting man is alone, though he has not planned it that way. Before he even began his journey, he was told by his teacher that in a village some miles upriver from Xi'an he would find a sure accomplice, a respected scholar named Mao, who shared the plotters' views and had money for the cause. But when he reached Mao's home he found only two of Mao's sons living there, both of whom were farmers; they informed him that their scholar-father had died six years before, and there was nothing they could do to help. And then there was the letter carrier's own cousin, an apparent believer in the quest, who traveled all the way with him from the south, to carry his baggage and keep him company. But two days ago the cousin panicked, now that the moment was so close, and fled without warning back to the south, taking one of the bedrolls and much of their baggage. So now there is no one to share the anxious watcher's thoughts.

It is almost noon when at last General Yue's sedan chair, with its accompanying retinue of bearers and outriders, can be seen making its way back along West Street. The man waits until they are almost opposite the Drum Tower, before running toward them across the road, brandishing his letter in the air. Instinctively Yue's retainers shout at the man to stop, and they form a protective ring around the general to block the stranger from approaching any closer.

From the seat of his sedan chair, General Yue stares out at the scene. The stranger is not dressed like the ordinary government underlings and office clerks, bustling around with correspondence for their superiors, with whom the general so often conducts his business. Nor does this man act like them—there is something unusual about his demeanor. Without leaving his chair, Yue makes a decision; he calls out to the retainers to bring him the letter the man is clutching.

They do so, and Yue glances at the envelope. A single look is all he needs to realize that he is in serious trouble. If this were an official letter, dealing with some detail of government, it would address him by his full name and title, as "Governor-general of the provinces of Shaanxi and Sichuan," or perhaps as "Commanding general of the Western Armies." But this letter, instead, is addressed to "The Commander-in-chief deputed by Heaven." In suspicious times, such as those Yue lives in, such a superscription is itself a danger sign. Ordering the retainers to arrest the stranger and hold him for questioning, Yue goes to his office and tells the staff there to leave him undisturbed.

When they are gone, he opens the envelope and begins to read. On the opening page, the writer of the letter identifies himself not with a name but by the mysterious title "Summer Calm, the Leaderless Wanderer of the Southern Seas"; the writer further states that the messenger who will deliver the letter to the general is named "Zhang the Luminous." As to the letter itself, everything is as General Yue has guessed and feared: a few lines suffice to show him that the contents are undiluted treason.

One

⬤

The General

General Yue Zhongqi has risen far and fast, which is what makes the present moment so dangerous for him. Born in 1686, the son of a general, Yue was a major at age twenty-five, a colonel at thirty-two, and was named commander-in-chief of Sichuan province at thirty-five. His string of military successes includes campaigns along the Tibetan border, in Kokonor, against mountain tribes in Xining, in China's westernmost province of Gansu, and on the borders of the far southern province of Yunnan. Now, in late October 1728, at the age of forty-two, not only is he governor-general of two provinces, and the regional commander-in-chief, but he has also been ennobled by a grateful emperor, and his own son in turn has been swiftly promoted to high office and is currently the acting governor of one of the strategic coastal provinces. The Yue family are rich; they hold huge estates in Gansu province in the far west, and in Sichuan to the south. The family inventories list dozens of properties held in the Yue name, great mansions with tiled roofs and multiple courtyards in several major cities, fine farmland scattered across several regions, and scores of caretakers and bailiffs who manage the estates when Yue Zhongqi is away on duty.

Yet despite his power and wealth, Yue Zhongqi knows he is totally at the emperor's mercy. Everything he has earned and won could vanish in an instant should the emperor doubt his loyalty. For the current emperors of China are the Manchus, warrior stock from the north, who conquered the armies of the floundering Ming dynasty in 1644 with their cavalry, established the Qing dynasty in its place, and have ruled the country ever since, constantly watchful to preserve their own prerogatives.

Another factor underlines the precariousness of General Yue's position: the burden of his family name. Yue Zhongqi is both blessed and cursed by being a distant descendant of another General Yue—Yue Fei—who six centuries earlier, in the time of the Song dynasty, tried to rally the Chinese of his own day to reclaim the lands they had lost in the north to barbarian conquerors. Yue Fei fought as long and as bravely as he could, until betrayed by his own countrymen and jealous courtiers. Imprisoned on a trumped-up charge, Yue Fei died in captivity, and the northern lands were lost. With time, Yue Fei's recklessness came to be seen as statesmanship, and his yearning plea to regain for China her "mountains and rivers" became a rallying cry for all Chinese people. Shrines to Yue Fei were erected in his native place. Plays and novels celebrated his passionate ambitions. Storytellers elaborated on his punctilious character and his prowess on the battlefield. They made their listeners weep as they recorded the warrior's courage amidst the carnage of war, and the perfidy of the political enemies who betrayed him. The Manchus who overthrew the Ming in 1644 were descendants of those same Jurchen tribesmen against whom Yue Fei fought for so long; thus, not surprisingly, Yue Fei's memory became once more a rallying cry for those who hated the Manchus. However loyal Yue Zhongqi may be to the current Manchu emperor, the popular belief is that he is primed for vengeance by virtue of his ancestral blood, and poised to restore China's former glories. General Yue knows this, and he knows that his emperor knows it.

Alone in his study, Yue Zhongqi moves to the heart of the letter that has just been handed to him. Some of it he has heard before and knows all too well, such as the passage hailing him as "the descendant of the Song dynasty martial prince Yue Fei," and urging him to "seize the chance to rise in revolt, and avenge the fates of the Song and Ming." "Once you have taken someone as your true ruler," the letter continues, "you should guard your relationship to that former person to the death. But instead you bow your head and compromise your loyalty by serving a bandit ruler." By serving the Manchus instead of keeping the faith with his illustrious ancestor, the current general Yue has compromised his very being: "A minister's choosing his ruler is like a woman following her husband. A man serving someone who is not truly his ruler, and thereby losing his moral character, is like a woman who has once been married and gets married for a second time."

But the letter by this man who calls himself Summer Calm also takes the familiar litany out into new terrain: "When the rulers of the Ming dynasty lost their virtuous ways, the land of China was submerged, the barbarians took advantage of our weakness to enter, and usurped our precious throne," he writes. "The barbarians are a different species from us, like animals; it is the Chinese who should stay in this land, and the barbarians who should be driven out." The reasons for this are obvious: "Heaven gives birth to humans and to things. The principle is one, though the manifestations are many. Those living on Chinese soil have the proper elements, their *yin* and their *yang* are in harmony, they possess virtue, they are human. Those outside the borders, in all four directions, they are oblique and vicious by nature, they are the barbarians. Below the barbarians come the animals."

Other passages in the letter speak of the portents darkening China's future as the country suffers under the barbarian Manchus' rule: "Heaven and earth are overturned, darkness prevails, there is no light." That is why, the letter continues, the Temple of Confucius recently burned down. That is why, for the last five or six years, floods and droughts in uneasy sequence have ravaged much of China, so that crops have been lost, the balance between hot and cold seasons has been destroyed, "mountains collapsed, rivers dried up." That is why "the five stars converged," "the Yellow River flowed clear," "*yin* was exhausted and *yang* began to rise."

In some passages, the letter's author reflects on the imbalances of a social order in which "the land has all been taken over by the rich—the rich get richer every day, and the poor get poorer." Summer Calm clearly separates himself from these wealthy families: "Living in the present day, and making my way in the present world, I have no intention of seeking profit or rank—these would defile me." Perhaps he is a farmer? "I live in seclusion on an empty mountain, with one or two like-minded friends, raising our chickens and growing melons." Yet if he is a farmer, he cares for old texts, old days, and has a sense of history. For the writer of this letter, nothing good in a scholarly or political sense has happened in China during the five centuries that have passed since the fall of that Song dynasty which Yue Fei fought so hard to preserve. In all that time, up to the present, only one scholar has "upheld the ideal," and that was the man whom the letter writer calls "The Master of the Eastern Sea."

As to the reigning emperor, Yongzheng, Summer Calm expresses nothing but disgust, and for General Yue's benefit he marshals the negative arguments: the emperor under whose rule they both are living has murdered several of his brothers, both older and younger; he has plotted against his parents; he persecutes his loyal ministers, and gives his ear only to sycophants; he is greedy for material gain, despite the richness with which he lives; he is ever eager to kill others, often drinks himself into oblivion, and cannot control his sexual passions. Could anyone be surprised that "the sky is shaking, the earth is angry; demons cry, gods howl"?

It is early afternoon by the time Yue Zhongqi finishes the letter. It has not been hard to read the letter in privacy, but many people have seen the letter delivered into his hands, and he must proceed with care. He will need unimpeachable witnesses if he is to question the messenger. If he were to investigate such an incredible document on his own, or to question the messenger in secret, even if he were to get the truth would anyone believe him?

The last time Yue Zhongqi found himself in a somewhat similar predicament was around fifteen months before, in early August 1727, when he was serving as the commanding general in the city of Chengdu, down in the southwest in Sichuan province. Just after noon, on August 4, a man was seen running wildly through the streets. He carried a stone in each hand, and shouted out for all to hear that a great upheaval was coming, that "Old Yue" would rise up with his cavalry and troops in Sichuan and Shaanxi provinces to overthrow the government. Within the very walls of Chengdu itself, secretly organized gangs would arise at the same time from their hidden bases near the city gates and would begin a bout of random killings.

That the city watchmen who first reported the incident and Yue's senior colleagues who investigated it all thought the man was mad was little solace to Yue Zhongqi himself. He still had to report the whole humiliating incident to the emperor, for he knew that his colleagues—even those among them he considered his friends—would be reporting it as well. Trivial though the incident might seem, both their careers and his depended on never concealing a single act that might be seen to threaten the regime. As Yue rather bitterly noted in his report to the emperor at that time, "If people are truly mad, there is nothing they cannot say, and no person they cannot destroy." And in a follow-up report Yue poured out his sense of anguish and guilt, lambasting himself for his failures as a general and as an official, confessing to financial and administrative errors and to mistakes in judgment, repeatedly referring to his own weakening health, and finally requesting to be relieved of all his duties.

Responding to Yue's reports in an edict issued later that same summer of 1727, Emperor Yongzheng handled the whole matter of the Chengdu incident with candor. Over the years, wrote the emperor, he had received numerous warnings of Yue Zhongqi's potential for disloyalty, warnings that were often linked to rumors that the general might seek to relive the triumphs of his ancestor Yue Fei. As emperor, he chose to ignore them all, and indeed had promoted Yue to ever-higher positions out of absolute confidence that the charges were groundless. His only regret was that these scurrilous accusations demeaned not only General Yue himself but also the loyal people of Sichuan and Shaanxi provinces, who formed the backbone of Yue's armies.

In a separate set of confidential comments for the general's eyes only, written in vermilion ink between the columns of Yue's impassioned outpourings, the emperor reassured Yue that he considered the charges Yue was directing against himself to be basically trivial matters, unworthy of further consideration. No one had mentioned them to the emperor before, and he did not care to know about them now. Yue should stay at his post, and get on with the work he had been appointed to do. Yue's poor health, however, was a real concern. Accordingly the emperor would send his own most trusted court doctor, Liu Yuduo, down to Chengdu, with a range of the medicines for which he was justly famous, to give Yue a thorough examination. Dr. Liu did indeed arrive in Chengdu, and spent three days checking the general's pulse rhythms, and in experimenting with different dosages of medication, before hitting on a formula that suited the general perfectly, brought an end to his nagging anxieties, and rebuilt his bodily strength.

Since the Chengdu case might leave rumors hovering in the air, rumors that could damage Yue's reputation and encourage doubts in the public's mind about the tranquillity of the region, Emperor Yongzheng also appointed a special investigator from the Ministry of Punishments to travel down to Chengdu and check things out for himself. Arriving in mid-September 1727, the investigator personally questioned the alleged madman, along with his relatives, anyone who had shared lodgings with him, and the members of the patrol that arrested him. The rigorous questioning—some of it under torture—revealed no instigators behind the scenes, and no traces of a concealed plot. It was clear that the madman, Lu, had acted alone while in a delirium caused by a protracted bout of malaria that had lasted over a month, leaving him weakened and desiccated. Lu had no memory at all of his actions in the street on that early August day. If there was any calculation behind his words and actions, it was that he had been driven to a state approaching madness even earlier, during a protracted struggle with the authorities to regain some land he had sold, under duress, to a brutal neighbor. The refusal of the various officials in the countryside where he lived to reopen his case had led Lu at last to Chengdu, in the hopes of catching the attention of the recently appointed general, Yue, who had a reputation for fairness. The investigator in 1727 also clarified some puzzling details in the case: for instance, Lu had been carrying a stone in each hand to drive away the wild dogs that followed him through the streets; the wildness of his gaze sprang from the delirium that fixed his eyes in an unyielding stare; once placed in a cart by the watchmen, to be conveyed to the city jail, all his energy evaporated, and he fell at once into a deep and trancelike sleep.

Yue Zhongqi was lucky that time, and apparently the case left no lingering resentments. But how can Yue report yet another case, of an oddly similar kind, not much more than a year after that earlier one, and still retain his emperor's confidence? His main hope for imperial understanding must be to keep the record limpidly clear, to have no suggestion of any hidden double-dealing. Only testimony from the most impeccable corroborating sources can be used. Lowly witnesses obviously will not do— for this is treason of the gravest kind. Twice Yue Zhongqi sends members of his personal staff to the second-ranking official in Shaanxi province, Governor Xilin, who also resides in Xi'an, asking him to report at once to the general's office. But the governor replies that he cannot come—he is out at the military training grounds in the northeastern part of the city, checking the martial skills of those taking the current round of military examinations. It would not be tactful in the circumstances for General Yue to order Governor Xilin to come, since the governor is a career Manchu bureaucrat, only one grade junior to General Yue, and the training ground is in the very middle of the "Manchu city" of Xi'an. That Manchu enclave was formed from the entire eastern half of the city after it was seized from the Chinese residents in 1646, fortified with its own inner walls, and made the permanent and protected residence area for five thousand Manchu garrison troops along with their more than fifteen thousand dependents.

Dipping, of necessity, one rung down in the bureaucratic hierarchy, Yue Zhongqi calls instead on the third-ranking official stationed in Xi'an, Judicial Commissioner Shise. This man's office is just across the road from the governor-general's compound, beside that same Drum Tower where the messenger had been waiting, and as it happens Shise is free, and is able to respond to Yue's call. After the two officials have consulted together briefly, Yue installs the commissioner in a room adjacent to the main office, so that he can hear everything that transpires without being seen. Once Shise is in position, General Yue summons the arrested messenger, "Zhang the Luminous," to his office, and offers him a cup of tea.

As they drink their tea together, Yue keeps his expression friendly and his words polite: Where is messenger Zhang from, how far did he have to travel to get to Xi'an, and how long did the journey take him? Where does Zhang's teacher, the "Leaderless Wanderer of the Southern Seas," live, and how can one get to see him? And more broadly, Yue Zhongqi asks, what factors induced Zhang's teacher to take the initiative to write such a letter, address it to General Yue, and arrange for its delivery in this particular manner?

Zhang is cautious. He has taken an oath, he says, never to reveal his teacher's whereabouts. What he can say is that his teacher lives in the far southeastern province of Guangdong, near the coast, protected by his numerous followers. Where does Zhang himself live? He spent his earlier years in Wuchang City, and elsewhere in the Hunan-Hubei region, but now he too lives with his teacher beside the southern seas. The journey to see General Yue took Zhang four months in all, as he made his way across southern China from Guangdong through Guizhou and Sichuan, and so northward to the city of Xi'an in Shaanxi. Why the choice of General Yue to receive this particular letter? Because both Zhang and his teacher had heard people tell how Yue was summoned three times to the court by Emperor Yongzheng, but refused to go. Thus they knew the general must be ready to revolt. The distressed economic condition of the southern provinces of China, and unusual heavenly portents, confirmed them in their belief that the time was ripe for bold action.

Pressed by Yue Zhongqi about those three summonses to court, messenger Zhang adds a curious twist to his story: "When I got to Shaanxi two weeks ago," he tells Yue, "I heard that the emperor never sent those three summonses for you to come to court; the story was baseless. Therefore I thought it might be better not to deliver the letter. But I had traveled so far that I could hardly return empty-handed. So I decided to deliver it anyway."

Trying to probe deeper into the motives lying behind the conspiracy, Yue returns to the economic arguments. Why was it that Zhang and his teacher thought that people were ready to rebel, he asks again? Was Shaanxi province not prosperous, as the messenger could see for himself? Shaanxi might be prosperous under General Yue, Zhang agrees, but Zhang's own home provinces of Hubei and Hunan were reeling from both floods and droughts. "Mere accidents of nature," replies Yue, "and certainly not things caused by human beings themselves." Besides, as he knows well, only a few small areas of Hunan and Hubei were affected by the bad weather, and the emperor has already sent relief to the stricken regions. "The government officials never know the people's real suffering," Zhang replies.

Shifting his ground again, Yue Zhongqi makes one more attempt to find out where the messenger and his teacher are really from. If Zhang will not tell him such basic details, Yue argues, how can he possibly know if this whole story is true or not? How can he be sure the whole thing is not an elaborate trap, in which Zhang has been primed by Yue's enemies to deliver a treasonous letter, so that they can see how Yue responds? (Something similar happened back in 1725 to Yue's predecessor in this very Shaanxi post, a man also at the peak of his power until undermined by a subordinate who lured him into acts of disloyalty and then turned him in. Yue was on the man's staff at the time, and knows all the dangerous details.) But Zhang does not rise to the bait, and swears that he will never reveal where he and his teacher live, even if the general kills him for his silence.

It is now three in the afternoon of October 28. Governor Xilin at last arrives, the military examinations being over. Yue goes out to greet him, and summarizes the impasse in which he finds himself. They decide that since the general is getting nowhere by politeness, they should turn to torture. The governor will conceal himself along with the judicial commissioner in the adjacent room, and the two will act as witnesses to what transpires.

But even when the torture instruments are used on Zhang, strong wooden presses that constrict hands and fingers or ankles and leg bones ever tighter, until they reach or pass the breaking point, he refuses to give the information the general demands. Zhang keeps repeating again and again through his cries of pain that his teacher lives down on the shores of the southern seas, where the borders of the provinces come together. The words are meaningless as a way of tracking down the conspirators, and after several hours the general realizes that Zhang will die if they continue any longer, and the mystery of the letter's origin will be unsolved. So he orders the messenger returned to his cell and arranges for the governor and judicial commissioner to return at dawn the following day, to take up their secret listening stations once again.

The whole of that next day, October 29, is spent in probing Zhang for hard facts, but to no avail. The general keeps the threat of torture in reserve, but does not resort to it again. Instead, he elaborates on what he said the day before about the need to prove Zhang was not a front man for some group of enemies determined to discredit Yue. Even the torture has its place in that enquiry, he adds, since how else could they have known whether Zhang was sincere? This time Yue openly says the name of his predecessor as governor-general and commander of the Western Armies, who had been betrayed by his own subordinates—the man was General Nian Gengyao, once the emperor's favorite but driven at the end to commit suicide on the emperor's orders. Doubtless Zhang and his fellows are planning the same kind of thing, the general observes, and why on earth should he trust this group of scholars apparently playing out the roles of wandering knights-errant? After the treatment he received the previous day, Zhang replies, it is hard for him to believe anything the general says to him. Such harsh treatment was logical, the general replies, since Zhang refused so consistently to tell the truth: "If you speak so fiercely to others, they are going to treat you with equal fierceness."

Zhang repeats his assertion that six provinces are ready to rise up in rebellion. Why six provinces? the general asks, and Zhang tells him that these are the same six that rose up in 1673 at the time of Wu Sangui's great rebellion against the Manchus, and they would surely rise again if given the proper leadership: "If you just give the word, all else will spring from that."

Yue probes the logic of the messenger's claims, winning debating points as he proves his superior knowledge of local conditions—it is, after all, the governor-general's responsibility to know such things—and regularly exposing great gaps in the messenger's information. But it is a circular and unproductive conversation. If there is a plot, its outline remains shadowy, its leader or leaders unknown. The last remarks from Zhang, as the evening comes upon them, are close to a threat: Many people now know, he reminds General Yue, of the torture used the day before. They would talk, as people always do. Their talk, and the reasons for it, would reach the emperor's ears and lead him to question the general about it. The general would then find himself in the deepest trouble.

Yue replies with unexpected candor: "For some time the emperor has known that people planning to rebel come to try and win an agreement from me; so naturally he doubts my true intentions, and takes his precautions. How can I ever have a day in which I am completely at peace?" But the messenger's threat has suggested its own solution, says the general: "Now that I am riding the tiger, I have no choice but to let you go. If outsiders do talk about this case, and the emperor decides to investigate, I'll just tell him that a group of naive scholars, under the illusion they were talking politics, got to saying crazy things. But after I gave them some tough questioning, I decided to let them go." The messenger is neither moved nor convinced: "Your words may sound logical, but I don't believe what you say. And since I came here ready to die, even if you were, in all sincerity, to set me free, I, in all sincerity, would not go." They are getting nowhere. Yue Zhongqi orders Zhang returned to his cell.

On the morning of October 30, seeing no other choice, Yue retires to his office and begins a report to his emperor. His rank entitles him to send a top-secret report, one that will initially be read by the emperor in person, before anyone in the bureaucracy has seen it. Such secret reports have to be written by the senior officials themselves, not by their secretaries, and must follow an exact format: an introductory title to show the content, followed by the main points sequentially arranged, terminating with general conclusions and suggestions for action. The paper, too, is standard for all senior officials: white, each sheet ten inches high and around two feet broad, folded into narrow leaves in a concertina fashion, which makes each report easy to scan through. The ink used is black, and the vertical lines of each official's calligraphy are spaced far enough apart to allow room for imperial notations in red ink between the lines, with more space at the end, after the date, for a lengthier comment should the emperor choose to make one.

For the introductory title to his report, Yue Zhongqi chooses unusual wording: "A Secret Report, Blunderingly Written, Which the Emperor Is Implored to Read with Compassion." As carefully as he can, Yue summarizes the delivery of the letter by Zhang the messenger at around noon on October 28, offers a sketch of the letter's contents, and presents a detailed account of the three phases of the interrogation across the afternoon and evening of the twenty-eighth, and on October 29. General Yue admits to the emperor that he has completely failed to solve the case—it has been in every sense "uncanny and elusive." Though he knows full well what his duty is to his ruler and his country, his capacities have proved inadequate to the task. All he can suggest now is that Zhang the messenger be sent to Beijing, where trusted officials of the emperor, skilled in interrogation, might be able to break through Zhang's walls of evasion.

By rights, Yue adds, he should be sending along a copy of the treasonous letter. But its contents are so wild and vile that he feels unable to send it for the emperor's perusal unless specifically ordered to do so. Accordingly, pending further instructions, he has put the letter in a sealed packet and deposited it with Governor Xilin, who will make sure it is not tampered with in any way. Governor Xilin, the general adds, who listened secretly to the second and third phases of the questioning, attests to the accuracy of this preliminary report, though Yue is sending it out under his own name. Messenger Zhang was also carrying two books when arrested, notes Yue. One was a handwritten copy of a work called "A Conspectus of Information for Attaining the Degree of Literary Licentiate," and the other was a printed book titled "Grasping the Essentials of the Classics, Illustrated with Commentary." These two have been sealed away for safekeeping.

The general entrusts his secret report to a special courier and orders it delivered at once to the emperor in Beijing. Just as there are meticulous rules for the format and presentation of secret reports, so are there similar rules for their dispatch. Most commonly the couriers are either trusted household retainers of the senior official concerned or else military officers on his staff. There are also government couriers attached to each of the various substations of the message-transmission system, which covers China like a tracery, linking key cities and transportation routes via an intricate system of post stations. One index of the dynasty's effectiveness is the speed with which messages can be delivered, for that depends in turn on maintaining stables and the necessary mounts which the couriers can use on the presentation of tallies: fast horses in the north, but also mules and donkeys for rugged terrain, and camels for the arid lands and deserts of the far west. In the southeast, crisscrossed by its myriad canals and rivers, the stables are replaced by a system of boats—various types, depending on the nature of the waterways. Inns where the couriers can sleep and get a meal are also part of the system. Yue Zhongqi does not mention in his report the name or rank of his courier, but we know the man traveled fast, leaving Xi'an at noon on October 30 and completing the 850-mile journey to Beijing by the fifth or sixth of November.

With the report written and dispatched, Yue Zhongqi can think more clearly about the case as a whole. Though the report he has just sent in may prove his honesty and patriotism, its contents suggest mainly a string of failures. And the solution he has offered the emperor is thin indeed. What if the Beijing interrogators succeed no better than he has, and Zhang the messenger were to die under their insistent questioning? How would that help to solve the case? And how would the solution he has offered in any way help to set the emperor's mind at ease?

As he reflects further, a possible line of action occurs to Yue Zhongqi. The messenger Zhang, wherever he might be from, is isolated and alone, frightened and in pain. Yet despite three protracted sessions of questioning, he has never let down his guard. Maybe a friendly face would accomplish what official sternness could not. General Yue knows and trusts a man named Li Yuan, formerly the supervisor of education in the eastern part of the city, whom he has just promoted to be acting magistrate. Li has not been in office long, and his path would not have crossed with Zhang the messenger. The general asks Li Yuan to come to his office, and sketches out his idea: Li Yuan will exchange his official robes for the simple clothes of a commoner, pretending to be one of Yue's household retainers. In this assumed role he will meet up with messenger Zhang, and attempt to get him to drop his guard. Li will find out what he can about the man, share local gossip, and also praise General Yue in the highest terms, as being a thoroughly trustworthy person. An unused room is found in one of the sprawling government compounds nearby, comfortably furnished, and Li Yuan is installed there. The messenger is thereupon released from his cell, and sent to spend the night in the same room, where Li Yuan is already waiting. Since the weather is cold, Yue has his retainers take warm furs over to the two men, and a plentiful supply of wine. He leaves the two men to talk, and drink, and sleep, and lets them laze away the next day too.

In the later afternoon of October 31, when it is already growing dark, Yue Zhongqi once against stations the judicial commissioner in an adjacent room, and has Zhang the messenger brought from his new quarters to the general's main office. With an air of absolute sincerity, Yue tells Zhang that he has been thinking about everything that has been said, and has decided to risk all and join the conspiracy. Zhang, perhaps softened by human friendship, by the warmth of the furs in the cold night, by wine, and by the good words he had been hearing about the general, accepts this pledge, though he also insists that the general back up his words by swearing a solemn oath never to betray Zhang and his teacher. General Yue swears that he will never divulge the information he is given.

Over the ensuing span of steady and courteous questioning, Zhang begins to yield up his formerly cherished secrets one by one. The true name of his teacher, "Summer Calm, the Leaderless Wanderer of the Southern Seas," is Zeng Jing. Zeng is currently not living anywhere near the southeast coast, but is at his home village of Putan, in Yongxing county, in the southeastern part of Hunan province. The messenger's own real name is Zhang Xi; originally from Hengzhou prefecture in Hunan, he has recently been living in the home of his teacher, Zeng Jing. Zhang Xi singles out four other men as central to his teacher's planning for the conspiracy. One, named Liu, is currently teaching in a local Hunan school, where he is famed for his knowledge of astronomy and his interest in military tactics. Another, Chen, of unknown address, is a self-proclaimed disciple of Liu. There is also a certain Qiao, another Hunanese, but from a different township, about whom Zhang knows no details. And there is a fourth man, from a completely different part of China: his name is Yan and he lives in Huzhou, a major commercial city in the distant coastal province of Zhejiang. Yan is especially esteemed for his skill in military tactics and knowledge of firearms.

Unwilling to push too far or too fast, Yue lets Zhang Xi go back to rest and relax with his newfound friend Li Yuan, and leaves the two undisturbed throughout the following morning, November 1. The general uses the time to write a second secret report to Emperor Yongzheng, outlining the nature of his deception, his swearing of the oath, and the results of his October 31 conversation with Zhang. As an attachment, he appends an annotated list of the six conspirators whose names are now definitely known, along with their places of residence when he has ascertained them. Yue's introductory title for this new report's contents is almost boastful: "A Secret Report on How the Rebel Has Spewed Out the Names of His Fellow Plotters." Choosing another courier, Yue sends him racing after the first toward Beijing. He will probably not be able to overtake the first courier, carrying the message of failure, but at least this second report should reach the court before the emperor has taken any action on the first.

General Yue lets Zhang Xi rest until twilight on November 1 before summoning him again. (Once again, the judicial commissioner is concealed as a witness in the next-door room.) With simulated eagerness and curiosity, Yue concentrates on the phrase Zhang used in their very first conversation, that the six potentially rebellious provinces would rise at once when the word was given: "If you just say the word, all else will follow," as Zhang had originally phrased it. What exactly does that mean in practical terms? asks Yue. Zhang answers elliptically: "It all depends on the state of mind the people are in; it is something ordained to happen."

Yue is not satisfied with such an answer. Things are not so bad in those provinces, he responds, and aid has been sent to the stricken areas. How could one possibly believe that it is all just a question of the people's mindset? "Surely you people must have an army ready, and supplies; then when you stage the rising in a given place, 'If someone just says the word all else will follow.'" Zhang's answer is defensive: "When I was with my own comrades, we just talked about general moral principles. I don't know about the rest of the specifics." "That was exactly why, in yesterday's conversation, I referred to you people as 'naive scholars,'" Yue retorts. "Because you are all so filled with bravado, you think you can change the world." Zhang replies that his teacher Zeng Jing, Liu, Yan, and the others he's mentioned "all possess huge talents that they are at the moment unable to use; but if you were to employ my teacher, what worries could you possibly have? As to exactly how in the case of Hunan and the other six provinces 'one word spoken would make all else follow,' only my teacher has everything worked out. I am merely a humble follower of his, and could never see the whole picture. I did no more than obey his instructions to give you the letter, and various other things he told me in person."

The rest of the discussion, however, is more productive of hard information. Zhang tells General Yue how one year ago, in the autumn, he traveled to Zhejiang province to visit the descendants of the deceased scholar Lü Liuliang, that being the true name of the "Master of the Eastern Sea" mentioned in the original letter to the general. Lü's grandchildren let

Zhang read Lü's journals and other works, and gave him copies of some of Lü's poems. Lü Liuliang had written powerful things, but his later descendants were not impressive people, Zhang felt.

Casually, Yue Zhongqi asks for the names and current homes of the people with whom Zhang Xi talked in Zhejiang, and also for the full names and locations of Zhang's father and other relatives. Though the day before Zhang steadfastly refused to give any information about his father's name and place of residence, he now gives the general all the information requested: His father's name is Zhang Xinhua, and he lives with his eldest son, Zhang Zhao, in a small village about forty miles away from the county town of Anren in southern Hunan. For a time, Zhang Xi's father held the junior literary degree of licentiate, which he had won in the local examinations, but the provincial authorities canceled his right to use the degree title after he was charged with being involved in a local disturbance. Thus he was no longer allowed to wear a scholar's robes. Zhang also had a younger male cousin, who had come with him all the way to Xi'an. But before the letter was delivered, this cousin panicked and set off for home on his own. Besides these family members, there were two men surnamed Che in the conspiracy, both originally from Hunan, who had changed their registered residence, and now lived in the city of Nanjing on the Yangzi River. A man from Jiangsu province, named Sun, lived in the same residence as the Che family. And there was a man called Shen, who was living in Zhejiang, and working with Yan, the expert in military strategy and firearms, whose name had been mentioned the previous day.

Suddenly, General Yue has all the information he can possibly have hoped for. He dismisses Zhang from his presence, and once more takes paper and brush, and writes out a third secret report for his emperor. He gives this one the introductory title "The Rebel Spews Out More." Yue summarizes the whole discussion he has just had with the messenger, and adds some thoughts of his own. Though he is not attempting to list the names and addresses of the Lü clan that he has gleaned from Zhang Xi— the best person to check that out, he tells the emperor, would be the current governor-general of Zhejiang province—he recalls that Lü Liuliang was fairly well known in the previous emperor's reign among the scholars from Zhejiang. Yue also has heard reports that one of Lü's grandsons somehow got implicated in an attempted rising by a renegade Buddhist monk called Yinian, and would certainly have been executed long ago had the late emperor not pardoned him, on the grounds that the Lü family was a scholarly one, not previously involved in any treasonous activities. General Yue also tells the emperor that after conducting a more thorough search of Zhang Xi's possessions, he has found some other handwritten copies of books tucked away there: one is a commentary on *The Book of Changes,* one a collection of selected poetry, and a third is a medical text. The general will keep the first and third of these items in safe storage, unless the emperor asks for them to be sent to Beijing. But since some of the poems in the collection are by Lü Liuliang, he will send those along right away, as an attachment to this latest report.

For the third time in six days Yue Zhongqi selects an express courier, and orders him to rush to Beijing—he will be carrying with him the secret report, the copy of Lü Liuliang's poems, and the annotated list of seven new names that brings the roster of conspirators up to thirteen. This courier will surely not overtake the previous two, but should arrive at the palace in time for the emperor to coordinate this report with the two earlier ones. The general has ascertained that there are named conspirators in at least three different provinces. It also seems to be a fact that in a total of six provinces, somehow, somewhere, armies are waiting to rise up when the right word is given.

It is exactly a week since a stranger ran toward General Yue's sedan chair with a letter, and the general brushed aside his retainers' caution and took the letter into his hands. Things have been dangerous for a time, but at last there is a chance that they are going to be all right. Nothing more can be extracted from the messenger Zhang Xi for now, and the need for deception is over. General Yue orders Zhang Xi removed from his comfortable quarters and sequestered in the most secure prison in Xi'an, the one under the direct control of the judicial commissioner himself. Messenger Zhang's brief days of fur and wine are over.

Two

The
Emperor

Emperor Yongzheng receives Yue Zhongqi's initial report on the conspiracy at the end of the first week in November. A meticulous administrator with a passion for detail, he reads it through carefully and in person, as he does all secret reports from the provinces, not leaving the task to his secretaries or the ministerial staff. Although none but the most senior provincial officials, those of the third grade and above in the nine-grade bureaucracy, are authorized to send in such reports for imperial eyes only, there are more than two hundred such officials, and the emperor receives dozens of secret reports every day. Much of his life is taken up with reading them, with writing his comments, and—in certain cases, if the matter is not too delicate—with passing the reports along to the senior ministers in the court bureaucracy, requesting their operational suggestions.

The emperor usually does this reading in one of two locations, within the Forbidden City itself or in the more relaxed garden palace grounds that his father built out in the northwest suburbs of Beijing, nestled among farms, with a clear view of the exquisite Western Hills. The secret reports are delivered to a special repository supervised by a select group of trusted eunuchs and guards officers, so they can be passed on to the emperor at any time of day or night, whether he is in the inner or outer quarters of the palaces. An ink stone is always ready on his table, with brushes and the vermilion ink that only the emperor may use for his notations on state documents. (All others write in black.) As he reads, he occasionally marks a passage with small circles for emphasis, or scrawls a quick comment above or between the lines. He normally reserves his longer remarks for the blank space left at the end of the report, writing swiftly, in cursive Chinese, the red ink swirling round the report's closing dateline, and contrasting sharply with the sober black of the report itself.

Given the expenses and time constraints of the courier system, the provincial senior officials normally send their secret reports to the emperor in batches. That way, he can read through a group from the same area all at once, and the replies can all be sent back at the same time, in the same dispatch box, in the care of the courier who brought them. Only ten days before this, for example, the emperor has received twelve reports from General Yue, in a single box, covering everything from problems with local commercial tax collection and various minor cases of banditry to major decisions about military logistics in the far west campaigns, the control of Muslims in Gansu, and the various ways to handle the envoys from the Dalai Lama, should they pass through Xi'an en route to Beijing. What is immediately surprising about Yue Zhongqi's report of October 30 detailing the messenger's arrest and interrogation is that it is sent on its own. The same is true of Yue's second report on the same case, that of November 1, which lists the initial group of six suspects. Clearly the case of the treasonous letter has been all-consuming to Yue, and he has had no time to respond to the other matters that are pending, however serious they may be.

By now, at the age of fifty, having spent six years on the throne, Emperor Yongzheng has read many accounts of treasonous actions, some of them implicating this same General Yue, as in the case of the Chengdu madman in 1727. He is used to accounts of strange behavior, veiled threats, and outrageous accusations, and names like "Summer Calm" and "Leaderless Wanderer of the Southern Seas" do not surprise him. Furthermore, Emperor Yongzheng's reading of General Yue's words is shaped by certain presumptions and colored by the long years he and the other princes spent waiting for their aging father to die. He has become at once a man of habit and a man with fierce obsessions. He has been convinced for years that people want to kill him, and he has ordered the killing of many in return, including three of his own brothers. This is no secret in the country at large. First to die, in January 1725, was the emperor's elder brother Yinreng, once named as the heir-apparent to the throne in the previous reign, whom Yongzheng since his own accession had kept incarcerated under harsh conditions in a Beijing prison. In the summer of 1726 two other imperial brothers died, the current emperor's eighth and ninth, whom he had never ceased to suspect of trying to oust him from the throne. Forced by Yongzheng even to give up their own names—one was made to call himself "Fat-as-a-Pig," and the other "Mean-as-a-Dog"—they perished within a week of each other. The ninth brother died first, apparently of fever compounded by dysentery, in a city just a few miles southeast of Beijing, after being chained hand and foot and literally bricked up in a stifling box of a hut, where food and water were made available to him only by a pulley that raised the supplies over the wall. The eighth brother died soon after, of an unexplained illness, but one that led people to believe that he had been poisoned. In neither case did the emperor permit any public show of grief or mourning by the dead men's family members.

Such events have fueled popular beliefs that Yongzheng must have usurped the throne and now seeks to destroy all possible rivals; and the aura of secrecy around him is deepened by the fact that in his six years of rule, he never once has gone on the great hunting trips to the north, or toured his vast domains to the west and south, as his late father so loved to do, and as he himself had occasionally done while a prince. And the emperor's own family line seems somehow marked for doom; of the nine sons and four daughters born to him by various consorts up to the end of 1728, all the girls and six of the boys have died from illness.

The emperor's public pronouncements show that he is always conscious of his ancestry as a member of the Manchu race, which conquered China eighty years before. Yongzheng is the third Manchu emperor to rule China since that conquest, and though he has never led a military campaign in person, he is constantly concerned with the politics that accompany border expansion and with strategies to defuse the angers of the indigenous tribes that dwell on China's frontiers or have been already partly absorbed into China proper. He gives enormous power to his favorite officials, both Chinese and Manchu, but watches them with endless care and infiltrates their staffs with spies who report back to him on his favorites' words and conduct. He strikes them down mercilessly if he feels they are wavering in their loyalty. He distrusts people from beyond the borders, whether Japanese merchants or Western missionaries, along with the Chinese middlemen who deal with them, and keeps a constant watch on their arrivals and departures.

Emperor Yongzheng believes most people are out for personal gain and need constant checking. He feels the morals of the nation are lax and must be corrected with a mixture of Confucian teachings and legal restraints. He believes in the messages implicit in natural portents, and seeks solace from his cares in religious disputation with eminent Buddhist priests. At the same time, often tired and ill, he invites traveling physicians to his court as well as Daoist adepts whose elixirs may give him back his strength. He has even commissioned his court painters to create a dozen portraits of him, each one representing him playing a different role: as Daoist magus, as musician, as warrior, as central Asian ruler, as scholar and recluse.

The news in Yue's reports that the conspirators' secret contacts have spread to Zhejiang province on the east coast, where Lü Liuliang made his home and where his surviving sons and grandsons still are living, strikes a special resonance in the emperor's mind. For he has developed a deep dislike for the people of Zhejiang, finding them malicious and supercilious. The greatest insults he has endured have come from Zhejiang men, and though he has killed them for it, he still bears the scars from their slights. To oversee the moral regeneration of the region, he has recently created a new office, that of "Supervisor of Public Morality for the Province of Zhejiang." No other province in the country has a special official designated in this way to be its moral guardian.

Despite these emotional concerns, the emperor makes no interlinear comments or emphasis marks on the preliminary section of General Yue's October 30 report. Only near the end, when Yue mentions that he has de-

cided not to send the treasonous letter on to Beijing unless specifically ordered to do so, lest its vile contents destroy the emperor's peace of mind,
does the emperor interject his own opinion: "When one hears the barking
of such dogs, the snarling of these wild beasts," he writes, "why should we
take any notice of them? Send the letter along, so I can take a leisurely
look."

But once he has finished the whole report, the emperor has plenty to
say, especially about the messenger called Zhang. A torrent of vermilion
words fills up the space left on the paper by Yue, the lines crammed closer
and closer together as the emperor nears the edges of the page:

"This is indeed a ridiculous business, and this man is really hateful.
The more I think about him, the less he seems to be like a typical troublemaker from our own land: when he talks about the state of the country at
the present time, he sounds like someone who knows nothing about how
things are handled in the government, and has never bothered to find out.
Perhaps he is one of the renegade Chinese, who have been living for years
in the Miao aboriginal outlands. If that's not it, maybe he is some kind of
rebel from overseas. Check out the way that he talks, and his accent. Does
he sound like a Hunanese? Judging from the way he behaves, the way he
carries himself, and his level of literary sophistication, what kind of person
does he seem to be? Does he seem the scholarly type, or more on the martial side? If he is just ordinary riffraff, you can chat with him at your
leisure, and find out easily enough." Obviously no one has to question
that this case is of crucial concern to General Yue's own self-interest, the
emperor remarks, and thus he understands why Yue felt compelled to act
firmly. But slower would have been better: "Why start to question the
man on the very first day, and move so quickly to using torture? If he had
the incredible nerve to get involved in this business, it is clear that he is one
of those who are unthinking about their fate and have ceased to fear death.
Even if you sent him to Beijing, he would behave the same way."

The key priority for General Yue must be to devise ways to get the
truth out of a man who has no reason to want to live. Writing swiftly
across the last page of Yue's report, the emperor suggests four strategies,
any or all of which might work. One is for Yue to appear relaxed and at
ease with the messenger, and to talk casually with him until the right line
of questioning begins to emerge. A second way is for Yue to hold the mes-

senger under secure guard, in the hopes that someone connected with the conspiracy will lose their nerve and come to try and find out what has happened to their coconspirator. It is unlikely that the messenger has been operating alone, and when or if such an accomplice appears, the newcomer can be arrested and minutely questioned. A third strategy is for Yue to appear to share his thoughts frankly with the messenger, and to tell the man he is still mulling over the case and wondering how to report it to the throne. Yue could appear puzzled, saying that the messenger must be either deranged or else have no foresight at all to think he could just attach himself to the general and say whatever came into his mind. After such initial remarks, Yue could proceed to outline the positive achievements of the present and the previous emperors, of the good fortune and prosperity they had brought to the country. How could the messenger reject all that goodness and concentrate only on groundless and poisonous thoughts? Surely somebody had been misleading him. From there the general could move to introduce the idea of accomplices—how could the messenger and his teacher be acting alone?—before suggesting that the two were being set up. The emperor even gives Yue some sample dialogue to try out on the messenger: "From what you have been saying, this affair is not limited to you and one or two other ignorant people. There must be others involved who know exactly what they are doing, and are playing with your lives as a part of their broader plans. Why not give me the names of these people who are sending you to your death?"

If none of those approaches work, concludes the emperor, Yue can try a fourth; elaborate flattery. Praise the messenger for being a heroic man, whose teacher must also be endowed with extraordinary powers, since at his call the people of six provinces will all arise. How many people there must be in this plot! "Why don't you just go back whence you came," the general could say, "and persuade all those people to return to their loyalties as true subjects of their country? Thus not only will you avoid being doomed to a bandit's death, but your own name would be enshrined for all time in the records of bamboo and silk."

The emperor has another report from Shaanxi on his table, also dated October 30. This one is written by Judicial Commissioner Shise, who spent so many late October hours concealed in the listening room provided by General Yue. On the basis of the conversations he overheard, writes Shise, he feels confident that he understands Zhang the messenger: "I studied that man carefully, he is truly crafty. This is obviously not just a plot limited to one or two people, there must be a much larger gang of these troublemakers." Shise finds no reason to doubt that the members of that extended gang are scattered throughout the province of Hunan, as well as in the southern coastal province of Guangdong. In stark contrast to the amount of time he has spent answering Yue, the emperor does not bother to grace Shise's report with any comment apart from the single word "noted." It is Yue who is the key figure here, and Shise's reflections are apparently of no great interest to the ruler.

That the emperor's very first response to the news of the conspiracy should be that Zhang—and perhaps his teacher, Summer Calm, as well—are somehow "un-Chinese" reflects his immediate preoccupations. Over the last couple of months the emperor has been having protracted discussions with various ministries and provincial officials on two related sets of problems. The first of these is the "renegade Chinese" who dwell in the tribal areas of the indigenous Miao peoples scattered across the provinces of Hunan and Guangxi; Chinese of this depraved kind often exploit the Miao, bilking them of their landholdings, inveigling them into spurious "native associations," and blocking those who seek a more creative partnership with the local Chinese authorities. The second deals with the problems of illegal trade and immigration between the coastal provinces of China and Japan, and of the difficulties of determining when there are legitimate reasons for travel—Buddhist personnel, for example, moving at the invitation of some devout Japanese patrons from their temples in China to one of Japan's great religious centers—and when the activities are used as cover for the smuggling of illegal goods and firearms, or of politically inflammatory literature, either between the mainland and Japan, or to and from the foreigners in Luzon, Java, and Siam.

Before there has even been time to reach the waiting courier with the emperor's lengthy endorsement to General Yue's October 30 report, Yue's second report, dated November 1, arrives at the palace, telling of the false oath, and the first breakthroughs in the case. This time, the emperor's composure cracks. When he reaches the point at which General Yue describes swearing an oath of loyalty to Zhang and his teacher, and promising to join them in their plot, the emperor marks red circles of emphasis next to the words "swearing an oath" and proceeds to pour out his thoughts to Yue: "Reading this report of the feigned and the true, I cannot stop the tears from running down my cheeks. Our sacred ancestors would surely view this oath that you personally swore as being a principled act; for it is bound to have the effect of warding off calamities, extinguishing crimes, bestowing good fortune, and prolonging people's lives. The joy that I feel is really hard to express in writing. I feel for you all the emotions that the sage rulers of old had for their loyal ministers, bound together in a felicity that can never be measured. How could anyone make even a rough comparison of the deep joy you brought to me by acting thus, on your own initiative, to help your emperor and to preserve the life of your country?"

Emperor Yongzheng's emotional response to Yue's report springs from other recent experiences of his, which have vividly taught him the political and strategic importance of the governor-generalship of Sichuan and Shaanxi, the position Yue now holds. This same region had provided the base for the grandiose ambitions of the first Chinese favorite of the emperor's reign, the scholar and official Nian Gengyao. For several years at the beginning of his reign the emperor plied Nian with the most lavish gifts and gestures of affection. Their bonds were all the stronger since Nian's younger sister was one of the emperor's most favored consorts— she bore him four of his thirteen children, one girl and three boys. So complete was the emperor's trust that he gave Nian the delicate and dangerous assignment of keeping watch over the previous emperor's fourteenth son, yet another of the brothers who Emperor Yongzheng feared was a major contender for his throne. This prince was Yongzheng's full blood brother, born to the same mother, a popular and capable man who at the peak of his power had coordinated China's campaigns in Tibet. When Emperor Yongzheng began to suspect this brother of implementing a plot, he exiled him to the isolated western city of Xining, in the territory controlled by Nian. Still later, suspecting his brother of treasonous collusion with Nian, Emperor Yongzheng recalled the fourteenth prince to Beijing and had him imprisoned. At the same time the emperor launched a series of attacks against Nian, charging him with corruption, disloyalty, greed, and vanity. Prominent among Nian's accusers in the early 1720s had been the rising young military officer Yue Zhongqi, who was awarded many of the same posts that were being systematically removed from Nian. Nian's life was spared as long as his sister lived, but the emperor stripped Nian of all his wealth and honors, even down to the presents he had recently bestowed on him. When Nian's sister died suddenly of illness, in the summer of 1726, the former favorite's fate was sealed. Nian was charged with ninety-two counts of dishonesty and malfeasance, and ordered to commit suicide.

Nian's house was searched after his arrest, and the emperor's agents found a strange manuscript there, entitled *Casual Notes of My Journey to the West.* The author was a man from Zhejiang named Wang Jingqi, a scholar from a respected family, who in 1724 had traveled west across China to Nian's headquarters in Xi'an, apparently in the hopes of finding employment. The manuscript had been his present to Nian. Though bearing an innocuous title, filled with wordplays and puns, and couched in the familiar form of a travel diary with daily entries, the *Casual Notes* were in fact scurrilous and polemical. Wang presented his journey as being a personal induction into a world of violence and misery, in which each day brought new surprises as he talked to a wide range of local people along the roads and at the inns where he stayed. Many spoke to him of the hardships caused by the protracted military campaigns in the region, not only of the mounds of bodies on the battlefields, but of the terrible treatment of the prisoners from the tribesmen fighting the Qing armies. They told him, too, of the women who were captured and raped, or parceled out among the officers and troops like chattels. Though the speakers often praised the prowess of Nian as commander-in-chief and the extraordinary courage of his young subordinate general, Yue Zhongqi, Wang remarked that however many victories those two won, the emperor never gave them suitable rewards, or even acknowledged their achievements publicly. They had every right to feel bitter at their treatment.

Wang's writings claimed to represent the feelings of the residents of the northwestern Chinese provinces, whose lands were mercilessly taxed to pay for the never-ending border campaigns. They died in as great numbers as the captive tribesmen, though their deaths came from starvation or despair, leaving their lands abandoned, their children sold, their womenfolk forced into lives of prostitution. Groups of bandits had sprung up throughout the region, adding to the miseries. According to Wang, the locals he met in western Shanxi, near the Yellow River, were full of stories, especially about the women bandits who formed their own gangs in many of the ravaged villages. Bound together by unbreakable ties of loyalty, toughened by suffering and by training, contemptuous of their men, each of these women had her own distinguishing martial skill, often reinforced by the nickname she had won for her prowess. Wang Jingqi wrote of "Emerald Woman" and the long spear she could hurl like a thunderbolt; of "Little Cloud," a genius with the broadsword, the flashing blade of which refracted the light like snowflakes. He told of "Jade Woman"—known also as the "divine-shouldered bowman" because of the immense power of her bow, and the distance and accuracy with which she could shoot her arrows—and her fellow archer "Purple Cloud," who always wore clothes of purple hue and carried a bow and arrows of the same color. There were many other women with special traits, such as those who could leap great distances into the air, those who could ride under the bellies of their galloping horses, those famous for their cruelty, those who dressed like men, those who had bound feet and yet moved with preternatural speed. There were other women, known in the area as the "rouged bandits," of whom the locals would speak to Wang only in whispers, or not at all, looking nervously round the inn for the omnipresent eavesdroppers.

Many of Wang's diary entries mocked both the present and the previous Manchu emperors for their gullibility and their parsimony, as well as for their endless wars. He was even harsher on the officials they trusted, rewarded, and promoted, presenting a rounded rogues' gallery of unctuous hypocrites at the highest levels of government—all clearly identified by family name, by native place, and by the date of their examination degrees—whose cruelty and excessive moralism drove innocent men and women to their deaths. Wang's roster of names included many of the country's most prominent officials over the previous forty years. Of those, none had risen higher than Zhang Pengge, holder of the highest examination degrees, president of several ministries in turn, grand secretary of the realm under both Emperor Yongzheng and his father, director of flood and river management, and special commissioner on countless imperial assignments. In Wang's account, Zhang (who died in 1725), far from being beyond criticism, was an oversexed and dishonest buffoon, coating himself with powder and rouge like the most tawdry actor. Wang wrote of Zhang hastening back home from a dawn audience with the emperor straight to his bedroom, where a naked maidservant was waiting for him. There, without even removing his court robes or official hat, Grand Secretary Zhang stood by the side of the bed and had his way with her, as the young woman curled her feet around his neck and shoulders.

"Seditiously false and maniacal," Emperor Yongzheng wrote across the manuscript when he was shown it. Wang had "ridiculed and reviled" the imperial family, and despite his advanced education and decent nurturing had proved to be "a rebel without any moral values." The emperor ordered that Wang Jingqi be executed immediately, along with his sons aged sixteen or older; Wang's womenfolk and his other children were to be exiled and enslaved. Nian's decision to keep Wang's manuscript in his personal possession, rather than handing it over to the state, was listed as one of the five "greatest crimes" out of the ninety-two with which he was charged before being ordered to commit suicide.

General Yue, of course, is fully aware of the emperor's sensitivity to any hint of further disloyalties within Shaanxi, and the content and tone of Yue's November report are designed to reassure the emperor that this particular general will not repeat the pattern of his predecessor. Yue has confessed to the receipt of the treasonous letter presented to him, not tried to stash it away. The armies of the northwest that Yue now commands will not be brought into the factional struggles still latent in the court between various princes and their political allies. Yue has kept his second report as short as possible, so that he can rush it to the emperor, and besides its inner message of total loyalty, proven by the broken oath, its real heart comes at the end, in the brief listing of the first six conspirators and of their hometowns or villages when known. Next to the list Emperor Yongzheng scrawls a second comment: "I am going to keep this list right here, and will personally arrange for some people to go and arrest them and take care of this matter. As to Zhang Xi, you can think up some way to ease his spirits, but at the same time you should keep him in detention."

In view of the importance he gives to this case, the emperor makes an exception to his own customary procedures and gives orders that a copy be made of Yue's two reports on the conspiracy, along with the imperial notations, and kept for future reference in the palace. Only when that has been done are the two original reports, now with the emperor's commentary, sealed in one dispatch box and handed over to Yue's waiting couriers.

As is always done when a dispatch box contains urgent material directly from the emperor, this one is wrapped in cloth of imperial yellow; the materials are hurried by the couriers across northern China and delivered to Yue at his Xi'an office on November 17. On receipt of the imperial messages, General Yue, as protocol demands, burns incense and prostrates himself on the ground in homage to his distant ruler, for the emperor's words carry the same symbolic weight as the emperor's person and must be acknowledged with due humility and awe.

By the next morning, overwhelmed with relief at the emperor's forgiving response to his involvement in such a dangerous case, and by the fact that the emperor's suggested way of teasing out the truth from the messenger coincides with the tactics he has ended up using, General Yue has already prepared the dispatch box for its return journey to the emperor: this time the box contains the original treasonous letter as written by Zeng Jing and presented by Zhang Xi, the various books on scholarly subjects found stashed away in Zhang Xi's luggage, and the general's own answers to the emperor's most pressing questions: Zhang Xi is definitely from Hunan, writes Yue, not from the southern coastal region, nor from one of the other outlying border areas about which the emperor enquired. Just as certainly, Zhang is no martial arts expert: he is weak and sickly in appearance, and has the look of someone interested only in cultural pursuits. He shows no sign of military skill at any level, nor does he manifest much initiative: in response to any substantive question on the conspiracy, Zhang always refers the interrogators to his teacher Zeng Jing.

Well before these additional items of information arrive at the end of November, however, the emperor has decided he must expand the circle of those who know about the case and can help in its solution. The trigger for this decision is his receipt of General Yue's third sequential report on the case, a report that increases the list of specific suspects to thirteen, including two or maybe more in Zhejiang, three currently residing in Jiangsu (though originally born outside that province), and the rest in Hunan. In addition, Yue's third report gives specific examples of passages from the Zhejiang scholar Lü Liuliang that appear to have had a profound influence on the conspirators in Hunan. And Yue has added a further detail, that one of Lü Liuliang's grandsons had been swept up in the excitement of the uprising led by the monk Yinian, which took place some twenty years before, in 1707. As all those who lived through that period know, Yinian had sought to rally his followers in loyalty to the fallen Ming dynasty; he issued proclamations dated according to the calendar of the defunct Ming dynasty, rather than using the calendar established by the current Qing dynasty, as the law demanded; his followers wore red turbans and carried replicas of Ming dynasty flags, and they swore blood oaths of loyalty to their leader and to each other. By late 1707 they were thousands strong, and familiar enough with military skills to kill Manchu cavalry sent against them and to create strong bases in the Zhejiang mountains. That rebellion had been crushed eventually by Qing troops, and General Yue reminds Emperor Yongzheng that after an extensive investigation the Lü family grandson was pardoned by the previous emperor, on the grounds that the young man was a scholar of Confucian morality, and was quite innocent of the practical evils of the world.

These additional details provided by General Yue give Emperor Yongzheng disconcerting examples of the intersections of scholarly endeavor with treasonous activities against the state, and heighten the sense of urgency that the case is generating in his mind. But widening the circle of those in the know must be combined with maintaining the highest levels of confidentiality. That way, there will be no chance of the conspirators in the provinces being alerted before they can be arrested by the authorities.

The balance is a delicate one. Public pronouncements about actions to be taken by the government are often printed in the *Capital Gazette,* a newsletter of official court actions and edicts printed in the capital under the supervision of the Grand Secretariat, and allegedly restricted to a readership of capital officials and those in the provinces with the rank of magistrate or above. But illegal leaks are always occurring, and information that should have stayed confidential is made available either by clerks in the metropolitan bureaus who sell the information to the printers of local newsletters or by the clerks in the provincial offices, who sell the latest issues of the *Gazette* to roving urban peddlers. The cheaply printed copies made available by either route become available to unauthorized readers all across the country. To lessen the risk of premature leaks, the court has imposed a time delay over the release of official news, but that is not always effective.

A solution to this quandary of how to combine some official involvement with the maintenance of secrecy often employed by Yongzheng is a direct and secret communication channel known as a "court letter." With his love for secrecy and efficiency, Emperor Yongzheng has developed this special device after a few years on the throne: When he feels that a court letter is the appropriate format, the emperor gives instructions to that effect to his three most trusted confidants at the highest level of the bureaucracy. Two of these men are Chinese career officials of exceptional loyalty and ability; the third is Emperor Yongzheng's own brother Yinxiang, the thirteenth son of the late emperor and eight years the current emperor's junior. (Because of his incorruptibility and his loyalty during the first difficult years of the succession struggles, Yinxiang is the only one of the royal brothers to have won Yongzheng's absolute confidence; he has been named a prince of the highest rank, and entrusted with virtually total control over the country's economy.) After receiving the emperor's oral instructions, the three men prepare a written version in the form of a court letter, and as soon as the emperor has approved the wording, they oversee the copying of the letter, and its distribution to a carefully monitored list of recipients. Thus several people can be reached at the same time, but confidentiality remains assured.

It is by this means, a court letter dated November 11, 1728, that the emperor informs a small number of senior provincial officials about the basic details of the emerging Zeng Jing case and of the strategy he has decided to follow. Along with the court letter, he sends each of them two attachments: one lists the names and locations of the thirteen conspirators, as divulged by the messenger in Xi'an; the second is a copy of General Yue's preliminary reports on the interrogation of the messenger Zhang Xi. The thirteen names will provide the focus for the second stage of the investigation, and they are accordingly subdivided by region. The emperor has decided that the three suspects identified as being residents of Nanjing or other cities in Jiangsu are to be rounded up and interrogated by the governor-general of the Yangzi provinces, an accomplished career official named Fan Shiyi. The Zhejiang names on the list will be handled by the governor-general of that province, Li Wei. It will also be Li Wei's responsibility to supervise the follow-up of all references to the Zhejiang-born Lü Liuliang's literary works, and to interrogate the surviving members of Lü's family, Lü Liuliang himself having died in 1683. Fan and Li Wei will work closely together, since their provinces share a common border.

Arresting the eight conspirators listed as living in Hunan province promises to be more complicated and more time-consuming. Not only is Hunan, the home base of the messenger Zhang Xi and his teacher Zeng Jing, the apparent center of the whole affair, it is also even farther away from Beijing than Jiangsu and Zhejiang; and the governor of Hunan, a man called Wang, is not an experienced senior administrator. Indeed, by an odd coincidence, he is the former supervisor of public morality for Zhejiang, only recently promoted to the Hunan post. Therefore the emperor decides to send Hailan, a Manchu military veteran who made his name long ago in the northwest wars of the 1690s, to serve in Hunan as a temporary imperial commissioner. It will be Hailan's responsibility to deliver the court letter in person to Governor Wang and thereafter to work alongside the governor in conducting the investigation.

By the evening of November 12, all three of these court letters are on their way. The documents for the governor-general of the Yangzi provinces, Fan Shiyi—whose office is in Nanjing, seven hundred and fifty miles to the southeast of Beijing and linked by a well-traveled route—are entrusted to mounted couriers from the Ministry of War. The Zhejiang governor-general, Li Wei, is headquartered in the city of Hangzhou, a distance of just over one thousand miles from Beijing, but in his case the logistics of communication turn out to be simpler. For Li Wei has recently sent a batch of confidential reports on various other matters to the emperor, and his own confidential courier, Colonel Tian, is at that moment in Beijing, waiting to take the reports and the emperor's endorsements back to his superior in Hangzhou. So it suffices to place the emperor's instructions, as relayed by the council of three in their court letter, along with the accompanying documents, inside a sealed wrapping, which in turn is locked inside the dispatch box carried by Colonel Tian. General Hailan carries the court letter and the backup documents in person, traveling on horseback, together with one of his trusted staff officers and a small entourage. They have the farthest to go, since it is just over twelve hundred miles to the Hunan capital of Changsha. There is no way for the emperor to gauge exactly how long each courier will take to reach his destination, but all of them will travel fast, and experience suggests that around ten days will be needed for the journeys to Nanjing and Hangzhou, and two weeks or a little more for Changsha. Assuming a week or so for each provincial investigation to get under way, and an equivalent stretch of time for the preliminary reports to be returned to Beijing, the emperor can expect it to be around a month before he receives any further substantive news on the case.

This enforced period of inactivity is broken on November 28, when Yongzheng receives the full version of Zeng Jing's treasonous letter, which he had ordered General Yue to send to him. General Yue's summary of the letter's contents and the few remarks about it that have been relayed from the messenger Zhang Xi have not prepared the emperor for the impact of the full document. It is not only the wildness of Zeng Jing's charges against him as both man and ruler that is astonishing, but also the remarkable range of apparently meticulous detail about the succession crisis of 1722, and the behavior at that time of the emperor and his brothers. The absurdity of Zeng Jing's arguments may be patent to the emperor, but they are phrased in an oddly convincing way; and if he is not simply to ignore them altogether, it will be necessary to produce counterarguments.

Within ten days of Yongzheng's receiving Zeng Jing's letter, his various reactions to it have taken on the outlines of a full and detailed rebuttal. As he notes at the beginning of his response, despite the range of the accusations he himself knows that his conscience is triply clear; in the light of Heaven, in the light of his late father, and before the many millions of people in China. But the vicious nature of the charges convinces him that Zeng Jing must have been drawing on some undisclosed sources; if he as emperor cannot track down those sources, and expose their basic fallacies to the world at large, then the ghostly miasma created by the conspirators' words will dominate the public mind. As a preliminary step to his end, he will start with the harshest of the charges: that he betrayed his own father by usurping the throne.

The more the emperor writes, the more he finds to say. He spells out the many occasions on which, before he ascended the throne, he showed his love and respect for his late father, Emperor Kangxi. He marshals the precise details of the days preceding his father's death, and the names and times that the other princes and imperial confidants attended his father as the end drew near. He describes the viciousness and recklessness of his brothers, both at that time and earlier, and describes how his father used to grieve over these princes' conduct, disowning some and bitterly criticizing others. He tells how his own decision to imprison several of his brothers sprang not from personal cruelty nor from a desire for revenge, but solely from his duties to his ancestors; and, far from seeking to kill the brothers who threatened him, he lavished the finest medical attention on them when they fell ill. Equally malicious and far from the truth were the stories that he had insulted his own mother and other senior palace women, or taken some of his brothers' consorts as his own: the emperor himself, and the many palace eunuchs who witnessed his visits, could testify to the dutiful conduct he displayed whenever he visited the women of the imperial family.

Turning to some of the other charges in Zeng Jing's letter, Yongzheng protests the charge that he is avaricious: What need has he for avarice when he has everything he needs in abundance? And how can he be accused of drinking to excess, he whose physical constitution makes it impossible for him to drink heavily, let alone to excess? Such charges came from misinterpreting the remarks of a general he had received in court audience who had worried over certain stories that were circulating about the emperor's health. In any case, writes Yongzheng, the ancient Chinese histories described how even the sage kings, Yao and Shun, enjoyed their drink, and the *Analects* recorded that Confucius himself drank without any inhibitions. Sex and women? From his childhood onward, the emperor observes, he never had much interest in sex, and in the years since he ascended the throne he has had only a few women serve him in the palace. Indeed "I have often said of myself there is no one in the country who dislikes sex as much as I do. I am one who truly believes in the phrase 'keep sex at a distance,' as the princes, the high officials, and my own personal retainers all know full well. Now there is this slander that I love sex: but what is this sex I am reported to love, and who are the people he says I dote on?" Other passages in the treasonous letter spread similar kinds of rumors that the emperor has betrayed many who worked for him with deep devotion—but to whom are they referring? To Nian Gengyao? Surely it is his brothers, not he himself, who are or have been guilty of all these acts as charged, and they or their eunuchs who have put the blame on him.

Nor is there any validity to Zeng Jing's arguments that the Manchus hate the Chinese and cause them misery. After all, it was not the Manchus but Chinese bandits who brought down the Ming dynasty and forced the last Ming emperor's suicide in 1644. Subsequently, it was the Manchus, although they had only around one hundred thousand troops, who destroyed the rebels and restored the country to order, bringing food to the people and peace to the towns. In all these labors, Chinese of good will worked alongside the Manchus. General Yue Zhongqi was just one example: a pillar of the nation, who in return had been rewarded with the highest office. It was the new Manchu rulers who gave continuity to the country by performing the sacrifices at the tombs of the former Ming emperors. It was the Manchus who offered famine relief when times were bad. One can see, writes the emperor, how in his letter Zeng Jing is twisting everything, even blaming the Manchus for the fire that badly damaged the Confucian temple. Yet one can also see, if one thinks historically, how the actions and writings of Zeng Jing and Zhang Xi, evil though they are, fit into the world of treasonous books and actions like those of the Zhejiang scholars Zha Siting and Wang Jingqi, or to the earlier Ming dynasty tradition of wild and reckless utterances pretending to pass as truth. But in the case of Zeng Jing at least, Heaven has been merciful, and has so arranged things that the full nature of Zeng Jing's thoughts has come to the emperor's attention. For that, one can only be grateful.

Once he has answered the specific charges in Zeng Jing's letter, the emperor returns to some of the broader considerations with which he began. There are a myriad people in the universe, he writes, who all share the simple rule that they respect their rulers and feel affection for their superiors; yet now comes this single rebel, with his ferocious nature, who alone "leaps beyond Heaven and earth, and cuts himself off from all the bonds, principles, and rules of human relationships." The lowest of creatures would never act as Zeng Jing has, "destroying the goodness of the nature with which Heaven endowed him." Logically, one would never believe that a single person could believe any of these wild charges, and yet "perhaps among the hundreds of millions of people there are one or two who do not understand the correct principles, and if they come across these rumors they may have their doubts aroused and be influenced by them. It is because of these people that I want to let the whole world know about this treacherous letter, and to tell them frankly about the goings-on at court, so that they understand them."

Yongzheng's final words on Zeng Jing's letter are more reflective than antagonistic, and reiterate his wish to share his thoughts with the country at large: "If I myself am making all this public because there is something that I don't have a clear conscience about, how would I be able to face my officials at court and in the provinces, or those who live across the country? Would I not then be using this document to deceive Heaven, deceive mankind, and deceive myself? I can say frankly that when I read this treasonous letter, I did not feel entirely angry—for because of these treasonous words I have gained a better understanding of the world. For several years now I have had no problems eating or sleeping; by keeping my heart both concerned and anxious about the ancestral altars and all living things, I have gained clarity about this world and about the future, and in the midst of my travails have attained great good fortune."

Obviously, to publicize the contents of Zeng Jing's letter along with these imperial responses will alert everyone to the conspiracy case, but the need for secrecy is now past. Hailan has reported his safe arrival in Changsha and outlined the steps he and Governor Wang Guodong have taken to arrest Zeng Jing and the other traitors. By now, as also in Jiangsu and Zhejiang, rounding up the suspects will have been completed, and in all three provinces the tough questioning will have begun. Yongzheng orders the Grand Secretariat staff to write out a fair copy of the thoughts he has drafted and they do so; the resulting document fills eighty-three pages. On the morning of December 11, he orders all the senior officials in Beijing—Manchu and Chinese, civilian and military—to assemble in the Forbidden City audience hall and has the document read aloud to them. That should take care of the treasonous letter for now. What happens next will depend on what he learns from the hunt under way in the provinces.

Three

The Messenger's Trail

Governor-general Fan is in his Nanjing office on the afternoon of November 23, when the Ministry of War courier arrives with the dispatch box wrapped in cloth of imperial yellow, containing the court letter. After making his ritual prostrations to Beijing, Fan reads through the letter and attachments and at once gets down to the business at hand. Though many of the details are still obscure, the basic structure of the task facing him is clear: the treasonous messenger Zhang Xi, after being interrogated in Xi'an, has produced a list of thirteen coconspirators (of whom Zhang himself is one). Three of the thirteen—two brothers called Che and a man named Sun—are listed as being residents of Jiangsu province, and thus fall under Fan's jurisdiction. Arresting those three is therefore Fan's responsibility.

Fan is a man of energy and determination, a member of the elite military unit called the Chinese Bordered Yellow Banner. The banner forces constitute the heart of the Qing dynasty's military establishment: there are eight banners in all, each identified by different borders and colors, and each subdivided according to the racial origins of the troops serving in them: Manchu, Mongol, and Chinese. Registration in a Chinese banner is an honor restricted to the descendants of those Chinese families that supported the Manchus during their conquest of China, and until recently Fan's career has been entirely in the military: he served as a company commander, regimental colonel, and general, before being transferred by the emperor into the civilian bureaucracy. Fan has never taken any of the literary examinations. Since he is a grandson of one of the most influential grand secretaries of the early Qing dynasty, son of a former president of the Ministry of War, and nephew of a famous patriot who gave his life to support the new dynasty during the massive rebellions of 1673, Fan's pedigree of loyalty is impeccable. Furthermore, in 1725 and 1726, as a garrison commander in north China, he was able to give Emperor Yongzheng invaluable information concerning the treasonous plans of some supporters of the emperor's feared and hated fourteenth brother. Perhaps for that reason, the emperor plucked Fan from his army post to be the acting governor-general of the three wealthy and populous Yangzi provinces of Jiangsu, Jiangxi, and Anhui, an astonishing promotion for a man with no other civilian administrative experience.

Fan's plan is straightforward and practical. By nightfall on the twenty-third, he has summoned a small group of trusted subordinates and army officers to his compound, divided them into two teams, and given them their orders. One team has an apparently simple task: all they have to do is go to the Che brothers' home within Nanjing, arrest the two men, and bring them in to the governor-general for questioning. The orders to the second team are slightly more complex: they are to travel to the city of Huaian, about one hundred miles north of Nanjing, to locate and arrest the man identified as Sun Keyong.

To the consternation of the Nanjing arrest squad, when they reach the Che residence they find only the older brother there; the younger brother has left home sometime before, escorting one of his daughters to the town where she is to be married. By an odd coincidence, that town is Huaian, for which the first squad of arresting officers has already departed. Determined to prevent this younger Che brother from escaping, Governor-general Fan rounds up the brother's family and has them sent under guard to Huaian, so they can help the arrest squad track him down.

So as not to waste time, Governor-general Fan summons the older Che brother to his compound. Following the same self-protective procedure that General Yue used in this case from the first moment, Fan has another senior official with him all the time, so there can be no talk of any kind of collusion with the arrested parties. Che Dingfeng is a scholar, he tells the interrogators, holder of the honorary "gongsheng" degree. Such a degree would entitle Che to study at the Imperial College in Beijing, should he so choose, but, as he tells his questioners, he prefers to spend his time at home in Nanjing, studying with his own brother.

The governor-general is quizzical: "So what fine books do you read? What important topics do you study? What special coterie of friends do you consort with?" When Che replies that he just proceeds in his own unclever and simple way, and consorts with few friends, Fan mocks his claims to simplicity, and asks what he knows about the man called Sun Keyong, described on the list of conspirators as a resident of Huaian. Again, calmly enough, Che replies that he did for a time have a man called Sun in his house as a tutor, but the man's name was Sun Yongke, not Sun Keyong, and his native place was Tongcheng in Anhui province, not Huaian. In any case the Sun whom he had hired turned out to be arrogant and impossible to get along with, so the Che family eased him out some time ago. Che has heard that Sun subsequently got a job tutoring for an official called Ren in Huaian, and maybe that is where the confusion about his native place springs from. Che has only seen Sun twice since then: once was last year, in the eighth month, when Sun came to pay his respects (rather late) at the birthday celebrations for Che's mother; the other was in the fall of the current year, when Sun stopped off at Nanjing on his way back to his native place of Tongcheng. Yes, a man called Zhang, from Anren county in Hunan, also dropped by during the birthday celebrations, though Che can not remember Zhang's full name.

Governor-general Fan guesses that the "official called Ren" is probably Ren Zongyan, an acquaintance who has recently retired to his home in Huaian after a career as a provincial administrator in Fujian. So for the third time he sends messengers to Huaian, this time to go to the Ren family compound and see if Sun is there. Given the size of the city of Huaian, and the ambiguity over Sun's real name, the first arrest party might have had difficulty locating their suspect. At the same time, to play it safe, Governor-general Fan sends a member of his staff to Tongcheng in Anhui province, about sixty miles to the northwest, to see if either a Sun Keyong or a Sun Yongke is registered as living there. If he is, he is to be arrested.

While waiting for his men to track down the younger Che brother and the tutor Sun, Governor-general Fan decides to make an exhaustive search of the Che family home in Nanjing. He goes in person, taking the judicial commissioner of the province with him, and they look through everything—"household utensils, pictures, registers, books, letters," as he itemizes them later to the emperor—in their hunt for subversive material. Their findings are slim, but useful. There are, for example, two bundles of miscellaneous documents, among which are ten unsigned poems. One of these poems, entitled "Occasional Writings for the New Year," contains the line "order comes out of chaos only if preordained by Heaven." This could perhaps be interpreted as an allegorical line belittling the emperor's powers as a ruler. But by far the most interesting discovery is the complete guest registration book for the birthday celebrations held in honor of the Che family matriarch, which took place in the eighth lunar month of the previous year. This guest registration list instantly confirms one major point: for there, clearly written, is the name of the messenger Zhang Xi, along with his courtesy name and the name of his native place, Anren county in Hunan province. This corroborates the messenger's own testimony about the timing of his visit to Nanjing the previous year, a visit that came after he had been to the Lü family's Zhejiang home to buy books. And, startlingly, among the roster of the various other guests who gathered for this auspicious occasion appear the names of the two Zhejiang province residents that Zhang Xi divulged just under a month before during his interrogation in Xi'an: one is a certain Yan Hongkui, described by the messenger Zhang as being "an expert in military strategy and firearms"; the other is a man called Shen, described by the messenger as being "Yan's disciple."

Pressed to explain the presence of these two men at his party, Che has a reasonable explanation: Yan has a reputation as a fine scholar, he tells Governor-general Fan, which was why they came to know him in the first place. Yan and the Che family used to exchange social visits on a fairly regular basis, so there was nothing surprising about his coming to the Che matriarch's birthday celebrations. It was because of this acquaintance that the Che brothers also hired Shen, one of Yan's former students, to be their family tutor. The messenger Zhang Xi, on the other hand, was quite a different case. The Che brothers hardly saw him at all in the lively bustle of the birthday celebrations. But because they shared Hunan roots with Zhang, because he was introduced by Yan and said he was in Nanjing to buy books, they let him stay with them for three days and then sent him on his way with a token gift of an ounce of silver for his travel expenses and some spare clothing. There was nothing more to it than that.

The younger Che brother, Che Dingben, who had taken his daughter off to Huaian to get married, is tracked down and brought back to Nanjing under arrest on December 2. The interrogators patiently take him over the same ground they have covered with his elder brother and his testimony replicates his elder brother's on almost every point. But in some instances the way that he answers questions already posed to his brother gives some new information to the interrogators. For instance, Che Dingben tells them that the Che brothers first met Sun Yongke, the tutor they hired the previous year and later fired for arrogance, in the house of Fang Bao. Anyone living in Nanjing in the 1720s, and remotely interested in literature, knows that Fang Bao, one of the country's most distinguished scholars, had been involved—almost fatally—in one of the most notorious cases of the previous reign. His mistake had been to write the preface for a historical collection that was later declared to contain treasonous materials. Condemned to death and then reprieved to spend years of exile in Manchuria, Fang Bao was finally pardoned, and came to live in retirement in Nanjing, although his native place, like Sun's, was Tongcheng. Che Dingben also confirms that the arrogant tutor Sun did go to Huaian to teach for the Ren family, but he adds that the interrogators will not find Sun there anymore: in the late summer of the present year Sun developed such a bad case of dysentery that he had to give up his job and returned to Tongcheng, his native place, to recuperate.

Che Dingben tenaciously and angrily denies that he ever had any contact with the messenger Zhang Xi, except for the most fleeting one at the time of his mother's birthday—he had never seen him before or since, and certainly never corresponded with Zhang, or plotted anything untoward.

He sticks to these denials, as does his brother, even when they are both put to the torture on December 6. He reiterates the line others have used: Why on earth should he scheme to work against an emperor known to be so virtuous? When challenged to explain why his name is on the suspects' list provided by Zhang Xi in Xi'an, Che Dingben erupts angrily: "At the time Zhang Xi came here he was just an aimless drifter with no roots. I certainly never got to like him, but I had no reason to hate him. He was just a vagrant wandering from place to place, and who later on wrote down the names of anyone he had met, completely at random, regardless of whether he knew their correct names or not." Zhang's muddle over tutor Sun's personal name and native place is typical of the man. If the interrogating officials do not believe him, why not send him to Hunan so he can confront Zhang Xi directly?

Che Dingben is right about tutor Sun. He is not in Huaian at all, but is arrested by the authorities in Tongcheng, and sent back to Nanjing under armed guard, arriving on December 8. Sun is indeed desperately ill with dysentery, a detail the governor-general's staff check carefully and enter in the official files. Nevertheless they proceed to interrogate him, as harshly as his condition permits, though Sun has little to add to what they already know. His true name is Sun Yongke, he says, and he has never heard of any Sun Keyong. When he was teaching at the Che house, he never ran into Zhang Xi, nor did he have any idea how Zhang came up with his name, even in a garbled version. He knew Lü Liuliang's former student Yan fairly well, for Yan came to visit the Che family quite often, but he knew nothing about Yan's alleged mastery of texts on military strategy and firearms. Since they overlapped as tutors in the Che family for some time, he of course knew Shen, though they were never close. When the interrogators show him a copy of the poem they have discovered, with the potentially treasonous line, Sun tells them that it is certainly written in Shen's calligraphy, though he has no idea who wrote the original poem. As to the topographical maps and books on astronomy that the authorities confiscated when they raided his home in Tongcheng, Sun observes, they were not arcane works, but ones publicly printed that he had bought less than a year before.

Despite lingering doubts about the disparities between this Sun's name and the one on the original list, Governor-general Fan concludes in the report he sends to the emperor on December 11 that he has decided to keep Sun under arrest. He is also holding the two Che brothers, and can certainly send them to Hunan to confront the conspirators there if the emperor thinks that is a good idea. It turns out that there is a third Che brother, older than the other two, who had previously been the educational commissioner of Fujian and is now living in retirement in Nanjing. But since this third Che is not on the original list and is not known to be implicated in the case in any way, they are leaving him alone for now.

The emperor makes no interlinear comments on the report itself, but at the conclusion he shares some brief thoughts with Fan: "Noted. The ringleaders of these criminals are all in Hunan, and I have recently sent a special imperial commissioner to that region to investigate. If you get hold of suspects from the Jiangsu area who are connected with this case, check them out quickly, cautiously, and secretly. Don't let them get away and cause further trouble."

Li Wei, the governor-general of Zhejiang, receives his copy of the court letter and the appended list of conspirators' names just one day after Fan, in the late evening of November 24, at his office compound in Hangzhou, on China's east coast. Though the emperor apparently has full confidence in Fan, he trusts Li Wei even more, and in an unusual gesture, prompted by the amount of banditry in the shared border of the regions administered by the two men, Li Wei has been given oversight of criminal arrests within the southern areas of Fan's own jurisdiction. The implication is that Fan is overextended by having to supervise the business of three different provinces, whereas Li Wei only has the single province of Zhejiang to administer, and thus has some time to spare to help his colleague.

In terms of trustworthiness, there seems to be nothing to separate the two men. Like Fan, Li is an efficient man, tough and tenacious, capable of rapid action. Now close to forty, tall and pockmarked, he is a career official who (like both General Yue and Governor-general Fan) has never sat for the examinations, but obtained his first post by purchase and rose quickly in the Beijing bureaucracy. Emperor Yongzheng spotted Li's abilities early in his reign, and sent him down to the southwest frontier province of Yunnan, with instructions not only to handle problems with the indigenous border peoples but also to report secretly on the activities of the Yunnan governor, whose loyalty the emperor doubted. Recalled from Yunnan and promoted to be governor of Zhejiang just at the time the emperor was coming to hate the province, Li Wei behaved sensibly and effectively, working without rancor alongside the newly appointed supervisor of public morality. When Li Wei fell ill for a period, so greatly was his work valued that the emperor insisted he send the eight characters of his birth horoscope to Beijing, so that experts there could calculate his chances for survival. The reading must have been encouraging, since shortly afterward Li Wei was given the title of Zhejiang governor-general, an unusual promotion that vaulted him to the uppermost levels in the bureaucracy.

Li Wei's task in Zhejiang is more complex than Fan's in Jiangsu; though he only has two named suspects from the original list to arrest—the one called Yan and the one called Shen—he also has an amorphous and overlapping assignment: nothing less than to round up an entire literary tradition, the scholarly legacy of Lü Liuliang, and to assess the depth to which Lü and his family have been spreading an anti-Manchu message, along with the extent to which the messenger Zhang Xi became enmeshed with them the previous year. Like Governor-general Fan the day before, Li Wei takes the challenge in stride as he reads the court letter, makes his own assessment of the situation, and summons a small group of trusted staff to his compound for consultations.

What doubtless gives Li Wei confidence as he prepares to move in on the family and library of Lü Liuliang is that he has handled an assignment rather similar to this two years before, in November 1726. He was new to the Zhejiang governorship then, having served only a year, when he received an urgent edict from Emperor Yongzheng. The edict informed him that an official from one of Zhejiang's most prominent families, Zha Siting, a brilliant scholar and career bureaucrat, currently serving as the chief examiner for the province of Jiangxi, had just been arrested on charges of treason. Zha's crime was that in one of the examination questions on the classical text *The Great Learning* he had told the students to comment on a phrase in Book One, Section Three, "where the people rest." Anyone could see, the charge ran, that this was not an innocent textual choice; for if one juxtaposed the first and the last characters of the four-character phrase, one came up with two characters that were recognizable as the reign name of the current emperor, but in each case missing the top stroke.

Zha Siting, in other words, had been luring the students to think of be-heading their emperor. Officials were methodically sorting through all the books and possessions that Zha had taken with him for his assignment as chief examiner, in search of incriminating evidence. The secret orders to Li Wei were that he should go at once to Zha's ancestral home in the north-ern Zhejiang river town of Haining and have it methodically searched for any traces of seditious works.

Li Wei obeyed the orders at once, learning not only how to cope with the unexpected—when the search party arrived at Zha's home it was night, a heavy-drinking party was in full swing, and a number of boats were moored outside the home's water entrance—but also how a search for in-criminating papers should be conducted: not only in the bookshelves and boxes of manuscripts, but in the table drawers, in crates and baskets, in the clothes stored in chests and cupboards, in the angles and corners of furni-ture and beds, in bowls and in bottles. By these means, the emperor an-nounced in a congratulatory edict, Governor Li Wei, along with the teams in Jiangxi, had found two volumes of "seditious and absurd diaries," along with answers to possible examination questions, written in tiny letters, tucked into the armpits of stored clothing, and complete sets of the key ex-amination texts written in equally small writing, presumably ready to be given to Zhejiang students so that they could excel in the exams. Zha's di-ary entries were found to be crammed with sarcastic remarks about the uselessness and sycophancy of the Confucian scholars training for the bu-reaucracy in the Beijing academies, and Zha had invented mocking alter-native phrases for their pompous-sounding official titles. In combination, these various kinds of texts, large and small, were taken to show the con-tempt Zha Siting felt for the scholarly world of his times, and for the cur-rent emperor and his late father, whose judgments on cultural and judicial matters Zha often mocked. The emperor ordered Zha's execution, but since Zha had died in prison during interrogation the sentence was changed to the desecration of his corpse and the exile and enslavement of his entire family.

Coming so soon after the discovery in Governor-general Nian Gengyao's home of the ribald and sardonic *Casual Notes* of Wang Jingqi, this event confirmed the emperor in his loathing of Zhejiang as a province. It was in retaliation for the contempt those writers had shown that he declared the entire province "degenerate," appointed a supervisor of public morality to bring Zhejiang back onto the right path, and forbade any students from Zhejiang to take the next round of the triennial national examinations. The emperor meant what he said, and in the examinations of 1727 not a single student from Zhejiang received the desperately coveted senior degree, compared to the thirty-five from the province who had passed in 1724. Though this entire episode thus damaged the province badly, it did nothing but good to Li Wei's own career.

As a result of the experience he gained at that time, Li Wei can now be clear-headed about the fact that Lü Liuliang is apparently being added by the emperor to a list of Zhejiang malcontents that already includes the monk Yinian, the writer Wang Jingqi, and examiner Zha. The messenger Zhang Xi, in Xi'an only a few weeks before, has mentioned several titles of poems and books by Lü Liuliang that he acquired on his Zhejiang journey in 1727: *Notes to Myself, Literary Works of Master Lü,* "Song of the Pines at Qian's Tomb," and "Songs of the Rivers and Mountains." General Yue, in one of the original secret reports that has now been copied and sent to Li Wei, summarized the testimony he had received from the messenger about the writings of Lü Liuliang and urged the emperor to instruct Li Wei to make the most thorough search possible of the Lü family homes so that nothing treasonous could any longer be hidden. Now that those suggestions have been transposed into orders directly from the emperor, Li Wei cannot afford to let the originals of these or any similar works be destroyed by members of Lü's family.

Late in the evening of November 24, 1728, directly after receiving the court letter and the accompanying documents from Beijing, Li Wei sends out orders summoning to his Hangzhou office three local officials whom he knows and trusts. Two of them are army officers, and the third is a magistrate from the same prefecture where the Lü family residences are located, in the town of Shimen on the Grand Canal. Li outlines the double task ahead and clarifies the basic priorities: there are two people on the list they have to arrest, named Yan and Shen, who live in the town of Huzhou some forty miles to the northwest. That task should be comparatively easy, though the list describes Yan as "an expert in military strategy and firearms," which might possibly cause difficulties for the arresting team. The other man, Shen, is described simply as "Yan's disciple."

At the same time, Li Wei's men have to effect an entry into the Lü family compound in Shimen, also about forty miles from Hangzhou, but to the northeast. Since in this case they are after manuscripts as well as people, and manuscripts can be swiftly destroyed, either with fire or with water, the governor-general cannot afford to run the risk of openly surrounding the Lü family home with a group of soldiers and official retainers, for that might alert those within to the impending danger. Instead, the arrest team should use a pattern of deception, which Li Wei spells out for them: before arriving at the Lü residence, the arresting officers should conceal their official ranks; once there, they should identify themselves as representatives from the court historiography office in Beijing, on a mission to make up certain gaps in the imperial collection. They should add that they have been authorized to pay cash awards for certain rare titles, and are particularly anxious to obtain two books, Lü Liuliang's *Notes to Myself* and the same author's *Literary Works of Master Lü*. Once inside the house, and given access to the library, they should express interest in seeing any other rare manuscripts or editions that the family might have stored away. Only when they have done this and are sure where all the manuscripts are kept, should they announce their true identities, and arrest the people in the house, and then bring them back to the governor-general's official compound for questioning.

Yan and Shen are arrested in Huzhou without any difficulties, and Colonel Wu, the senior member of the investigative team, reports back almost at once that the rest of the plan has worked beautifully. His group reached the main Lü residence on November 26 and were greeted by two of Lü Liuliang's sons, along with several grandsons and in-laws. Having explained their scholarly mission, they were welcomed into the house, where they were shown two volumes of Lü's *Notes to Myself* and two different collections of Lü's literary works, which had been assembled and published by members of the family. But that was not all: there were three volumes of other literary works by Lü Liuliang, for which the printing blocks had not yet been carved, along with batches of unpublished poems and various works on ritual practices, including a daily record of the family's implementation of the rites. There were also six volumes of Lü's miscellaneous journals and diaries. Secure in the knowledge that the arrest group had prevented the destruction of the key materials, Colonel Wu impounded all the written material and sealed off the library. The various adult male members of the Lü family on the premises—seven in all—were arrested and were now being brought to Hangzhou for questioning.

It turns out that the two sons of Lü Liuliang who welcomed Colonel Wu to the family library are the only ones of Lü Liuliang's nine sons still living. Li Wei interrogates them immediately. At each session, he has with him his Zhejiang second-in-command, who in the absence of one of his colleagues is serving as both the financial and the judicial commissioner of the province. This fellow-interrogator, though junior to Li Wei in the bureaucracy, is even closer to the emperor: he has served in the imperial household on a number of confidential assignments, and his daughter is a junior consort of the emperor's favorite son.

The elder of Lü Liuliang's surviving sons is not helpful. He was the fourth of his father's sons, he tells the interrogators, and he is sixty-eight years old. "I am an elderly man, and childless. Since there is nothing I am any good at doing, I just stay at home. Last year, in the eighth lunar month, a man from Hunan called Zhang Xi did come to our house, to take a look at my father's surviving writings. Since my ninth brother, Lü Yizhong, had him to stay here, I saw him a few times, but our conversation was inconsequential, and there was no rebellious talk."

This younger brother, the ninth son of Lü Liuliang, is full of information for his questioners. He confirms that his father died forty-five years ago, on October 3, 1683, and that his father's grandfather had, long before, married a woman from a collateral branch of the Ming dynasty ruling house. Lü Liuliang formally enrolled in the state Confucian school in 1654, but failed to pass the annual qualifying exams in 1666, and hence lost his official student status. Despite this disappointment his father always continued to study, and his reputation as an acute expert in the field of Confucian moral philosophy spread far beyond Zhejiang. And despite Lü Liuliang's own failure within the official examination system, he steered all his sons who reached maturity (his fifth and eighth sons died in childhood) successfully to obtain the basic-level licentiate's degree. Twenty-three years after Lü Liuliang had died, his eldest son brought honor on the entire family by obtaining the highest degree; he was placed—as proof of his scholarly brilliance—second in the top class among all the competing students in the nation. This eldest son was immediately appointed to the

Hanlin Academy—the government research center in Beijing for the study of the Confucian classics—but died of illness less than two years later. None of the other Lü brothers were able to rise so high.

The surviving members of the Lü family all know the extent of Lü Liuliang's reputation, the ninth son continues, which is why they were not surprised that Zhang Xi should come all the way from Hunan asking to see Lü's books and manuscripts. Many years before, Lü Liuliang had established a bookshop, the Firmament Bookstore, and his descendants had kept it going. It was there that they sold printed editions of some of Lü's works, though they had never carved the printing blocks for Lü's collected poetry, nor had they published his diaries. But they did sometimes show those manuscripts to visitors, as they had done in the case of Zhang Xi. They had also given Zhang Xi the name and address of their father's one surviving student, Yan Hongkui, since Zhang had said he would like to meet someone who had studied with Lü Liuliang. The interrogators know that Yan Hongkui is one of the thirteen people on their list, and that he has already been arrested.

What of four specific books, Li Wei asks, what of the *Notes to Myself*, *Literary Works of Master Lü*, and the poetry collections containing "Song of the Pines at Qian's Tomb" and "Songs of the Rivers and Mountains"? What was their exact provenance, and how were they distributed? All Lü Liuliang's manuscripts led a wandering life over the last forty or more years, replies the ninth son. They were borrowed by local scholars, or copied by married relatives of the family, some of whom wrote their own prefaces or changed the contents around. There were two variant versions of the *Notes to Myself*, for instance, one of which was edited by friends and relatives locally, the second of which was created out of Lü Liuliang's own diaries by Lü's former student Yan Hongkui, who lived in Huzhou and kept his own copies of his edition in his own home. The *Literary Works of Master Lü* had been compiled by outsiders, who paid for the printing blocks themselves and also gave the author the fulsome title "Master Lü," something the family itself would never have presumed to do.

But there were other manuscript copies of the same collected works also in circulation. The two poems Li Wei mentioned were written by Lü Liuliang long ago, and had been circulated in a celebrated anthology of poetry compiled in the 1670s by one of Lü's friends. That same friend, incidentally, was one of those who had worked at editing Lü's *Notes to Myself*. "I just want to point out," the ninth son tells his interrogators, "that when the officials came to us, everyone in our household, all my brothers' sons and their in-laws, were either serving this dynasty as officials, or else studying for the exams; none of us has shown a trace of unorthodox views. It was just that when Zhang Xi came to see the books we had at home, I improperly let him see some of my father's draft poems along with his diary. That is why I deserve the death penalty." Neither of the interrogators contradicts him.

The picture here of a respectable scholarly family, struggling to make a decent life under the Qing dynasty, is reinforced by the interrogation of the oldest surviving grandson of Lü Liuliang. The eldest son of the eldest son—it was his father who performed so brilliantly in the exams of 1706 and died so tragically two years later—Lü Yili tells the interrogators of the hard-earned degree as a senior licentiate that he had just been awarded in 1723. It was a degree he had never really expected to attain, since the year after his father's death he had been accused of being an accomplice in the Ming loyalist uprising led by Yinian, who claimed to be a descendant of the last Ming emperor. Lü Yili tells the interrogators how in 1708 his house was regularly searched, and he was constantly questioned about his ancestor's earlier marriage into the Ming family, and about his own deceased father's possible involvement in the uprising. But even when questioned by an imperial commissioner sent from Beijing to suppress the upheaval, Lü Yili always refused to admit to things he had not done. Finally, he was confronted face-to-face with the captured false claimant and was questioned under torture, but he managed to convince the court that he had never met the man. He subsequently received a complete pardon. Ever since then he had been working at his studies. He knew nothing of Zhang Xi, and had not been in the house when Zhang came calling: "When I got back, people told me it was my ninth uncle Lü Yizhong who saw him and invited him to stay. As to what those two talked about, I have not the faintest idea."

Going to the back files in the governor-general's Hangzhou office, Li Wei finds the official affidavit written in 1708 by a Manchu special commissioner named Mudan. In that document, Mudan wrote that he was convinced Lü Yili was not lying, and ordered him cleared of all charges.

Perhaps sensing some resentment of his ninth uncle in Lü Yili's closing remark, or some hint of a willingness to cooperate with the enquiry, Li Wei acts on a hunch: he has one of his staff escort the grandson back to the family library in Shimen, where the books and manuscripts have all been placed under seal for security, to make a further search. Sifting through the materials, Lü Yili produces a draft copy of his grandfather's poems, along with more volumes of his grandfather's diary.

In addition to interrogating the three senior members of the Lü family, Li Wei has also been questioning the two listed suspects, Yan and Shen. Yan Hongkui proves to be a cooperative witness. He tells the interrogators he is seventy-four years old and is a holder of the licentiate's degree; he never advanced to a higher degree, though two of his nephews both attained the topmost literary degree, *jinshi,* and are serving as officials. Yan's story of how his name came to be on the list of coconspirators seems convincing enough: "I have no sons or grandsons, and live at home, where I teach and practice medicine. I knew nothing whatever about Zeng Jing, but in the eighth month of 1727 a Hunan man named Zhang Xi came to my place from the Lü home in a search for any books by my teacher Lü Liuliang, or for former students of his. He said he wanted to study with me, and that he was a disciple of Zeng Jing, a teacher in Hunan, who had about twenty students there, and was known as the master of Putan. Zhang Xi drew parallels between his teacher and Confucius." Though Zhang Xi expressed his eagerness to study with Yan, particularly the sayings of Confucius, and such classical texts as *The Book of Changes* and *The Supreme Ultimate,* Yan was not impressed: "I could see that his scholarship was mediocre, and could not refrain from making some rather cutting comments."

Yan testifies that on the eleventh day of the eighth lunar month, Zhang Xi said he had to move on to Nanjing, to visit a friend. Perhaps glad to be rid of him, but also pushed by the logic of hospitality, Yan told his visitor that one of his former students named Shen was in fact in Nanjing at the time, teaching in the home of two brothers called Che. Since the Che family were originally from Hunan province and had moved to Nanjing not too long before, Yan supposed they would receive Zhang warmly. Yan also, he tells his interrogators, thought it would be good for Zhang Xi to get some sense of what good scholarship was really like, and this former student of his would be just the person to show him. Nothing in any of these conversations was in any way treasonous, or even controversial, said Yan. He and Zhang just talked about texts and about interpretive problems at the level at which Zhang could sustain such a discussion. Yan himself, he wanted his interrogators to know, had always been loyal to the dynasty. Indeed, in 1723, the first year of the current emperor's reign, he had been invited by one of the grand secretaries to take a job in the Beijing editorial offices where a group of scholars were currently working to compile the official history of the fallen Ming dynasty. Only the sudden onset of a serious illness had prevented him from going.

Li Wei is always thorough. Though there is no particular reason to doubt Yan's story, he has his subordinates check through Yan's engagement diary for the year 1727; there they do find a reference to the arrival of Zhang Xi on the fifth day of the eighth lunar month, and his departure on the eleventh. They also track through the files in the Zhejiang governor's office, until they find a report from the then governor to the Ministry of Rituals, stating that Yan Hongkui was unfortunately too sick to take on the Beijing editorial assignment. As far as anyone can tell, Yan's knowledge of the military arts comes entirely from classical texts, and he has no personal experience of warfare.

The student Shen, of whom Yan spoke so warmly and whose name is also one of the thirteen on the original list, is interrogated immediately after his teacher. His full name is Shen Zaikuan, and it is true he was teaching at the Che home in Nanjing in the eighth month of the previous year, when Zhang Xi came to call. Since Zhang Xi carried a note of introduction from Shen's former teacher, of course Shen received him cordially, as did the Che brothers. But it did not take Shen long to see that Zhang Xi was not in any way a serious scholar—his remarks about philosophical principles made little sense, and when asked to support them with quotations from classical texts he was quite unable to do so. When it was obviously time for Zhang Xi to depart, Shen gave him a handful of copper coins— worth about a third of an ounce of silver—along with a couple of poems he thought Zhang would be interested in.

But these fleeting contacts, Shen protests, do not mean the two men talked about anything treasonous. Why on earth should they do so? Shen has been a stipendiary student of the government for over twenty years, and he expects to accomplish great things. It is true that when searched he had several books on astronomy and geography in his possession, along with some on medicine, but these were topics he enjoyed studying; they had no especial practical applications. Shen knows—as does Yan—that the men who arrested them have searched their homes thoroughly and have removed quantities of their draft writings, diaries, poems, and casual essays, as well as more polished works and a wide selection of works by Lü Liuliang. Li Wei also tells Shen to write out from memory the two poems he gave to Zhang on his visit the previous year, and enters Shen's renderings in the official file on the case.

Li Wei completes this batch of interrogations by December 2, 1728, and by the next day has prepared a summary of all the salient points in the form of a lengthy report, which he sends off to the emperor in the care of another of his staff officers, Colonel Huang. On the problems of the literary and philosophical implications of all these texts they are discovering, Li Wei tells the emperor, he is not enough of a scholar to comment with any precision. But from what he has seen so far, a good many of the allegedly dangerous writings do not seem very different from those produced by many scholars, including the most distinguished ones, over the previous several centuries. The most important difference might be that these scholars from the Lü family, along with their friends and former students, seem to have been using their scholarly investigations of philosophical principles as a cover for exploring and spreading their own disruptive ideas, rather than attempting to advance the moral level of the people as a whole.

Three days after dispatching his report, Li Wei makes a supplementary decision: he takes the five suspects who seem to him the most potentially dangerous—Lü Liuliang's two surviving sons, Lü's oldest grandson, Lü's last surviving student, Yan, and Yan's favorite student, Shen—and sends them off, tightly bound and under a special military escort, to Beijing, so that they can be reexamined by the ministerial staff there. And with the five men he sends a broad selection of their written works, both printed and in manuscript, along with various other writings found in their possession.

But, as Li Wei tells the emperor in a follow-up report, it is impractical to send all the other members of the Lü family he has located along to Beijing at the same time, since the numbers are constantly increasing as he tracks down more and more of them: initially he identified seven, but that number has already swelled to twenty-three, living in seven adjacent households. These numbers do not include those who have left the clan home for some reason as children, and now live elsewhere. Instead of being sent to Beijing, these other family members will all be kept under guard in Zhejiang, along with their families and their property, until Li Wei receives further instructions from the emperor. Similarly, the number of books accumulated in the Lü family library is unfortunately so huge that there is no possibility of sending them all to Beijing. Instead, Li Wei has ordered the local magistrate to head up a four-man team to go methodically through everything. The published classical and historical texts would be screened and stored away under seal. Once the survey and inventory are completed, the various other draft manuscripts that are emerging would be handed to the governor-general, and he would peruse them in person, before sending them on to the emperor in Beijing.

Li Wei is on a boat, checking out problems of river conservancy and flood control, when an imperial courier from Beijing catches up with him, bringing two new packages from the capital. One is a special present of the most coveted of informal imperial gifts, a batch of the celebrated musk melons from Hami, an oasis town on the farthest western edge of the Chinese domains in central Asia. The second is another of the special imperial dispatch boxes, covered in yellow silk. Inside is a copy of the whole of Zeng Jing's treasonous letter, in the exact form it was presented to General Yue in Xi'an just over six weeks before. It is not untypical of Emperor Yongzheng, when he is grateful to a trusted official for serving him well, to send special gifts as a way of expressing his gratitude. But in this case the symbolism behind the double present is particularly apt: in one box, the sweetest taste that the country has to offer; in the other, the pure and uncensored version of treason's darkest face.

Four

In Hunan

General Hailan, carrying with him the emperor's court letter and the list of suspects, enters the Hunan capital of Changsha in the early afternoon of November 28. Passing through the massive gates into the inner walled city, he makes his way at once to the official residence of the Hunan governor, and after the necessary formalities they move into a detailed discussion of the task ahead of them. The challenges are considerable. They have seven suspects to track down, and Hunan is a huge province. It is, also, as soon as one leaves the prosperous Changsha region and heads down to the south, in many ways a wild frontier province: a place of fast streams and narrow valleys, where steep forested hills blend imperceptibly into massive mountain ranges, of almost inaccessible small market towns and isolated villages, of great tracts of sparsely farmed upland where the indigenous Miao peoples make their home. And according to the information yielded up by Zhang Xi during his interrogations in Xi'an—that being the only indicator of the probable whereabouts of the conspirators available to Hailan and Governor Wang—both the chief conspirator, Zeng Jing, and the incriminated members of the Zhang family are all down in the mountainous southeast of the province, where the going is roughest.

The geographical details are naturally central to the two officials' planning. Like the other provinces of China, Hunan is divided up into circuits and prefectures, each containing a number of separate counties controlled by state-appointed magistrates. The counties in turn are subdivided into scores of smaller administrative zones, under the nominal supervision of the heads of the local tax collection agencies; and in each of those subdistricts one finds clusters of small villages, watched over by headmen appointed to supervise local security. According to the documents brought to Changsha by General Hailan, the chief conspirator, Zeng Jing, lives in Yongxing county, in a village called Putan. The standard records of all the Hunan counties, on file in Changsha, show Hailan and Governor Wang that Yongxing is around 190 miles from Changsha, if one takes the land route. The journey by water, even if appearing easier on paper, is in fact far longer, due to the rivers' meanderings—over 350 miles in all—and is, besides, upstream, for the main rivers here all flow northward, up to the Yangzi River and its tributaries.

Yongxing county is further subdivided into twenty wards, and though the village of Putan is not itself marked on the local maps, the indications are that it lies in the mountainous nineteenth ward, situated in the northeastern part of the county. This particular ward is over twenty-five miles of hard traveling from the county town of Yongxing, but within easy reach of Anren county, home to the messenger Zhang Xi and his family. The military garrison in Yongxing is small, only fifty soldiers commanded by a single sublieutenant, and the few soldiers stationed there are likely to be poorly trained locals, scattered in ones or twos at road junctions, river crossings, and rural markets. They would hardly be of much use in quelling a major insurrection, and there is no guarantee they would not spread the word about any impending government forays into their area. Clearly, other troops will have to be brought in from the main provincial garrisons, and close liaison established with the magistrate of Yongxing as the noose around Zeng Jing is tightened.

The Anren county home of the Zhang family is easier to pinpoint.

During his interrogation by General Yue, the conspirator Zhang Xi not only stated that his whole family were living in the Anren village of Pengtang—where Zeng Jing taught school for many years—but gave a precise location for his home village that would make it easy to find: Pengtang, he testified, lay on the axis between the county town of Anren and the neighboring town of Ling to the southeast, being forty miles from Anren and seven from Ling. To the officials planning the roundup of the conspirators, however, the closeness of this village to Zeng Jing's home suggests other possible problems: even if neither Zeng Jing nor the other members of the Zhang family are yet aware of Zhang Xi's arrest and interrogation in Xi'an—that news has been made available only to a handful of senior officials—the transcripts of Governor Yue's reports to the emperor show clearly that Zhang Kan, the cousin who accompanied Zhang Xi on his teacher's orders, ran away from Xi'an in a panic. He may well be almost home in Anren by now, ready to share the news of the disastrous escapade with his family. In any case, news of an arrest party striking in Putan will be hard to conceal from villagers in Pengtang, and vice versa.

By nine o'clock in the evening of November 28, Hailan and Governor Wang have come up with a plan of action and a division of responsibilities. The seven suspects they have been ordered to arrest live in three different parts of the province—four in the southeast, two in the far south, and one in northern Hunan, in the Dongting Lake flatlands, near the Yangzi River. But even though Zeng and the three Zhangs are living so near each other that a single arrest squad might snare them all, given their importance to the case Hailan and the governor decide it is safer to appoint two teams to round them up, and so they assemble four arresting teams in all. One squad, assigned to arrest Zeng Jing himself, at his home in Yongxing county, will be commanded by Captain Han, the staff officer whom general Hailan brought with him from Beijing; this officer will be accompanied in his assignment by the adjutant-major of the Hunan governor's garrison forces, as well as by the acting head of the department in which both Yongxing and Anren are located. The other squads are to be led by teams of equivalent rank and prestige drawn from the Hunan civil and military establishments, the most prominent official among them being the prefect of Changsha, who leads the group sent to arrest the members of Zhang Xi's family.

The following four days are occupied in putting together the pieces of this plan, in moving men into position, and in ascertaining that it is both safe and feasible to proceed with the resources the governor has available. Some nervousness is not surprising, since as far as Hailan and Governor Wang can tell from the information made available to them in Zhang Xi's preliminary confessions, Hunan is a province wracked with problems, suffused with discontent, where unknown numbers of people are awaiting the call to arms. Other potential dangers are lurking: there are rumors about the popularity in the region of Buddhist "White Lotus" teachings, which can galvanize people with their religious message of imminent salvation; there may be followers of esoteric and mystical Daoist practices, who believe in the overlays of quietism and social activism and whose movements and emotions are hard to anticipate. And there are those indigenous Miao tribesmen spread across many areas of the province, and the renegade Chinese who live among them.

By December 1, the plan is operational: the squad assigned to arrest the conspirator in northern Hunan has coordinated its moves with the regional military commander of the Dongting Lake garrison; and the three squads that will be operating in the south and southeast have shared their plans with the military commander in Hengzhou, a city south of Changsha, where a sizable garrison of provincial troops is stationed. The orders issued by the governor leave little to chance: "meticulous search and arrest" in each area will be achieved by "strong military force." The governor has also sent secret instructions to the magistrates in each of the four counties where the conspirators are believed to be residing, as well as to the magistrates of the counties adjacent to them: they are told to put whatever troops they have on alert, either for local defense, should insurrection break out, or to deal with any accomplices of the conspirators who might suddenly appear. Especially important here is the magistrate of Yongxing county, a career civilian official from Shandong named Dai; holder of the second-highest examination degree, Dai has already won a reputation for administrative ability and for solving difficult cases, including those involving homicide. A courier is sent to brief him on the case, and he at once makes preparations to prevent Zeng Jing's escape.

In the event, perhaps influenced by local conditions of which we have no record, but most probably because Pengtang village is more accessible to troops than Putan, the decision is made to arrest the Zhang family on December 2 and to move against Zeng Jing two days later, once all the Zhangs have been successfully rounded up. The first task proves simple enough, and the Zhangs are surrounded and captured without any struggle. This despite the fact that their cousin Zhang Kan, after his headlong flight back south from Xi'an, had arrived home in Pengtang just the day before, and surely must have been queried on his adventures by his clansmen. But if he was, no one heeded him, and in any case he would have had no knowledge of Zhang Xi's torture and confession, which took place some days after his flight. Once all the Zhangs have been rounded up, the three principal suspects—the messenger's father, cousin, and elder brother—are shipped off to Changsha under heavy guard. The other family members are held in the Anren county prison, their property is sealed off, and the local officials begin an intensive search through the Zhangs' manuscripts and possessions.

The squad deputed to arrest Zeng Jing is in position at Putan village in Yongxing county by December 4, and their operation is equally swift and trouble-free. But it might well not have been so, since alone among all the suspects in the conspiracy, Zeng Jing seems to have anticipated his own arrest and to have made at least a rhetorical gesture of resistance. Perhaps, despite the careful government security, he heard something of the unusual troop movements in the area, or of the arrest of the Zhang family. Perhaps someone told him that Zhang Xi's cousin had just reached home in Anren county after fleeing from Xi'an, perhaps it was just a fatalistic awareness that something had gone badly wrong with his plans. According to one of the officers, Zeng cried out, "The Master of Putan dies here," as the raiding force entered his house: apparently he was determined to commit suicide, or to be cut down in the attempt. But as Hailan reported to the emperor later, "It was as if Heaven itself took away his will to act." The arresting officers also note that Zeng Jing has adorned his clothes with matching couplets of calligraphy, and when he is searched they find other texts written on his undergarments, in which (using an alternate name for his native village) he calls himself "the one who has brought the Way to Baitan." Such writings are often inscribed on the inside of burial garments by those anticipating death, so that they can be correctly identified in the underworld.

But Zeng Jing neither takes his own life nor is himself harmed. Instead, his family—including his mother and his sons (his wife is already dead from illness some time before)—are arrested and held in prison by Magistrate Dai, and their now empty house is sealed. Zeng himself is taken, under heavy guard, to the provincial capital. The arresting party required only three or four days to reach his home, but they take eleven days for the journey back to Changsha, alert to any attempt his followers may make to release him. Again, nothing happens, and by the time Zeng is brought in to the provincial capital, the other suspects have all been rounded up and their interrogations are under way.

As soon as Zeng Jing reaches Changsha, Hailan and the governor break off their other questioning and begin to interrogate him. "I am fifty years old," Zeng Jing tells them, "and live in Yongxing county. Once I held the scholarly status of literary licentiate, but because I was ranked at the fifth level in the reexaminations, the degree was taken from me. Writing that letter was something I thought of several years ago, and was determined to carry out. It was only this year that I discussed how to do it with my student Zhang Xi. Zhang Xi pledged his house and land to get the money for the travel expenses. This year, on June 14, he set off on his journey; it was I who told Zhang Kan to go along with him." But why Zhang Kan, the interrogators ask? Was he some kind of an intellectual companion? Zeng Jing's answer is a resounding denial. "For the kind of topics that I was dealing with in that letter, it is essential that one have some real learning, so that one can discuss the problems with others. Zhang Kan is someone who has no learning whatsoever, why on earth should I want to discuss anything with him? He is an ignoramus." And Zhang Xi's father, Zhang Xinhua? "He just knew that his son was going on a journey to Sichuan and Shaanxi to deliver a letter; he didn't want to know anything about the matters discussed in the letter. There are few people of real learning in Yongxing county; and since I live in the mountains, a long way from the county town, I rarely had a chance to meet such people."

This gives the interrogators a natural way to probe Zeng Jing for the exact roles of those who influenced him in his rural backwater. What kind of inspirations did he find? There was teacher Liu, Zeng tells them, the supervisor of the Yongxing county school when Zeng Jing was an enrolled student there, whose knowledge of moral philosophy and skill at astron-

omy won Zeng's admiration. But Liu, holder of an advanced literary degree and a rigorist in matters of principle and ritual, became enraged at
Zeng's unorthodox interpretations of moral questions and cursed him
roundly; and now Liu was retired and lived too far away for Zeng to have
a chance to try out his ideas on him, even if he wished to. Liu had a student
called Chen, who lived as a companion with his teacher and was a man of
considerable scholarship.

In addition, there was a local scholar called Qiao, whom Zeng did not
know in person but whose published essays showed true depth of learning; Zeng Jing yearned to discuss the great Song dynasty moral philosophers such as the Cheng brothers or Zhu Xi with a man of that caliber.
That was why, Zeng Jing tells his questioners, when he came across some
essays by Lü Liuliang, he was so moved and encouraged by the way Lü
revered the great moral philosophers, and shunned those writers of the
past whom Zeng also found superficial. "Thus I came to admire Lü Liuliang," says Zeng, "and last year Zhang Xi made a trip to Zhejiang to acquire more books by Lü. So it was I learned that scholars in Huzhou like
Yan Hongkui and Shen Zaikuan had all imbibed the truth from Lü Liuliang, and must surely be true men of learning."

He and Zhang Xi talked all this over many times, Zeng tells his questioners, and felt that if their plan succeeded it would be greatly to their advantage to make use of scholars such as these. But Zeng never met the
Zhejiang scholars face-to-face: "We hatched no plots together, and formed
no gang." The same was true of other students from his own Yongxing
county with whom Zeng had a chance to talk and share his views. "They
might know the type of issues discussed in the letter, but they made no
schemes with me. I acted by myself, and I take the responsibility. I don't
let anyone else take the blame, for it is not good to incriminate others."
The questioners probe for more information on the scholars mentioned
by name in Zeng's manuscript *Knowledge of the New*. It turns out Zeng has
never even met many of the people he lists as allies in his moral quest, and
some of the leads are cold, like a ninety-six-year-old from Anhui province,
now deceased. But others have curious resonances: one man mentioned
there turns out to be the editor of a literary collection of Lü Liuliang's
works that Zeng has in his possession; another has shown his zeal for the
works of Lü Liuliang by traveling to Lü's former home (just as Zhang Xi

did), where he paid the formidable sum of eighty ounces of silver for some works by Lü that he coveted.

If there was no plot and no prior agreement among any of these people, General Hailan asks, what was meant by that phrase "in six provinces, at just one word all else will follow"? "That was something Zhang Xi and I talked over together," replies Zeng. "We saw that the sickness of the times was spreading everywhere, as it would if Heaven itself was ill at ease. We realized Heaven must feel the same as we did, and so we used a phrase like that. There was no thought-out plan."

Not surprisingly, the six Hunanese who have been arrested along with Zeng show little enthusiasm for the man who has brought them to this pass. The sixty-year-old Liu, Zeng Jing's former teacher and supervisor of the Yongxing county school for the period from 1713 to 1723, praised by both Zeng and Zhang for the depth of his scholarship and his knowledge of military tactics and astronomy, has a modest view of his own skills and of his former pupil's judgment. "Because I studied the *Book of Historical Documents* when I was young," he tells his interrogators, "and thus got a smattering of knowledge about diagramming the stars, Zeng Jing thought I knew all about astronomy. As for my book entitled *Illustration of Philosophical Principles* in eight sections, that in fact is all lifted from the former sage Zhu Xi. All I did to it was add some commentary and have some copies printed, as an aid in teaching the candidates for the military licentiate's degree. How does that add up to a mastery of military strategy?" Zeng Jing's mistake had been in thinking that reading these basic books was proof of advanced knowledge of the particular fields. Checking over these various books, as Liu asks them to do, the interrogators find nothing unorthodox whatsoever, let alone treasonous. Liu's student Chen also denies all knowledge of any of the contents of Zeng Jing's letter.

The local scholar called Qiao, whom Zeng had praised even more highly, is skeptical about both Zeng and Supervisor Liu. Qiao is seventy-two years old, he tells his interrogators, and has been a registered government student on stipend for twenty-eight years. But just this year, because he was poor and also fell seriously ill, he failed the requalifying exam and thus was deprived of his student status. He has never held any public office, he says, nor taken long journeys to study the ways of the world. He is a man who likes to keep his thoughts to himself; his main pastimes are reading and teaching. "But Zeng Jing and Zhang Xi came to my home some time ago, when I was away, and took several of the books from my collection, apparently to make copies of them." Qiao has no idea what made them do such a thing. As for "teacher Liu" says Qiao, he was able to read and write but that was about it—he was certainly not a distinguished scholar. Qiao wrote a few prefaces for him, at his request, and some occasional pieces, but that was all. Qiao concludes defiantly: "That's the truth. If you don't believe it, round up those people, and have them confront me face-to-face; or better still, have a couple of people masquerade as me, and then bring in Zeng Jing and his accomplice, and ask them which of us is the real Qiao. That way I'll be exonerated."

Despite these claims to innocence by the seventy-two-year-old, the officials still order a thorough search of Qiao's books and possessions. They come up with nothing at all even conceivably incriminating, except for a single poem written on a painted likeness of the founding emperor of the Ming dynasty. And as Qiao tells them when challenged, he did not even write the poem; it was written several centuries before, by a scholar from the same area of Hunan that Qiao lived in now.

Closer to the heart of the case are the three relatives of the messenger Zhang Xi whose names were all included on the initial list of thirteen: Zhang's father, elder brother, and cousin. For a day or two after he was captured in Xi'an back in October, Zhang protected his father by concealing both his name and native place, but after General Yue swore the false oath, the father's real name and residence came tumbling out, along with so much other information. Now all of them have been caught and can be questioned at the Hunan officials' leisure.

Zhang Xi's father, though ill and frail, is forthright about his views of the conspirators, his own son included. He is sixty years old, he tells the interrogators, and in 1695, at the age of twenty-seven, was admitted as a student in the county school. But because he could not pass the qualifying exams he lost his student status. Some time ago he changed his name from its original form, Zhang Shihuang—"Jade of Office Zhang"—to his current name, Zhang Xinhua, "New China Zhang." The arrested messenger Zhang Xi is his second son, and the father is bitter about his son's behavior: "He began to study with Zeng Jing in Yongxing county, and after a while his words became so boastful and shameless that I kicked him out of

the house. So he went off to live with Zeng's family. Earlier this year he
came back home and pawned off his land and house, saying he had to go
to Sichuan and Shaanxi to deliver a letter. Because I could not prevent my
stupid son from being pushed into this lawless action by Zeng Jing, I deserve to die." There is much more the interrogators want to ask the father,
they report to the emperor, but he is so ill they are convinced he will die if
put to the torture, or else starve himself to death in despair. Since his death
at this stage would solve nothing, they have stopped questioning him for
now, and have ordered the Hunan judicial commissioner to keep him under constant observation.

Zhang Xi's older brother Zhang Zhao is crisp with his questioners:
"Zhang Xi is my younger brother. For the last couple of years he's been off
living with Zeng Jing in Yongxing county. All I know about is farming. I
have no idea at all what those people have been up to." The interrogators
enter his statement in the record, and do not push him to elaborate. But
from the third of the arrested Zhang family relatives, Zhang Xi's cousin
Zhang Kan, they get a barrage of new information. For some time he'd regarded Zeng Jing as his "teacher-father," he tells them, and admired his
cousin Zhang Xi for his knowledge of medicine. In the fifth lunar month
of the current year, Zeng Jing's eldest son and Zhang Xi came together to
visit Zhang Kan, with a proposition: they would give him several ounces
of silver if he would serve as the companion and baggage carrier for Zhang
Xi on his upcoming trip to Sichuan and Shaanxi. They told him that "good
prospects lay ahead," though Zhang Kan was not clear what they meant
by that. But he agreed to take the job. He and Zhang Xi reached Shaanxi
on October 16, 1728, and Zhang Xi told his cousin to proceed at once to
the tomb of the fabled early ruler King Wen, to gather some of the wild
milfoil stalks that grew on top of it, these being the plants most valued in
divination. Zhang Kan was back in Xi'an with the stalks by October 26,
but was shaken to learn that his cousin intended to deliver a letter in person to the governor-general's office. Panic-stricken that he might be considered an accomplice and put to death, Zhang Kan shouldered his bedroll
and headed for home. "I know nothing about what Zhang Xi did after that
day," he adds. Zhang Kan had made his own way back south to Anren by
road and river, covering the six hundred miles in thirty-six days, and
reached home safely on December 1; but the very day after his return, he

was arrested during the officials' raid on his family. "That whole business was carried through by Zeng Jing and Zhang Xi," Zhang Kan concludes. "I knew nothing about it, and beg for forgiveness." Tortured, he sticks to the same story.

While the interrogations are under way, teams of investigators search carefully through the homes and possessions of all arrested suspects; to their surprise, they make their most important finds in the home of the Zhang family, who have so insistently, though in different ways, denied all knowledge of the contents of the treasonous letter or Zeng's other written materials. Secreted among the Zhangs' possessions are not only copies of the two treasonous books written by Zeng Jing himself, the *Knowledge of the New* and *Record of Hidden Things,* and some short texts on how to make sacrifices to Heaven and to one's ancestors, but also the entire draft of the treasonous letter that Zhang Xi delivered to General Yue in October. Why on earth did the Zhangs have these at home, when Zhang Xi was in prison in Xi'an?

Summoned back for further interrogation, Zhang Kan admits he carried the books back with him from Xi'an, but claims he did so unwittingly: the books and manuscripts had been taken to Xi'an by Zhang Xi, who hid them for safety inside Zhang Kan's bedroll. When Zhang Kan fled precipitously, he had simply shouldered the bedroll with its ballast of texts. "I never knew anything at all about the books' contents," Zhang adds. For clarification, he suggests, the interrogators should question Zeng Jing again. The interrogators do, and Zeng Jing takes full responsibility: "Everything written in those books was said by me. How would I let Zhang Xi take a role in something like that?"

Having read through the two books written by Zeng Jing, the interrogators tell the emperor, they remain so shocked and disgusted at the wild and treasonous contents that they dare not send them along with their report. Instead they have sealed them away for safekeeping and request permission to burn them. The drafts of these treasonous books have not yielded any important additions to the list of conspirators. Anxious to share these findings with the emperor, the Hunan interrogators write out their report in mid-December and send it to Beijing in the care of one of the Hunan army officers. As soon as he receives it, the emperor forwards the news to General Yue. "Here's something really strange—Zhang Kan had only been home for a single day when he was arrested by the special commissioner's staff. Of all those people listed by Zhang Xi, not a single one is now missing, and every one of them has been arrested. I tell you this to please you."

If this message shows his satisfaction with the way the case is being handled, the emperor does not share that pleasure with the Hunan officials. Indeed, for some time he has been skeptical of their ability to handle the details of the investigation, and as early as December 3 has made the decision to send to Hunan someone more skilled in investigative techniques than the former morality supervisor or the elderly general. His choice is Hangyilu, a young Manchu career official from the Manchu Bordered Red Banner, recently named vice-president of the Ministry of Punishments, and expert in handling delicate negotiations. At his December 3 briefing, the emperor gives Hangyilu a series of options that echo those already sent to General Yue in the case of Zhang Xi: on arrival in Changsha, Hangyilu should seek to break Zeng Jing's composure by reminding the conspirator of the remarkable achievements of both the late and the current emperors in bringing peace and prosperity to China, and should urge Zeng to explain what it was about the country or its government that could possibly merit the extremist measures Zeng had apparently been willing to undertake. But Hangyilu and the Hunan officials should also concentrate as much as possible on finding the origins of the treacherous words that were being spread by Zeng Jing and the others identified so far. They should be patient and methodical in this, following up all promising leads, including those that might be found in the treasonous writings themselves. At the same time, the emperor gives Hangyilu an oral edict for immediate relay to the Hunan governor, Wang: How is it possible that after only one year of Wang's governorship in Hunan the people could have become quite so unruly there? Wang is to exert all his efforts to reform the province, and to redeem himself by turning things around and halting the slide of Hunan into lawlessness.

Hangyilu reaches Changsha on December 26 and delivers his instructions to the special commissioner and the governor; and at once the three men begin applying the new tactics suggested by the emperor. Zeng Jing is summoned back again, this time to a close security room in the governor's own office compound. There, he is reminded of the emperor's benevolence, warned of the power of life and death that the three men have over him, and pressed to explain the exact motives that lay behind his wild acts and writings. On some matters Zeng speaks cogently, as Hangyilu probes deeper. He wrote the book *Record of Hidden Things*, Zeng explains, as a kind of extended briefing paper for Zhang Xi on his journey to Shaanxi: "When I sent Zhang Xi on his journey, it was just a confidential matter between us—we were not going to waste our secrets on other people, or have them participate or share in it with us. In this way, if we succeeded, we would reap the profit; if we failed, we would come to no harm. So in the *Record of Hidden Things* I reiterated to Zhang Xi that he should make enquiries all along the road; if what he heard did not accord with what he had been told back home, then he was to come back at once, and we would make a different plan. He was not to act lightly. It was not as if we had a firm plan, in which having arranged everything thus and so we had to act exactly in that way. We had no fellow plotters. My book can serve as proof of that."

Following up these remarks with another round of questions put to all those arrested so far as well as to those who can be located from among the people mentioned by name in Zeng Jing's two books either as inspirations or potential accomplices, the interrogators have to admit that Zeng might be right. None of the others admit to being privy to any of the information presented by Zeng Jing in his own writings and his treasonous letter.

But on the question of his deeper motives and what exactly he was hoping to achieve by all this plotting, Zeng's answers, even if gratifying at one level to his interrogators, are completely useless at another. As the interrogators report to the emperor: "He fell into a wild fit of weeping, and prostrated himself on the floor again and again. He seemed to us like a man recovering from a drunken stupor, or awakening from a dream. But when we began to press him for details of each item mentioned in his treasonous letter, this criminal's replies were so vague they left us nothing to hold on to, they were either totally wrong or completely made up; however much we questioned him, nothing had substance." The only solution, the interrogators decide, is to abandon spoken questions altogether: "We gave him paper and brushes, and ordered said criminal to write out his own detailed confession."

It is a laborious process, in frightening conditions, but Zeng Jing begins to draw his thoughts together:

"I was born in the eighteenth year of the Emperor Kangxi's reign [1679], and grew up in a mountain valley near the border of Hunan province. Down to my grandfather's time, my family had been accumulating good deeds through generations. We often hear of families practicing charity for three generations, but my grandfather's may be called 'a family accumulating charitable deeds for ten generations.'

"In my childhood, I followed my father's instructions to study. I aspired to realize the Way of the Sages and of the Great Learning, hoping to live up to the expectations of the court by exerting myself in actual practices. However, I lived in a secluded mountain valley where men of letters did not go, and my father died early. As the family was poor, and our household small, I could not possibly travel far to seek improvement from learned scholars, and there was no scholar, teacher, or benevolent friend in my neighborhood who could correct me. The place I lived was far from town. There were almost no commercial transactions, and if there were occasionally, people used grain as the medium. Not only were coins not used, even silver was rarely seen. The poor people gained no profit from their products, and there was nowhere they could exchange their goods for silver. All they used was grain. Only the rich families that accumulated plenty of grain would try various ways to sell their grain for silver. As to coins, we used neither those of the Kangxi nor the Yongzheng reigns.

"Chen Meiding was a commoner in Anren county. He died of old age in the fifty-second year of the Kangxi reign [1713]; my father-in-law Chen Guoheng, younger brother of Chen Meiding, was a commoner too. He died of illness in the forty-sixth year of the Kangxi reign [1707]. His son, too poor to support himself, moved to Sichuan province in the fifty-seventh year of the Kangxi reign [1718]. As to Chen Meiding's son, I do not know if he is still alive now. Chen Meiding was my elder uncle-in-law. I married his niece, Chen Guoheng's daughter, when I was seventeen, and went to live with his family when I was eighteen.

"As my father-in-law came out to greet me, [Chen Meiding] pointed at me and said, 'This is a conscientious gentleman from a respectable family, one who values poetry and propriety. Among all the things that my third brother has done in his life, only the choice of a son-in-law shows his insight is superior to others under Heaven.' He also said, 'The sagacious son-in-law has the virtue to benefit the world and the magnanimity of a prime minister.' All his life he held a very low opinion of the present world, and frequently expressed his nostalgia for the clothing and culture of the previous dynasty.

"When I went to the main town [of Chenzhou] to take the examinations, I encountered a collection of the exemplary examination answers written [by the scholars] of our dynasty and selected by Lü Liuliang, along with his comments on various topics and essays written by the *jinshi* degree holders on nonexamination occasions. Upon seeing that his comments on these topics were based on the classical commentaries, and his writings modeled on the major masters, I was won over because they suited my crude nature, and mistook him for a top personage of our dynasty, and as an authority against whom to judge all statements and arguments. In fact, at that time, I knew nothing of his personality or his deeds. Lü Liuliang's literary commentaries are prevalent in our society. Most of those who study for the civil service examinations model their essays on those on which he has commented, and regard his interpretations as conclusive. Until I reached middle age, I continued to believe Lü Liuliang was a leading master in literary circles; since many of his ideas corresponded with mine, I could not help being drawn to him, and mistakenly taking him as my guide to self-cultivation.

"I had been taught the classics as a child, and when I read the chapter in the *Book of Mencius* in which Duke Tengwen asked about the governance of the state, and discussed the equal-field system, I felt happy at heart, thinking privately that it should be practiced in our own time. Since then, I often asked people about it, but none of them said it could be practiced today. I heard that, and felt unhappy. Later, I read Lü Liuliang's comments on that chapter, and was surprised that he thought it could be put into practice. He even said that the equal-field system from the days when there was less central power was indispensable to the proper ruling of the world. Once the equal-field and decentralized system was revived, one could then expect the world to be ruled properly. His words spoke directly to my heart. From then on, I was deeply convinced by Lü Liuliang's words, and my heart clung to this dead practice.

"When the edict announcing the death of the late emperor [Kangxi] arrived, even in the deep mountains and remote valleys there were none who did not run around and cry out loud as if their own parents had died. Even someone as stupid, stubborn, and ignorant as I stopped eating, cried bitterly and loudly, wore white [clothes of mourning] in the deep mountains, and observed the mourning rituals to the last detail. At that time all those feelings surfaced unconsciously and involuntarily, rather than deliberately.

"In the third year of Emperor Yongzheng's reign [1725] we began to talk about moving to the west. At the time, we meant no more than that. I lived in an isolated and out-of-the-way place in a mountain valley; for miles around there were only farmers and no literate people. When my father was alive, he used to think of moving elsewhere, but could never do anything about it. In recent years, as population has increased, farmland has risen in price, but my family, with its small household and scant resources, was unable to make the move. Later, two students, Zhang Xi and Liao Yi, came to study with me. They wandered back and forth and could not settle down. Both of them were also from very poor families. According to messages sent back by those who had already gone to Sichuan, farmland was cheap there. So Zhang Xi, Liao Yi, and I discussed moving to Sichuan and finding a quiet place to migrate to, where we could settle down and farm. I thought of taking Zhang Xi and Liao Yi with me, so they could carry out their intention of studying. So we made our plans to travel to Sichuan.

"Departing on the twenty-fifth day of the seventh lunar month [September 1, 1725], we arrived in Changsha by boat, and took a walk around the town. I had never traveled before, except for one trip to Chenzhou to take the examinations, but otherwise had not been anywhere. To our surprise, we saw a poster in Changsha which talked about "five stars strung together like pearls, with the sun and moon in conjunction." We were overjoyed, thinking that a better world was coming, and the equal-field system would at last be revived. People would be needed to revive that system, but it was hard to tell what might happen to us when they came to choose the people. And once that equal-field system was revived we would be able to settle down anywhere. So why should we move the whole family to Sichuan? We gave up our plan to move to Sichuan, and got ready to return.

"At that time the only plan we had was that we should go to the capital and submit a letter with our ideas, but we hesitated and could not decide, because various rumors from traitorous villains had filled our hearts with doubts. So instead, we went on to Mount Yuelu near Changsha to see the scenery, and came home via Xiangtan. We did not meet anyone else, nor say anything improper. We arrived home on the third day of the ninth lunar month [October 8, 1725].

"In the following two years, the harvests were not good. As flood disasters continued year after year, rice and other grain prices rose. Life was hard for the people, and many of them tried to escape the famine and floods. We then began to suspect that the auguries of 'five stars strung together like pearls, with the sun and moon in conjunction' probably meant something else.

"My two books, *Knowledge of the New* and *Record of Hidden Things,* record every bit of my wild heart. Though these two books have different titles, they were not composed or embellished with any specific goals in mind. In the *Knowledge of the New* I followed [the Tang dynasty philosopher] Zhang Hengqu's words that 'once the mind is illuminated, one should record the thoughts right away.' So I jotted down everything I got to know and see every day, no matter whether fine or crude, right or wrong, so that I might read it over and examine the good and bad points in what I had learned. I did not check my arguments carefully, or embellish my writing. I just wrote things down casually, in plain language. The *Record of Hidden Things* was nothing but my instructions to Zhang Xi. I did not want to tell him openly, lest other people should hear it, but I was also worried that he might not remember. That was why I wrote those things down on paper. When enough of them had accumulated, I gave them a title. It was just my private instructions to him. Now both books have been found, and submitted for review by the emperor.

"In the fourth and fifth years of Emperor Yongzheng's reign [1726–27] many people moved to Sichuan from Hubei, Hunan, and Guangdong. Occasionally they passed by my door. They told me that in the west there was a Mr. Yue who took good care of the common people, and that in the west the people loved him and were most willing to obey him. The commoners who told me this did not know the full name or official titles of Mr. Yue."

The three interrogators in Hunan cannot wait for Zeng Jing to finish before reporting to the emperor, so as he writes, they do the same, gathering together everything they now have: the transcripts of the new round of confessions, Zeng's *Knowledge of the New* and *Record of Hidden Things,* the original rough draft of his treasonous letter, an introductory pamphlet on classical learning for small children that he wrote sometime in the past, several guides and indices to the Lü family collections of Lü Liuliang's works that Lü's ninth son had given to Zhang Xi on his previous visit, a fan with inscriptions by Zeng Jing, the works confiscated from the scholars he emulated and admired as a student, and the strips of writing that he had secreted in his clothing at the time of his arrest, when he had declared his intention to commit suicide. All of these are packed into a group of specially sealed boxes, and consigned on January 7, 1729, to the care of a local officer, Lieutenant Wu, who will deliver them safely to the emperor in Beijing. After reading the report and the confession transcripts, the emperor writes that "the testimony by these rebels shows them to be completely laughable people."

Nevertheless it is obvious to the emperor that despite his earlier instructions, and even with the help of Hangyilu, the Hunan interrogators have not been successful in finding out how Zeng Jing got hold of the wild stories from which he fabricated the various charges included in his letter to General Yue and those in his own two briefing books for the messenger Zhang Xi. The emperor knows his Hunan interrogators can do better, for he has recently received a lengthy new report from General Yue in Xi'an, dated December 14, 1728, that shows how insistent questioning can begin to get to the heart of the problem.

Despite the fact that Zhang Xi was in total despair and dangerously ill, weeping and berating himself for his stupid actions, the general kept up the pressure, demanding that Zhang concentrate on recalling the precise moments at which he heard the most damaging of the charges against the emperor. Finally Zhang responded: "Last year, when I made my journey from Hunan to Zhejiang, I traveled by boat, and it was my fellow passengers who told me these things." What class of people were these passengers, the general asked; where did they live, what were their names? They were just people who happened to be on the same boat, said Zhang. They were ordinary traveling merchants. It never occurred to him to ask their names, or where they lived. Then what did they look like? the general asked. "Everyone was talking in great excitement," said Zhang. "I can remember the words they said, but I can't remember the people themselves." Had Zhang heard similar wild tales in Yunnan and Guizhou? He had never been in those provinces, said Zhang. Then what about on the journey through Sichuan and on to Shaanxi? That was this year, Zhang replied, and he had taken the overland route. He hadn't heard such talk on that trip—in fact, people had been complimentary to the emperor, leaving Zhang perplexed. He asked them what about the current emperor was so good, but their answers were unclear and contradictory.

Zhang understood nothing about the emperor and his conscientiousness as a ruler, responded the general, and Zhang's obstinacy would have tried the patience of even the ancient sage kings Yao and Shun: "If the travelers on the boat really said the things you have reported," he told Zhang, "then it's because people like you deluded them." If what the general said about the emperor's virtues was indeed true, countered Zhang, and it was Zhang and his teacher Zeng Jing who were the deluded ones, then "obviously there could be no way of drawing significance from what was said on the boat."

Concluding his December 14 report to the emperor on this long conversation with the prisoner, General Yue reflected on the way rumors spread in general: one person said something, someone else misheard it and repeated it, someone heard the new version for the first time and believed it to be true. A good recent example, Yue observed, was the rumors swirling around that the current emperor was a heavy drinker, rumors that Zeng Jing himself had picked up: an initial statement by a senior official, reported in the *Capital Gazette,* that the emperor now found wine bad for his health, had been transformed by the rumor mill into the fact that the emperor drank immoderately. Even senior officials could not get such things right, commented the general, they "cannot accurately report the conversations that have taken place, but distort them to such an incredible degree. That is just the kind of story the riffraff trump up as they loiter around in the marketplace. The news that Zeng Jing and some others had the nerve to plot a major uprising, and the degrading and outrageous things that they said, have now also been spread abroad everywhere. Despite all my detailed questioning of Zhang Xi, I still don't believe I have got at the whole truth. If those people who he says were talking to him on the boat really do exist, then they must have been told these things by some other malcontents on some earlier occasion."

Only nine days later, Yue Zhongqi gets fresh evidence of how swiftly and damagingly rumors can grow. Stories are now swirling in Xi'an that the general has secretly been in league with Zhang Xi all along. How else, says the rumor mill, can one explain the lenient treatment given to Zhang Xi during the interrogations, his release from jail during that period, and his convivial meetings with members of Yue's staff? Disturbingly, senior military officers in the area seem to think there may be something to such charges. These stories, too, General Yue feels he must pass on to his ruler.

The general's ruminations on rumor, and the receipt of the report from Hunan, prompt the emperor to compose a new court letter in late January 1729, which he sends through Prince Yi to the Hunan interrogators: "When I first read Zeng Jing and Zhang Xi's treasonous letter sent to me by Yue Zhongqi," runs the emperor's message, "it was impossible for me not to smile. I could not imagine where they got those weird and reckless ideas. But when Zeng Jing composed that letter, he must have been influenced by rumors created and circulated by crafty and rebellious people, schemers and deceivers. I feel we have no choice but to dissect and clarify these rumors item by item, and to make our findings known to the people as a whole." The emperor continues that he has only that very day received the report of Hangyilu's follow-up interrogations, and therefore has not yet had a chance to think through all the details. But he has got the drift clearly enough. Naturally if his character and actions were even a minute bit as Zeng Jing described them in his treasonous writings, then the whole country would be seething with the desire to rebel just like Zeng Jing. So the interrogators are to push Zeng Jing for the source of every rumor, with the goal of tracking down which ones he created himself and which he got from other people. "If Zeng Jing cannot give us the exact names of those people, he must have at least a general idea of where they were from and where they were going and what route they were taking."

Brought in for a third intensive round of interrogation, Zeng Jing again weeps abjectly and begs for mercy. But once he has clearly understood the central focus of the new message from the emperor, he becomes calmer and begins to concentrate: "The schoolhouse where I used to teach," he tells his inquisitors, "was in Pengtang village, by the side of the road that runs to the Anren county town. I would often hear stories from people traveling up or down that road, though it is the truth that I did not ask them for their exact names, or where they lived. Nor would I have dared to recklessly tell others the things that I heard. But there was one occasion, on the last day of May in 1723, that a stranger came to my schoolhouse. He told me his name was Wang Shu, and his courtesy name was Yanshan, and that he had obtained the *jinshi* degree at the examinations of 1706. For a time he served as a reading tutor for the fourteenth prince. I was scared that he must be a senior official, and so did not dare question him in detail. Because he said his son was currently a military commander in Sichuan and Shaanxi, I thought he might be Yue Zhongqi's father. I entered this item in my book *Knowledge of the New* and told Zhang Xi to investigate. Apart from this one man, I cannot identify any specific person who was spreading rumors." Where was this Wang Shu from, the interrogators ask, how old was he, what did he look like? Zeng Jing never found out the name of Wang Shu's hometown, he replies, but he got the impression Wang was from Jiangsu or Zhejiang; Wang "looked to be in his late forties then, so now he must be around fifty; he was fairly short, stout, with a sparse beard." Despite the clarity of these details, Zeng cannot recall the names of anyone else from whom he heard wild stories.

Even if Zeng can remember no more, there is no doubt in the minds of the Hunan interrogators that this new information changes the nature of the case: it now appears that some of the darkest rumors about the emperor are stemming from the holder of the highest literary degree in the land—a degree he attained in the very same year as Lü Liuliang's eldest son—and not only that, but from a man who has been a tutor to the emperor's most hated rival, the fourteenth prince, his fourteenth blood brother, imprisoned now in a Beijing palace compound. Thus this new information would seem to fulfill all the emperor's recently stated criteria for the kinds of memories he wants his interrogators to dig out from the minds of the conspirators.

Yet for some reason, the officials in Hunan do not race the news to the emperor at once. Part of the reason for their delay may be that they are trying to get even more out of the suddenly forthcoming Zeng Jing, whether about Wang Shu himself, the stories he told, or people traveling with him. Another reason is that in the early months of 1729, pursuant to the emperor's orders, various suspects from different parts of China are slowly converging on Changsha, so that their stories can be double-checked against Zeng Jing's: General Yue sends Zhang Xi back to Hunan on January 19, and he reaches Changsha exactly one month later; the Che brothers and their former tutor Sun, dispatched from Nanjing by Governor-general Fan Shiyi, only reach the Hunan capital on February 26. And each in turn is then reinterrogated by officials eager to prove their diligence to the emperor.

So not until April 7, 1729, is everything ready for the journey to Beijing and the procession makes its way out through the great gates of Changsha. It is a strange cortege, composed of all those whom fate and Zeng Jing have thrown together: the heavily fettered prisoners, the groups of guards who surround each of them, the three senior local officials—two military and one civilian—who will be in charge of security and the detailed arrangements of food and lodging, and presiding over all the veteran General Hailan and the rising Vice-president Hangyilu. There is Zeng Jing himself, along with his seventy-seven-year-old mother and his two sons, who have also been arrested and made to accompany him. There is Zhang Xi, still sick and frail, sent back to Changsha some weeks before by General Yue, now being rerouted once again. There are Zhang's father, his elder brother, and his cousin. There are the Hunan scholars mentioned in Zeng Jing's treasonous writings. There are the two Che brothers from Nanjing, sent to Changsha not long before so they could confront Zhang Xi and Zeng Jing face-to-face as they requested. And there is the erstwhile Che family tutor Sun, still ill and weak from dysentery. "Noted," writes the emperor across the end of the lengthy report in which the Hunan interrogators summarize all the details of their meticulous planning, designed to prevent the faintest chance of escape by any of the suspects, and tell him of the completion of Zeng Jing's written confession and of the new lead to the *jinshi* candidate Wang Shu. "In just a few days you will all be here in Beijing."

Five

*The
Phoenix
Song*

While the team of Hunan investigators intensify their questioning, groups of officials in Zhejiang and Beijing are going methodically through all the writings of Lü Liuliang and his followers, and passing their findings on to the emperor. As Yongzheng reads this new material, any impression he may have had of Lü Liuliang as a conventional commentator on the classical canon fades away. In its place, Lü's letters and diaries bring the outline of someone different into view: a Chinese man passionately attached to his ancestral race, filled with anguish at what he perceives as the destruction of his people and his culture, and suffused with mockery and hatred for the Manchu masters of his country and the Chinese collaborators who serve them.

It is true that Lü's life is firmly in the past. Born in 1629, he was a young student when the Ming dynasty collapsed in 1644 and the Manchus moved into Beijing's Forbidden City, establishing the Qing dynasty in its place. And Lü died in 1683, when both the current emperor, Yongzheng, and the conspirator Zeng Jing were only four years old. Yet though Lü had continued to study under the Qing and had even taken the lower-level examinations, writing well-received commentaries on the ancient Chinese texts collectively known as the Confucian canon and publishing samples of exemplary examination answers by other Chinese scholars, from the tone of Lü's informal and private writings one might believe he had spent his whole life in loyal and devoted service to the Ming. The bitterness of Lü's ironic commentaries on the Manchu conquerors, though written half a century before, could well make one believe he knew all about the hazards of the current emperor's world. The more Emperor Yongzheng reads, the angrier he gets.

Many passages in Lü's writings described the reactions of him and his friends to the Manchu edict of 1645, which had ordered all Chinese adult males to shave their foreheads and braid their hair in back, according to the Manchus' own customary style. The Manchus also expected the Chinese people to adopt the different robes and clothing styles of their new masters. In one such diary entry, Lü wrote of a friend he called Shen, who defied the Manchu order. For a decade after the conquest, Shen refused to leave his home, or to allow any guests to visit him there. All through that time Shen continued to wear his Ming dynasty robes, and kept his own full head of hair untrimmed in the Ming style, held in place by a hair net and adorned with an ornamental cap. Shen also forbade his children to seek any office or accept any favors from the Manchus. But Shen's son was anxious to make a career for himself under the new dynasty and to receive a tablet of honor for his widowed sister. So one night he got his father drunk, and shaved the old man's head while he was sleeping. On awakening in his shorn state, Shen wept inconsolably. All he could do was to pass his time in writing about the old days and the values he had cherished. But the son, fearful that the writings might be discovered, burned his father's works.

In his diaries and letters, Lü kept special words of scorn for the Chinese sycophants and collaborators who joined forces with the Qing. One such Chinese scholar boasted that he joined the Manchus as soon as he could in 1644, and over the next few years wrote all the edicts that the Manchus issued in the Yangzi valley regions. Lü mocked this turncoat's pretentious couplet, that thanks to these actions "the whole world is unified, and the constellations all in place; / Rites and music thrive, warfare fades away." Such poetic exaggerations simply made decent men sneer, said Lü. In a similar vein Lü wrote of Chinese city dwellers who jammed the streets to see off an effective Manchu official when he left their area for a new posting. To Lü, their actions merely showed how swiftly people's yearnings for food and drink pushed aside their other moral feelings. And when a friend showed him an "ode" he had composed to celebrate a rebellious region recently "pacified" by the Manchus, Lü refused to read it unless the man dropped the word "pacified" and changed "ode" to "lament."

Lü used a striking image to summarize his own private stance. As he wrote in a letter to a friend: "Someone was walking down the road when he heard a candy seller calling, 'Trade your worn-out caps for candy.' The man took off his cap and hid it away, only to hear the candy seller calling, 'Trade your torn old hair nets for candy.' So the man hid his hair net away as well. At which the candy man cried out, 'Trade your bushy hair for candy.' Exasperated and flustered, the man shouted back, 'Why do you push me so hard?'" As Lü concluded to his friend, "That's why I had my whole head shaved, to stop the pressures from the candy man." All Chinese of that time knew that shaving one's whole head in emulation of the Buddhist monks might be a gesture taken out of religious conviction, but was more likely in the context of the times to be done in order to make it impossible to carry out the Manchu state's order that one braid one's hair as a gesture of obedience. More directly, one of Lü's diary entries contained the words, "I am determined to die as a recluse in the mountains. If pushed to take the special examinations, I will shave my head and become a monk." Such an action was the only one that made sense in a world where, as Lü wrote in a poem that Zeng Jing later quoted, "Even the children are taken aback by the new clothing and hats."

Lü was just a teenager when the Ming fell, but he was a grown man when the last legitimate Ming contender for the throne—the self-styled Emperor Yongli—was hunted down and killed by Manchu troops, along with his young son, on the Burmese border in 1662. Lü often commented in diary entries on the plight of the Ming fugitives, and on this tragic moment he had a detailed entry: When Emperor Yongli was captured, wrote Lü, both the victorious Manchus and the Chinese troops were deeply moved. "The heir-apparent urged his horse forward, and pointed his riding whip toward the east. The Manchu and Chinese troops drawn up in ranks on the eastern side all knelt. He pointed to the west, and those to the west knelt. On the day he was executed, Heaven and earth turned dark, the sun and moon lost their light. For a hundred miles, thunder roared above all the temples of the god of war." Quite apart from the critical tone of the whole passage, just to refer to the Ming fugitive as "Emperor Yongli" instead of calling him the "the falsely designated Yongli" was a crime punishable by death, as Lü would have known full well.

In rather similar fashion, Lü Liuliang kept track in his diaries of key events from the great rebellion of the Chinese turncoat general, Wu Sangui, which began in 1673 and continued until 1681, shortly before Lü's death. Lü took note of the people's reactions to Wu's initial rebellious stance, pondered whether Wu at sixty-one might not perhaps be perceived as too old to lead a successful rising, and reflected on the ingenuity with which Wu chose to announce his own imperial claims at an hour, day, month, and year that all contained the same auspicious cyclical character *yin*. And in many passages Lü referred curtly to Emperor Kangxi—who smashed that rebellion and was the current emperor's father—merely as "Kangxi," rather than by his full and honorific imperial titles. In mocking asides, Lü spoke of Kangxi's stinginess, of how the ruler would steal the salaries of his own officials, and even keep for himself the gifts of satin offered to his court painters by wealthy princely patrons.

As he reads, Emperor Yongzheng could note how auguries and portents filled Lü's writings and were used as a device to comment on the shifting political and economic scene. One of Lü's diary entries spoke of a "strange red wind, that blew for three days through the capital of Beijing," turning the faces of those it touched a similar shade of red. In another, Lü noted "a great star, large as a bowl, followed by a trail of tiny stars like a comet." There was one afternoon when "rays of sunlight darted to and fro, as if struggling with a black sun"; and another day when "three suns appeared together in the sky, one bright, one still and white, one small and red and constantly in motion." Torrential rains, spectacular lightning flashes, protracted roars of thunder, all found their place in Lü's musings and made him uneasy for the future of his country.

In one unusually long and detailed diary entry, the auguries took a different form: there Lü wrote of a phoenix that had alighted at a town in Henan province, before whom all the other birds gathered in homage. Two red birds of unusual size screened the phoenix with their bodies. Its own feathers were of five colors, blended together, and its cry was like the courtly music of olden times. Uneasy at the sudden visitation, the local people tried to drive their oxen forward, to scare the bird away, but the cattle trembled and refused to move. The roads were covered with the bodies of lifeless birds, and dead golden carp lay scattered across the ground. Chinese of Lü's day all knew that the color red was the color associated with the fallen Ming dynasty, and that a phoenix alighting always portended some major change in the world. As Lü wrote after the diary entry, in a follow-up invocation to the phoenix itself: "If morals have not all collapsed, you usually do not come. Your brilliance lies in your singing of the Way. That suddenly we hear you must mean a sage is born."

The scholarly, the elliptical, and the overtly critical elements blended in Lü's voluminous literary works, so that when Governor-general Li Wei had first glanced through them he did not even notice the most destructive passages. Nor did General Yue see anything especially wrong with the poems by Lü Liuliang that the messenger Zhang Xi had brought with him the previous October to Xi'an. It was Zhang Xi himself who pointed out to the general that he might think differently if he read poems by Lü Liuliang like the "Song of the Pines at Qian's Tomb," or the "Songs of the Rivers and Mountains." Now that the emperor could read these poems at leisure, they too yielded up their message to him, as they had before to Zeng Jing and his followers. Thus the "Song of the Pines" might seem, on quick reading, to be a mere reflection by Lü Liuliang on the old and knotted pine trees that grew around the tomb of a long-dead scholar. But the great age of the pines led Lü to comment that they must have been alive at the time of the Yuan dynasty. The Yuan, as the emperor and all Lü's readers knew, was the dynastic name taken by the Mongols, who destroyed the last remnants of the fallen imperial house of Song in 1279; the Chinese suffered under what they considered this "barbarian" yoke for almost a century, until the Mongols were ousted in their turn, in 1368, by the founder of the Ming dynasty. Thus it was in three brief lines on life under the Yuan that Lü made his political point: "Though it lasted only a few decades, / The Heavens were wrenched apart and the earth pillaged, / There was nowhere left for men." Any anti-Manchu reader would relate to the implied parallels in those lines between the Mongols and the Manchus, and could apply them to the times in which he lived.

Lü's poem "Songs of the Rivers and Mountains" was far longer, and the historical references more elaborate, but again one could see why Zeng Jing and his messenger, in their agitated mood during the 1720s, found Lü's words so powerful. In this poem the rivers and mountains were painted ones, as rendered by an artist born under the Song but watching his beloved dynasty slipping under the control of the Mongol Yuan; his painting was thus two things at once, a lyrical landscape and a lament for the times gone by. Lü wrote of how other loyalist followers of the fallen Song, forced to live under the Mongol conquerors, echoed the painter's sentiments in poems they inscribed around the borders of the landscape scroll. But later, when the Yuan dynasty fell in its turn to the conquering Ming, those loyal to the defeated Mongols wrote their laments for the world *they* had lost on the same painting. Thus the painting Lü Liuliang commemorated in his poem was a multilayered one, of regrets across the ages for a loss of dynastic ties. But it was an ambiguous mourning, since no one knew the exact date of the painting, nor even the dates on which most of the poems already appended to it were written. And the figures one could faintly see, scattered through the painted landscape, were dressed neither in the rough clothing and straw hats of the mountain recluses nor in the court robes of those who had agreed to serve a new dynasty. As Lü wrote in his poem, if they were Song figures, they must have been shamed for their rivers and mountains, which they had allowed to fall under Mongol rule. If they were Ming figures, they must have raised their wine cups aloft in happiness, and been "mad with joy" to see their mountains and rivers once more in Chinese hands. They would have felt like "the blind who regained their sight, or cripples who could walk again." But if they were figures from the fallen Yuan, grieving for the departure of their Mongol masters, then they must be those who had lost all sense of discrimination, all sense of right and wrong: they were "beetles enjoying a meal of snake's brains, or rats feasting on excrement."

The yearning for "the return of China's rivers and mountains" had been one of the rallying cries of the patriot general Yue Fei as the Song first yielded to the conquering Jurchen, and with poems such as these, and the kind of diary entries that the Lü family had let Zhang Xi examine, one could begin to understand how the Hunan conspirators had pieced together their views on race. In those same spring months of 1729, the emperor gained a new kind of context in which to read Zeng Jing's own books *Knowledge of the New* and *Record of Hidden Things,* which had just been sent to him. Was it because of Lü Liuliang that Zeng Jing had written, "Outside China proper there are barbarians on four sides. Those who are closer to the Chinese heartland still have a little humanity, but the further away they live, the closer to animals they become"? Was it because of Lü's stimulus that Zeng told his followers, "Between humans and barbarians there can exist no distinctions such as that of rulers and ministers"? If that were true, then so was Zeng Jing's conclusion: "The ethical obligations between ruler and ministers cannot be dispensed with even for a day. How can there be a nation without a ruler under Heaven! As the philosopher Mencius wrote, 'Those who know no father or ruler are animals.' Yet even animals have rulers and ministers. Even bees and ants know how to obey and follow. Now we have lived for over eighty years without a ruler. There is no choice but to search the whole land for a brilliant and wise man to come and be the ruler."

Zeng made it clear in his own writings that at the end of the Ming dynasty the throne should have gone to a man steeped in learning like Lü Liuliang, rather than to a foreign barbarian or to one of the "local thugs" or so-called worldly men of valor who had so often taken over China in the past. It was "scholars like us," wrote Zeng, "who know best how to be emperor." The way to solve China's problems was to restore the once-existing form of government, whereby the sages of old both ruled with modesty and integrity and held the barbarians at bay. Those earlier rulers had known that barbarians had to be "killed or hacked down—what talk was there of leniency?" To Zeng, anyone could see the simple logic of the situation: "The barbarians stole the throne and defiled China, like robbers who plunder a family's possessions, drive out the master, and seize the house. Once all the family members, who were away at the time, hear the news, they are entitled to chase the robbers away." Now that Lü Liuliang was no longer living, might it not be possible that Zeng Jing himself could "rise on the current" and revive the blessed days of the revered Three Dynasties of antiquity?

Yet it was obviously not only Lü Liuliang's words that had given Zeng Jing and his followers such grandiose ideas. On his trip to Zhejiang, Zhang Xi had spent several days with Lü's former student and current disciple Yan Hongkui. Yan was the self-appointed guardian of many of Lü's works, including his informal journals, and had made them available to Zhang Xi. Yan's own diaries, seized by Governor-general Li Wei in the Zhejiang winter raids, yielded up to investigators another jumbled mass of dark portents and unconcealed critiques of the ruling Manchus. When arrested, Yan told the investigators he was seventy-four, so he must have been born in 1654, exactly a decade after the Ming dynasty was overthrown. Yet obviously he considered himself as much a Ming loyalist as did his teacher Lü Liuliang. Like his teacher, Yan wrote in his diaries of the attitudes of those near his home in northern Zhejiang to the orders given by the Manchus on clothing and hairstyle. Yan wrote approvingly of a friend who for his whole life under the Manchu rule dressed in clothes with the straight collars of the old style Ming robes, and always wore a mourning head covering to show his grief at the death of the last Ming emperor. Another of Yan's friends passed his whole life after 1644 dressed in full mourning and never would cut his hair in the Manchu style, despite the personal risks of his defiance. Yan himself always had worn a special hat of archaic design known as a "hat of unity," which like the "unity headbands" of an earlier day was meant to express a yearning for better times; a good many of the local people had copied him, Yan noted in satisfaction. When reading through the works of the famous Ming loyalist Gu Yanwu, Yan had been delighted to see that Gu also discussed the same form of headgear, and claimed that it had been worn three centuries earlier by no less a personage than the founder of the Ming dynasty himself.

Like Lü Liuliang before him and Zeng Jing later, Yan was fascinated by local portents, and his diary entries were filled with episodes from the reigns of the emperors Kangxi and Yongzheng that had roused his interest. In one extended passage, Yan wrote of an earthquake that struck just north of the Great Wall, on a winter's day. The quake's effect was felt across an area of thirty miles: rocks were hurled high into the air, and the earth belched flames. All the people fled from their homes. A few days later terrible floods hit the northern area of Rehe—where the Manchu emperors had their summer palaces and hunting grounds—and more than twenty thousand Manchus were drowned. All of this, wrote Yan, could be linked to the hopes for a Ming restoration, as was shown by the dream of a female servant in the household of an official in Beijing, which Yan also recorded. In her dream the woman saw three lords sitting on the dais in a great reception hall. Suddenly people cried out that the Ming pretender, Zhu the Third, was coming. As the three lords came down the steps to welcome him, they saw that his face was streaming blood. The bloodstained figure demanded that they grant him three streams of black water, and at last they consented. On such and such a day, they vowed, the floods would come.

Other auguries had more bureaucratic provenance. Yan wrote of one first circulated by staff in the Imperial Bureau of Astronomy: the officials there predicted a certain stellar conjunction that, they warned, was a harbinger of civil war, a war that would divide the country between the southwest and the east. Armies would spring up in the midst of cities, and since the color of the constellation would be white, the color of mourning in China, the ruling dynasty must perish. Yan also claimed to have heard of a great Manchu official in Jiangnan who shared the feelings against the dynasty of the Chinese scholars living in his region. To underline the disjointed nature of the times, Yan recorded anomalies of nature whenever he was told them: a rooster that laid eggs; dogs giving birth to snakes; turtles bearing their young as fully fledged creatures, not as eggs; frogs that ate humans. Mixed in with such diary entries were Yan's records of his conversations with friends as they mulled over the actions and sayings of sage rulers long ago and mused on the virtuous conduct of recluses in the past who refused the throne when offered it. And in his diaries Yan inserted records of visitors from afar: among them one concerning a man called Zhang Xi, who came from distant Hunan, bringing word of his revered teacher Zeng Jing, the "Master of Putan."

Fortunately for Emperor Yongzheng, the negative weight of all these dangerous portents was offset by proof of Heaven's blessing. In those same early months of 1729, he received news from Governor-general Ortai, in the far southwestern province of Yunnan, that gave him cheer. Ortai reported that on the last day of the tenth lunar month of the previous year—the emperor's fiftieth birthday—glorious five-colored clouds were seen circling the sun for many hours above one of Yunnan's most sacred shrines. The amazing sight, repeated the following day, could be seen by countless people across a great range of countryside. Clearly, Ortai wrote, this was a "completely unprecedented omen of good fortune." Gratified, for Ortai was one of his most trusted senior officials and the first to whom he had sent a copy of Zeng Jing's treasonous letter, the emperor reported this phenomenon to his court officials. They in turn begged him to order that the auspicious sightings be included in the official history of the realm.

On February 6, 1729, the emperor agreed to their request: "In giving my permission to enter this event in the official historical record, it is not my intention to be boastful to the public. Rather, it is because this shows how the principle of the relationship between Heaven and man is swift and reciprocal." A few days after issuing this edict, the emperor announced the promotion of Ortai to high rank in the Manchu aristocracy, and promotions across the board for all officials of magistrates' rank and above who were serving in the southwest under Ortai's jurisdiction. In mid-March, citing a wide range of classical precedents, the emperor ordered the construction of imposing new temples to the Lord of Clouds and the Lord of Rain. The projects were to be jointly supervised by the Ministry of Rituals and the Ministry of Public Works. Over the course of 1729, sixteen more reports of auspicious cloud sightings flowed in to the emperor, from Yunnan, Guizhou, Shanxi, and Sichuan. There had been no parallel for such signs of heavenly harmony with a ruling emperor under this or any previous dynasty.

But the matter of portents was not merely a simple one of ousting one batch with another. The emperor could use the powerful institutions under his control to spread the news of those favorable to him, but news of unfavorable ones could always be spread by unpredictable rumors. Nor was it necessarily enemies of the state who would hide dark stories in their private diaries, or place the omens' origins in the court Astronomy Bureau to lend them credence. As the Fujian governor-general, Gao Qizhuo, wrote to the emperor in a secret report of April 30, 1729, similar rumors had just been making their way across a swathe of China from Beijing to Zhejiang, and had ended up in his own domain. It happened that in March the personal retainers of two senior officials—the director-general of grain transport, and the morality supervisor for Zhejiang—ran into each other just south of Beijing. They had both been delivering their masters' secret reports to the emperor and were now on their way home to Hangzhou. Naturally enough, they agreed to make the long journey back south in each other's company. In Shandong province they were joined by a third man neither of them had met before, named Ma. Like them, Ma was the retainer of a senior official, in his case the supervising intendant of one of the circuits in the province of Fujian. The three men traveled together by the land route for a while, and then switched to a boat for the journey down the Grand Canal. They had reached Yangzhou, some miles north of the junction with the Yangzi River, when Ma told the other two a disturbing tale. While waiting in Beijing to make the journey home, he heard that the court astronomers had observed a strange phenomenon: their calculations showed that the Ziwei star—the northernmost star in the Plough, believed by many to be the home of the Lord of Heaven—would soon be positioned exactly over Fujian. The omen was not good. To propitiate the heavenly forces, Ma told his traveling companions, the emperor had ordered that every male child in Fujian province aged three to nine must be slain, and imperial agents were even now speeding to Fujian to carry out the order. Ma was telling his two companions this news, because he knew at least one of them was a native of Fujian and might have family there. Shortly after this, Ma left the two retainers and continued on his own way south. As soon as they reached their own home base in Hangzhou, the two reported the conversation to their superiors, who in turn informed the governor-general, Li Wei.

Despite the fact that he was making final plans for his trip north to see the emperor and was busy arranging myriad details with those deputed temporarily to take over his duties, Governor-general Li Wei made the time to coordinate an investigation of this strange rumor with the senior officials in Fujian and Shandong. Ma was arrested and interrogated. Though pleading guilty to spreading the story about the impending slaughter of the children, he denied that he was its source. He had heard the tale from a man called Zhang, whom he met on the road in Shandong. Zhang was not too hard to trace, since he had identified himself as the personal retainer of a certain investigative censor in the north, and it did not take long to find an incumbent in that office who had a retainer named Zhang. But when located and arrested, Zhang also denied that he was the source. He had heard about the story from a man named Yucheng, whose native place was in the city of Guilin, far down in the south. Yucheng was traced and arrested, but said he heard the story from another man, a native of Guangxi. The search was now continuing.

On the eve of his departure from Changsha, Zeng Jing had also provided hard evidence concerning the source of stories harmful to the emperor and the dynasty. In that deposition, passed on to Beijing by his interrogators, Zeng Jing had stated that the source of the negative rumors he had heard was a holder of the 1706 *jinshi* degree named Wang Shu, who stopped by Zeng's schoolhouse back in May 1723. This Wang Shu claimed that he had, at some earlier stage, been a tutor or reading companion to the fourteenth prince, Emperor Yongzheng's younger brother; Wang also mentioned that his son was a commander with the army in the southwest.

Certainly there was nothing inherently improbable about such a story. The old Emperor Kangxi had wanted all his sons to be fluent in the Chinese language and familiar with the Chinese textual tradition, while at the same time remaining true to their Manchu heritage and culture; thus, most of the Manchu princes had studied with Chinese reading companions at one time or another. The current emperor, Yongzheng, while still a prince, had been assisted by the later disgraced general, Nian Gengyao, a *jinshi* degree recipient of 1700. The third prince studied for years with Chen Menglei, *jinshi* of 1670, who helped him to amass an immense library of scholarly books; together the prince and his scholarly adviser compiled a major encyclopedia. The current governor of Guangxi province had previously spent several years as a retainer on the staff of the twelfth prince. The eighth prince (killed on Emperor Yongzheng's orders in 1726) had even left the financial management of his immense fortune to his Chinese tutor, a *jinshi* recipient from 1709. And the ninth prince, also killed by the current emperor, had been tutored by one of the country's most celebrated classical scholars, He Cho, who had been awarded the highest literary degree by an act of imperial grace in 1703. Though the fourteenth prince had no such stellar scholars in his entourage, he had a variety of Chinese friends and associates. One of these men had even been arrested and executed for suggesting that the fourteenth prince was the old emperor's lawful heir, and that the current emperor, Yongzheng, should be deposed. Might not other people have the same idea? Perhaps a scholar from a princely family, now fallen on evil days?

The only trouble, as the Beijing investigators soon found out, was that nobody called Wang Shu had passed the *jinshi* examinations in 1706. There was a Wang Shu who passed high on the list of *jinshi* candidates in 1712, but he appeared to have been an exemplary bureaucrat, an expert in financial matters, a fine classical scholar, and a master of calligraphy. He was never the tutor to a prince. Nor did he have a son serving with the southwestern armies. This Wang Shu was sixty-two years old and had recently retired to his ancestral home in Jiangsu to attend to the burial of his parents. It was true that he had a reputation for being outspoken, but he did not sound like the kind of person to circulate wild rumors about his emperor in far-away Hunan. If the man who had claimed to be Wang Shu was not Wang Shu, then who was he? And where was he? Unless Zeng Jing had made the whole thing up, which did not seem likely, then presumably someone was using the real Wang Shu's name—and with it the prestige conferred by the attainment of the *jinshi* degree—to give credibility to his anti-Manchu stories.

If the emperor has learned one thing from all this, it is that every rumor is started by someone, whether by mishearing of an idle conversation or through deliberate malice. And rumors are likely to spread whenever their path is left unchecked. General Yue summarized the predicament succinctly: the "degrading and outrageous things" that the conspirators said and wrote, and the news that they had planned an uprising, were now "spread abroad everywhere." What does this do to the emperor's ability to rule? Musing in writing at the end of another secret report from Governor-general Ortai that he is about to return, Emperor Yongzheng asks his confidant about the appropriate response to all the bitter things contained in Zeng Jing's treasonous letter: "If, according to his arguments, I am not qualified to be the emperor of the great Qing state, then what am I supposed to do about it?" Or, to put it in rather different words, how does one silence the song of a phoenix?

Six

*Talking
Back*

The astonishing and unsettling words of Lü Liuliang and his disciples absorb much of Emperor Yongzheng's attention in the early months of 1729, but in mid-April he is pulled sharply back to the details of the Zeng Jing case itself. For it is at that time that he learns not only that the entire group of conspirators assembled in Hunan is at last on the road to Beijing, but also that Zeng Jing has admitted meeting a senior scholar named Wang Shu, a former confidant of the emperor's fourteenth brother. The news shifts his mind to the eighty-three-page edict he drafted the previous December, denouncing not only the content of Zeng's treasonous letter, but purporting also to give a concise and accurate history of the succession crisis.

Since that lengthy document was read to the assembled Beijing officials on December 11, it has entered a kind of limbo. Despite Yongzheng's statement that he intended to circulate the rebuttal far and wide, in order to prevent any potential doubters being won over by Zeng Jing's wild words, the document has never been distributed across the country in any formal way. One copy has been transcribed by the court diarists, and entered into the confidential imperial record, but that source is not open to other readers. And a capsule version of the diatribe—focused on the messenger's delivery of the treasonous letter to General Yue—has been released for inclusion in the *Capital Gazette,* and hence to some extent entered the public domain. But the *Gazette*'s sparse coverage has merely provided further material for the omnipresent rumor mill.

How then to proceed? The emperor's first impulse is to send a copy of the edict down to Ortai, the governor-general of the provinces in the far southwest. Since the death of Nian Gengyao, Ortai has become the emperor's closest confidant: a member of a noble Manchu family, the direct descendant of a Manchu military hero of the conquest period, and yet also fluent in Chinese and the recipient of the second-highest literary degree, Ortai's comments on practical problems are always full of sense, and he knows how to boost his emperor's spirits, as in the case of the auspicious birthday clouds reported in February. Fortunately, one of Ortai's own confidential couriers, Baoyu, is in Beijing, and on April 20 Emperor Yongzheng has given him a copy of the rebuttal, sealed in the imperial yellow dispatch box, to deliver to his master. Along with the document go generous presents for Ortai: two imperial-style robes trimmed with ermine, a box of dried fruits, and a box of milk cakes. Baoyu is also given a parting present for himself, ten taels of silver, to speed him on his way. The rebuttal edict is in Ortai's hands on May 12, along with an additional personal note from the emperor: "This edict was written in response to the traitor Zeng Jing. I plan to share it with the whole country, so I've sent a copy for you to look at. As soon as all the conspirators have reached Beijing and been carefully examined, I'll issue another edict."

But on April 21, only one day after dispatching the preliminary version of the document to Ortai, the emperor gives the Grand Secretariat a set of instructions on circulating the lengthy edict: they are to order their clerical personnel to write out several hundred fair copies of the December rebuttal, a sufficient number to provide each of the provincial governors (there are a total of seventeen) with nine copies—one for himself, one for each of the three commissioners serving under him (those dealing with finance, justice, and education), and three for the area garrison commanders stationed in his province. Each governor's two remaining copies will be spares: either these can be given to members of the governors' staffs for multiple recopying, or else the governors can pass them on to their local artisan-printers. (In accord with the contemporary practice, the printers would place these spare copies facedown on wooden blocks and carve around the written characters; these carved blocks of reversed characters would then be inked and used to produce a positive printed version.) These new copies would be passed on to the junior civil and military officials in every province, with a view to meeting the emperor's goal of having his words "distributed so as to reach the fullest number of people possible, down to the poorest villages and meanest homes." Senior officials serving in Beijing, governors-general supervising several provinces, and others temporarily stationed out in the provinces would also get their own sets.

Though such a distribution of the details of a treason case to a massive circle of readers across China is unusual, the emperor and his advisers are surely aware that a similar technique was used by the founding emperor of the Ming dynasty, Zhu Yuanzhang, in the 1380s and 1390s, late in his reign, when he wished all his subjects to know the depth of his political enemies' perfidy. In a world in which the Hunan conspirators and Lü's followers seem determined to present the early Ming rulers as paragons of Chinese moral virtue, it is certainly apt to use that Ming precedent to spread an accurate account of the real facts of Qing history, and lay the wilder rumors to rest.

By late April, the mass copying is under way. As each set of nine is completed, it is handed over to the governors' couriers, if they happen to be in Beijing, or to special messengers from the documents office of the Ministry of War, who will hand-deliver each set to its destination. The system works smoothly, the date of receipt being a function of the distance to be covered: for instance, the director-general of irrigation and flood control, who is stationed in north China, receives his copies on June 2; the governor of Guangxi, in the deep southwest, does not receive his set of nine until July 4.

Not surprisingly, the most detailed comments Yongzheng gets back are from Ortai. After expressing his gratitude for the emperor's trust, his awe at the emperor's thoroughness, and his revulsion at Zeng Jing's writings and behavior, Ortai adds some more personal comments of his own. One cannot deny that among the ruling Manchus, he writes in his responses to the emperor, there have been some who were ignorant or shameless, just as there have been others who were conscientious and intelligent and drew their models from the finest examples of statecraft in China's past. But in dealing with this case, everyone faced special problems: "When Zeng Jing fabricated these mendacious writings, bombastic and crazed, he secretly distributed them among his criminal accomplices, and thoroughly stirred up the senior officials. I think that the reason he could do this, and get as far as he did, was because this affair spread gradually, and also there was a source for what transpired. For instance, how could the vile slanders directed against the emperor have such an impact, unless they either started within the court and spread out from there, or started among the Manchus and spread out from them to the Chinese? It is the very absence of firm proof that makes me think this must be so. The basic goal pursued by the emperor's disgraced brothers Acina and Sesshe has become transposed into the words used by Zeng Jing."

Any group of outlaws or ignorant bumpkins has the capacity to spread slurs about the dynasty, continues Ortai, but they would never follow up with their charges to this kind of extent: "I suspect that when Zeng Jing says he is expressing the deep-felt but hidden grudges of the Chinese people, he is just using them as a pretext." Though the Manchus have ruled China well and responsibly for over eighty years, Ortai notes shrewdly, the country has never truly come together: "The hearts and thoughts of the Chinese are not yet at one with ours, and the Manchus themselves have yet to come up with any truly great achievements." Ortai admits that these are depressing reflections. The emperor agrees, running a series of red marks for emphasis along this particular passage, and writing, "I too sigh and weep over this."

Ortai concludes his response with some fatalistic thoughts: humans are not created in isolation, he writes, but live on earth alongside the birds and beasts. As the emperor has himself written, even among the birds and beasts there are evil and predatory creatures, as there are among humans. A man like Zeng Jing is like the lowest form of such birds and beasts, but nevertheless lives in the midst of his fellow humans. "The emperor's edict is both honest and compassionate," Ortai observes, "but you also question yourself and blame yourself. It is not just on account of Zeng Jing, but for the hundreds of millions of Chinese people, officials and commoners alike, that you are making all this known, both in Beijing and in the country at large." The emperor responds briefly and affectionately: "Since I myself am comfortable with this, don't be too upset about it yourself. When one encounters something as bizarre as this, one just has to find a special way to handle it, as you will see."

While the emperor's impassioned words against his brothers and Zeng Jing are spreading across China, Zeng Jing himself, now in prison in Beijing, is subjected to continuing interrogations. Most of the time he is questioned by Hangyilu, who has traveled back with the batch of conspirators from Hunan. Now that Zeng Jing and all the other conspirators identified so far are in prisons in Beijing, they can be cross-questioned by day or night. Every suspect can be presented with stories told by the others or confronted with outside witnesses face-to-face. Memories can be stirred and prodded. The interrogators have faith that no one can hide the truth forever.

Sometime between June 15 and June 20, Zeng Jing at last gives Hangyilu what he has been waiting for. What Zeng Jing now tells his interrogators is that, in addition to the stories told him by the fake Wang Shu, he had received damning information about the court and the emperor's character from two other separate groups of people, and at different times. The stories about the emperor's sexual improprieties, especially his taking of concubines from his own disgraced elder brother Yinreng, came from various condemned prisoners who were being escorted in the summer of 1727 down the road to Hengzhou city that passed near Zeng Jing's schoolhouse. The stories about General Yue's criticisms of the ruling emperor, on the other hand, along with other elaborate and dramatic tales of politics in the capital, came to Zeng at various times between 1723 and 1728, from neighbors living near his home. Though he does not remember the names of any of the prisoners, Zeng Jing does now remember the names of some of those neighbors: one is a licentiate from Anren named He; another is a local doctor named Chen, who practices medicine in the eighteenth ward of Yongxing county. Both licentiate He and doctor Chen, when talking with Zeng, named a third man as being the source of their information: a professional geomancer and fortune-teller from Chaling called Chen Dixi.

Informed of this new development, the emperor at once composes a court letter, which is hurried by military courier to Governor Wang Guodong in Hunan province, reaching him in early July. Wang is ordered to proceed immediately on two fronts: he is to check the Hunan government files for the names of all condemned criminals who traveled down the Hengzhou road to exile in Guangxi province in the summer of 1727; and he is to arrest the other three men named by Zeng Jing and to investigate them. He is to make Dr. Chen and the licentiate itemize every single story they told to Zeng Jing; they are also to list the circumstances, and the exact location, in which they first heard the stories from geomancer Chen. The governor is to record all their answers in detail. He is also to tell the three suspects of the serious danger they are in, and of the terrible punishments they might suffer. But at the same time he can reassure them that they will be considered guiltless if they were just the purveyors of rumors passed on to them by others, and can name the exact people who told them the original stories. If they close up about their sources, they will be interrogated under torture. If they refuse to talk under torture, Governor Wang is to ship them off under guard to Beijing so they can be confronted by Zeng Jing face-to-face.

A similar message, about tracing any condemned criminals traveling down the Hengzhou road in the summer of 1727, is rushed to the Guangxi governor for his immediate attention, since it was to the malarial districts of his province that these particular prisoners had been exiled. The senior officials conducting the investigation are specifically warned by the emperor not to punish people who merely report that they *heard* wild rumors—punishing those innocent bystanders would only lead to everyone keeping their mouths tight shut.

Pending the results of these new enquiries, Yongzheng launches a set of three linked rhetorical assaults against Lü Liuliang and his two main disciples, Yan Hongkui and Yan's pupil Shen. As each one is completed, the findings are issued to the court in the form of an edict, echoing the way that news of Zeng Jing's treasonous letter has been spread, though not at the same length and without the same complex pattern of mass distribution being put into effect. The idea of disclosure rather than concealment has come to fascinate Yongzheng: how much better to appear to reveal all, and then demolish the parts of the story one does not like, than to pretend nothing has happened and let the rumors build.

The first of this new batch of charges to be presented is the one against Lü's last surviving student, Yan Hongkui, which Yongzheng orders presented to the court on July 9, 1729. In the interests of brevity, the emperor makes no attempt to address all the complex intellectual issues in Yan's literary works or even to repeat all the passages in Yan's diaries that have upset him. There are simply too many, he observes, most of them inaccurate and worthless—the absurd nature of Yan's descriptions can be seen especially vividly in the more recent diary entries, those from 1716 to 1728, when the emperor has his own clear memories of the particular period being described. There is only one entry, notes the emperor, in which Yan caught an element of the truth, and that is the passage on the flood of 1709. Therefore, he would concentrate on a rebuttal of that item, for by proving the errors there, the errors elsewhere would become all the more glaringly apparent.

It was indeed true, the emperor notes, that a serious flood occurred in the Rehe region during July 1709, as Yan had written. But the flood happened not because the bloodstained figure of some Ming pretender persuaded the guardian spirits to unleash their torrents of dark water, but because of a perfectly predictable rise in the local river levels owing to heavy rains. Emperor Kangxi was in the area at the time and had naturally made sure that his camp was pitched on safe, high ground. Not a single one of the seasoned troops and officials traveling with the emperor was caught by surprise when the river flooded, nor were any of the local residents, who were used to such sudden changes in the river levels. It was only some of the artisans from the capital, brought along on the journey to look after the emperor's needs, who had panicked at the sight of the rising waters and constructed clumsy rafts, to which they clung in a desperate attempt to paddle their way to safety. Some of those rafts hit submerged rocks, and as a result some people were indeed drowned. By coincidence, continues Emperor Yongzheng, in that same month of 1709, he traveled from Beijing to visit his father in Rehe, along with a hundred or so guards and retainers. He could testify from his own memory that in the other areas affected by the flood there was no panic, and no one died of drowning.

What a ridiculous story it was to say that twenty thousand Manchus had died. In an area like Rehe people were all mixed together, regardless of race. How on earth could just Manchus have drowned and nobody else?

Perhaps even more absurd than Yan's retelling of history, the emperor continues, are Yan Hongkui's pretensions to be seen as some kind of Ming loyalist or recluse, a martyr to his beliefs. Lü Liuliang had at least been *born* in the Ming era, and had an ancestor who had married into the Ming imperial family. But Yan had not been born until the 1650s, well after the Manchu conquest. Not only Yan's father, but even his grandfather had spent years living peacefully under Qing rule. "What conceivable reason did Yan Hongkui have to link himself to the Ming rulers, or to their state?" the emperor asks. The rottenness of Yan himself was shown by the way he had turned down the graciously extended invitation that he help with the composition of the Ming dynastic history and by his fawning behavior to a visitor from far away like Zhang Xi. As the emperor writes in his July 9 edict, Yan "treated the summons to help the emperor as if it could just be sloughed off like outgrown clothes. And yet for the messenger from a rebellious imposter such as Zeng Jing he rushes off all kinds of letters as if they were the closest friends. Even when they are a thousand miles apart, they breathe in the same air together." Yan Hongkui was a troublemaker, one who "dreamed of the clash of arms even in prosperous times." Furthermore, Yan "licked up the spittle of Lü Liuliang." Let all the senior officials reflect on the appropriate punishments for Yan. A day later, Yongzheng issues a rather similar edict, mocking the even more absurd Ming loyalist pretensions of Yan's student Shen, who had not even been alive when Lü was teaching yet filled his own draft poems with slurs and innuendoes clearly designed to bring the Qing dynasty into disrepute. Shen should be intensively questioned and a suitable penalty be decided upon by the Ministry of Punishments.

The emperor reserves the most important attack, that against Lü Liuliang, for the end, issuing it in the form of an edict on July 16. For this final assault he returns from the fairly relaxed environment of the summer palace west of Beijing to the great halls of the Forbidden City. This time his arguments are detailed and comprehensive and contain a subtle shift in direction. Whereas in both the initial December attack on Zeng Jing and the two recent edicts on Yan and Shen the emperor had seemed to suggest that he regarded Lü and Zeng as being guilty of similar types of treasonous behavior, in this July edict he begins to formulate a rather different strategy, one that presents the two principal figures as a study in contrasts: "Lü Liuliang was born in the cultured region of Zhejiang," Emperor Yongzheng tells his officials, "among readers and scholars. Lü did not start off in a mountainous and impoverished area, as Zeng had to, growing up obstinate and ignorant. Besides which, Zeng Jing limited his criticisms to my own person. In contrast, Lü Liuliang directed his slanders at the moral reputation of my late father. Zeng Jing's slander and abuse sprang from his ignorantly listening to the swirling rumors; whereas Lü Liuliang's crazed charges came from within his very being. Thus Lü Liuliang's guilt is of the vilest kind, far worse than that of Zeng Jing." There is a clear trail, the emperor points out, running from Lü Liuliang's writings to the collapse of the whole moral fabric of Zhejiang province, to the viciousness of Zha Siting and Wang Jingqi, and to the various more recent examples of wild rumors, such as the stories of imminent mass slaughter, which have led thousands to flee for their lives. For Lü was the kind of man who "loves chaos and takes joy from catastrophe."

The emperor mocks Lü Liuliang's claim to be some kind of morally upright loyalist supporter of the fallen Ming regime. Apparently the marriage of one of his ancestors to a distant member of the Ming ruling family had gone to his head. Lü was indeed born "during the waning years of the Ming dynasty," the emperor observes, yet when the first assaults were launched against Beijing, "Lü Liuliang was still just a boy. It was only after our dynasty was founded that he really began his education, and started to mature as a scholar, and it was in the [first Qing] emperor's, Shunzhi's, reign that he took the examinations and became a registered student on stipend." At that time Lü showed no sympathies for the miseries of those caught up in the conquest, but simply continued in his pattern of subsidized study and career ambitions. Only when Lü failed the triennial reexaminations in 1667, and thus lost his sheltered degree status, did he suddenly discover his reverence for the Ming and begin to express hatred for the Qing; only then did he start to issue wild statements about totally shaving his head and retiring to live the life of a monk or hermit in the mountains. A decade later some of those who admired Lü's scholarly abilities—despite his examination failure—recommended Lü for a special examination being held by imperial grace, but Lü refused to even consider the offer. Has there ever been anyone quite like Lü Liuliang before, the emperor asks, "such a spreader of weird tales, so utterly without shame, so laughable yet so despicable?" Lü wrote his treasonous books and spread his vicious stories, but in fact "he was nothing more than a peddler of essays and a hawker of books, always seeking fame and financial profit, and even daring to mock the virtues of his own emperor." Lü's writings, like his diaries, whether spread abroad or stashed away, are all despicable, as the emperor knows from reading through them.

In this edict, Emperor Yongzheng does not try to quote all the passages by Lü that disturb or shock him. He concentrates instead on the ways that Lü belittled the dynasty that had raised and fed him with its virtues, given him home and nourishment, and enabled him to raise his sons and grandsons. Lü never used the correct and honorable names for the Qing dynasty and its rulers, the emperor points out; instead, he used a whole range of casual or belittling words, calling the Manchu rulers "northerners," "Beijing dwellers," or simply "those people." In contrast, Lü used honorific forms when referring to Ming pretenders, and even for the rebellious turncoat, General Wu Sangui.

The emperor spends considerable space in the edict trying to undercut the logic of Lü's account of the Qing troops in the southwest falling on their knees before the Ming pretender on his horse. In reality, writes the emperor, the fugitive pretender lived amidst vagabonds and bandits. He caused harm to the poor peasants around him, his troops deserted him, and he himself went into hiding in Burma. It was the Burmese ruler who later handed over the pretender to the powerful Qing forces. That was the sum of the whole sorry story, declares the emperor: no one fell in homage before anyone's horse. Lü's involved descriptions in his diaries and essays of natural portents had no more significance than this groundless tale. His writings showed that Lü was incapable of realizing that some natural disasters were bound to afflict China at intervals, in all previous historical periods just as in the Qing. Such crises were obviously not just phenomena of the times in which Lü was living. The true measure of a dynasty lay in its ability to help those afflicted by hardship, and in this the previous emperor, Kangxi, had excelled. In the present day, officials like Governor-general Li Wei were working to restore prosperity to Zhejiang province, even as the sickness spread by Lü Liuliang continued to infect the whole region. The honest endeavors of such officials made it all the more shameful that it should be someone like Lü Liuliang who claimed to follow the great tradition of Confucian reformist thinking and was constantly invoking the great masters of the past in his own writings and edited works. "When I first came to the throne," the emperor writes, "I knew nothing at all about the writings that Lü Liuliang had transmitted. Yet the full measure of the damage he caused stirred up the anger of humans and the gods, Heaven and earth had no way to contain it, so that Zeng Jing was drawn to write his letter to Governor-general Yue Zhongqi."

Though of course Zeng Jing's behavior has been outrageous—after all he spread wild stories of his own and planned to launch an insurrection—who was to say it was worse than Lü's hypocrisy? Or that Zeng was any worse than Lü Liuliang's sons and grandsons, who instead of making a bonfire of the wooden blocks from which Lü's works were printed and of the writings themselves, instead lovingly preserved them and distributed them ever more widely? "Anyone in the entire country," the emperor concludes, "official or scholar, who had a shred of decency within them, would grind their teeth together, and their hair would stand on end. Whether one is an emperor or an official, it is self-evident and inescapable when someone chooses not to uphold the honored rituals of Heaven and earth." Therefore, every senior official in the metropolitan bureaucracy, and in the upper tiers of the provincial officialdom, should reflect on the penalties that should be imposed on the deceased Lü Liuliang and on his still living relatives, not just his sons and grandsons but also all other collateral relatives. Having reflected, they should report back their conclusions.

Despite the emperor's specific request for advice on the appropriate punishments for Lü Liuliang and his followers, the summer continues to glide by and no suggestions from the bureaucracy are forthcoming. During the same summer months, however, news on the condemned criminals who passed down the Anren and Hengzhou roads at the times mentioned by Zeng Jing, and the pinpointing of their current whereabouts, begins to filter back to Beijing. With the Guangxi governor coordinating their findings, the southern governors piece together their information on the various convicts, the routes they followed, where they stayed and ate, and the behavior of their military escorts.

By the end of August 1729, the Guangxi governor can report that in the two summer months of 1727 specifically mentioned by Zeng Jing—the fifth and sixth in the lunar calendar—eight condemned criminals passed down the Hengzhou road with their guards. Two of the eight have since died. Two of the six survivors, a former keeper of the palace tea-storehouse and his six-year-old son, proved to be consistently peaceful and law-abiding since reaching Guangxi. The other four are all eunuchs from various princely palaces in Beijing and have a mixed record: one has never been reported as saying anything untoward; one has a reputation for being outspoken and unruly, though all the paperwork was not in on him yet, and it was hard to be clear about his record; the last two, Cui and Ma, were clearly troublemakers, frequently uttering remarks that were either on the edge of treasonous or full of grudging resentment against those who had found them guilty. The Guangxi governor's staff has located two other eunuchs, not on the summer list, one sent into exile in December 1726 and one in November 1727, who both had a record of being outspoken and sharp-tongued. Especially after being given food and liquor, some of these eunuchs spoke in an utterly reckless fashion, praising their former princely masters and claiming insistently that they had been wronged. Following another urgent message from Prince Yi, the five considered most likely to have spread the subversive rumors are sent under guard to Beijing.

In a frank notation on the Guangxi governor's report, Emperor Yongzheng writes: "You handled this very well. According to the confessions of the various listed criminals, these sorts of rumors have been spreading their poison for several years now. It's impossible to say how many gullible country folk believe this sort of thing. All one can do is strive to bring an end to it. We cannot afford to ignore any of the places to which criminals such as these are sent, and when we are dealing with someone like [my eighth brother] Acina, who was disloyal, unfilial, lawless, and unworthy of being an official, we have to check out every detail. Our edicts must be made known to everybody, and cannot just be allowed to drift. You used to be in the service of [my twelfth brother] Yintao, and though I have given you high office I know that you cannot claim to be ignorant of the kind of behavior my elder and younger brothers engaged in. Watch out!"

As the emperor does his own checking and draws the details together, all kinds of things begin to fall into place for him: as he explains in a follow-up edict, "The convicts exiled to Guangxi from the capital in the last few years have mostly been the eunuchs and retainers of my eighth, ninth, tenth, and fourteenth brothers." The eunuchs already identified as the most rebellious by the Guangxi governor in his report were all once in the service of those brothers who hated the emperor the most. It was these eunuchs who now sought to avenge their dead or humiliated masters. In the emperor's words, "Wherever they went they complained of being wronged, and they told their slanders to whomsoever they met." This was known to the guards who accompanied them and to the staff in the lodgings where they stayed overnight. Whenever they entered a village store or a township they would call out to the people: "All of you come over and hear the news about the new emperor. We have been wronged. We want to tell you so that you can tell others." Some of the eunuchs also said, "They can accuse us of this crime or that, but how can they seal our mouths?"

While the Guangxi exiles are being tracked down, Governor Wang struggles with the second item in the emperor's edict, the order to arrest the three men mentioned in Zeng Jing's latest confession. As always, he moves methodically, carefully checking things out with the military officials and the magistrates in each of the counties involved. Dr. Chen is arrested first, at his home in Yongxing county. Yes, says the doctor, he had met Zeng Jing. It was about five or six years ago: Zeng Jing's wife was seriously ill, and Zeng called in Dr. Chen to treat her. Naturally the two men got to know each other and talked about nonmedical matters as well as about the patient's condition; in some of those conversations, Dr. Chen passed on to Zeng Jing the stories told by the geomancer Chen Dixi. But in fact, though Dr. Chen relayed some of the geomancer's stories, he had never met the man in person. The doctor had been told the geomancer's stories, including the one about General Yue's courage in standing up to the emperor, by a military licentiate whom the doctor was treating in nearby Anren county. That had been about a year before the doctor was called in to treat Zeng Jing's wife.

The second person Zeng Jing has named, licentiate He Lizhong, is also arrested without any trouble, though Zeng had recalled his name in rather a garbled form. He Lizhong had seen Zeng Jing at intervals over the years, he tells Governor Wang, but the two of them could hardly be considered friends. A year ago he and Zeng ran into each other at the funeral ceremonies for licentiate He's son-in-law. Zeng Jing remarked, rather bluntly, that the deceased had been a man of shallow judgment. Licentiate He responded that few people nowadays had much judgment, except of course for the currently reigning emperor. Even the emperor let his officials break the basic rules of protocol, for instance, allowing a senior official to submit a highly critical report and not punishing him for it. But such remarks "were just to make conversation," says the licentiate; "it was not some rumor that I created. I heard it from one of my clansmen, and he said that he had heard it from geomancer Chen."

Geomancer Chen is not hard to find either, though he is living in most inhospitable terrain, in Chaling, east of Anren county, in the mountainous Jiangxi border region. When presented with the roster of names—the doctor, the licentiate, the clansman—he tells the interrogators he knows none of those men well. But it is true that the previous autumn he was called in to the aforementioned clansman's house to use his divination skills in *fengshui* to make some prognostications for him. While he was there carrying out his assignment, he heard the clansman's brother-in-law Zhang chatting about some rumors circulating in Sichuan province. According to those rumors, a certain General Yue had sent in a report critical of the emperor and urging the ruler to improve his conduct and to practice more benevolence. That same brother-in-law, Zhang, had also told his listeners that people in Sichuan were talking about a poem written on the wall of one of their local temples. The temple was a shrine to the memory of Zhuge Liang, the canny political organizer and military strategist of a previous era fourteen hundred years in the past, whose adventures were celebrated in China's popular fiction and histories. Zhuge Liang had dreamed of reuniting the war-torn and fragmented China of his own time, but had been frustrated by the ambitions of rival rulers. The brother-in-law had memorized the poem and recited it to his audience. The geomancer, too, could still remember it clearly:

Oh Zhuge Liang, little is left of your dreams of unity.
On every side the flowers are scattered, the trees have fallen.
The troops of Qin and Chu reach across the land,
East and West beyond the borders, desolation spreads.
From Qin and Jin the armies come, marching to Yan and Zhao.
As autumn fades even the crows can find no food.
Everyone across the land is about to perish;
All countrymen must arm themselves with swords and spears.
You ask who will live to see the good days come again?
Only those who hide out in the mountain caves.

Governor Wang tries to pin the various witnesses down more tightly, but
however rigorous his questioning, a coherent analysis always eludes him.
As he tells the emperor sadly, no two testimonies seem to agree, and no one
will admit to being the first to hear the poem or the stories about General
Yue. What should have been fact-finding cross-examinations of different
witnesses keep ending up as protracted bouts of mutual recriminations.

The emperor's reply to Governor Wang is angry and contemptuous:
"The people in the area you administer are making up stories like this, yet
you neither investigate them thoroughly nor report them promptly. Hearing of what has been going on down there I first send a special commissioner to conduct a thorough trial, and yet you still don't get to the heart
of what these scoundrels are up to. Now on top of that I even send you a
list of prime suspects from Beijing. Originally I feared that treacherous
people might hear wild rumors and spread them far and wide, so I asked
you to take quick and effective measures to investigate all this. But even
with those who have been investigated and have had their confessions
taken, you shift the work over to others and keep procrastinating, and
never seem to find out who really said what. How can we call you a governor of skill, merit, loyalty, or efficiency?" Governor Wang might as well
send the whole batch of these new prisoners off to Beijing for further interrogation, the emperor concludes, and as more suspects turn up, they
can be dispatched to the capital in their turn.

Governor Wang has been joined in his investigations by a new colleague, one whose recent appointment by the emperor implies a further

rebuke of Wang's incompetence. For this man holds the newly announced post of supervisor of public morality for the province of Hunan, and the emperor is clearly implying that Hunan now is in as parlous a state as Zhejiang was three years before, when Wang was first named morality supervisor there. Now, in the late summer of 1729, Governor Wang and his new colleague try to get back into the emperor's good graces by providing evidence of a dramatic breakthrough in the case. Their confidence is based on the fact that a Hunanese man has unexpectedly presented a petition to the morality supervisor in which he testifies that the master of the Changsha post station is a close friend of Zeng Jing's and has long kept in touch with Zeng through an exchange of letters. The excited officials report this news to the emperor without checking the story in detail, and are soon forced to confess that the whole thing is a fabrication. The post station director has never had any contact with Zeng Jing at any time, and the petitioner is a disgruntled former employee of his who sought through this dramatic accusation to gain imperial preferment.

Nor do they have any better fortune with their reexamination of geomancer Chen, which they undertake after receiving the emperor's scathing rebuke. At first, their progress seems patent: Chen now tells them that all his various stories about the different people in southeast Hunan who fed him the wild rumors were lies: he had simply accused all those people whom he disliked, either because they had been callous to him when he was ill, or because they had threatened him with violence. The real truth is that he heard the story about General Yue's reprimands to the emperor in the summer of the previous year, 1728. The geomancer had gone to the city of Hengzhou to buy some silk thread for his mother. Since it was a hot day, he sat down in a little pavilion to enjoy the breeze, rest his feet, and drink a cup of tea. As he sat there relaxing, he saw four men, tall soldierly-looking types, in riding jackets of military cut, along with a fifth man, clearly their baggage carrier. The geomancer could hear what they were saying: they were telling each other stories about General Yue's courage in facing down the emperor. The geomancer did not dare question them in detail or ask them their names, because they spoke with the authoritative accents of the official class, and he feared they might be bannermen from the imperial army in the capital. But he did ask the baggage handler where they were going and the man replied, "To the city."

As to the poem on Zhuge Liang that he recited at his first interrogation, he had not in fact heard that from one of his Hunan neighbors. That had also been a lie. He had read it during a separate trip to Hengzhou, the previous October. This time he had gone to the city to buy a cooking pot, but was distracted by a crowd he saw gathered at Fellow Students' Bridge. The center of their attention was a bewhiskered, white-haired Daoist with a gourd on his back. The man looked ninety years old but assured the crowd he was a hundred. The old man had posted a sign on the bridge, "Rain-cloud Daoist, Expert in Physiognomy." Another sign announced that for eight copper coins he would read your future. The geomancer joined the line to get a reading, and while waiting his turn saw the Zhuge Liang poem written on a sheet of paper and posted on the bridge. It was from thus idly reading it over a few times that he had come to remember it. The Daoist was from Sichuan, or so he said. As a fellow professional, the geomancer had to admit that the old Daoist gave an admirably clear reading of his character.

These retold stories are strange indeed, and this time the emperor makes no specific comment to his Hunan officials. He neither scolds nor praises them, nor does he order them to hunt down a one-hundred-year-old man with a gourd on his back. Instead, he keeps his own counsel. The geomancer will be in Beijing shortly, to join the growing roster of those available for detailed questioning.

There is one other figure whom the emperor has not forgotten: the man, whoever he is, who back in 1723 was using the name Wang Shu and falsely claiming to have earned the precious *jinshi* degree. How to find this man in the vastness of China? Emperor Yongzheng has an idea: he orders the Ministry of Personnel, which supervises and coordinates all bureaucratic appointments, to check through their files and see if they can find someone who has gone missing, someone who might plausibly claim to have passed the *jinshi* exams and to have served as a reading tutor to a prince of the realm. There cannot be too many people matching that description.

There are not many, but there is one, a Suzhou man named Wang Zhuo. This Wang had been serving as a military official in the southwest corner of Hubei province, just across the border from Hunan, when he lost his job by attrition after a bureaucratic reorganization at the end of the previous reign. According to the regulations, Wang should have reapplied to Beijing for another posting, but he never did. Instead, he vanished. Alerted by Prince Yi and the other senior grand secretaries, the Hunan governor coordinates an intensive search with the officials in Hubei. They are eventually able to track down Wang Zhuo, arrest him, and send him under guard to Beijing. There he is handed over to Hangyilu, previously in charge of the Hunan investigations into Zeng Jing's conspiracy, now co-ordinating all levels of the case in Beijing. Hangyilu takes Wang Zhuo in person to the imprisoned Zeng Jing, to see if he is the man Zeng talked to back in 1723. He is not. Zeng Jing has never seen him before in his life.

An alternative theory emerges: the false Wang Shu might be a person who once knew, or even worked for, the real Wang Shu. But questioned at his home in the lakeside city of Wuxi, where he is now living in retirement, the real Wang Shu cannot recall anyone he has employed as a secretary or family tutor over the years who was Hunanese or who matches the description proffered by Zeng Jing. Sometime that summer, an artist in Beijing is commissioned by the investigators to paint a portrait that will come as close as possible to the description given by Zeng Jing of the false Wang Shu. The portrait is circulated among all those who might have encountered the false Wang Shu at some time or another, but none of them can make a positive identification.

It has been a protracted hunt, and there are still numerous questions that remain unanswered. But the loose ends worry Emperor Yongzheng less by summer's end than they did at its beginning. As he told Ortai in May, "When one encounters something as bizarre as this, one just has to find a special way to handle it, as you will see." As summer glides by, the emperor has been giving substance to those enigmatic words: Quietly and steadily he has been turning Zeng Jing.

Seven

Summer
Lessons

In June 1729, Emperor Yongzheng, besides preparing his diatribe against Lü Liuliang and ordering the immediate follow-up on Zeng Jing's revelations concerning the exiled eunuchs, the geomancer, and Dr. Chen, also receives back Governor-general Ortai's response to the draft of his lengthy December edict. There is no specific indication that Yongzheng regrets writing that astonishingly frank document and ordering it so widely distributed, but his subsequent actions show that he has been reflecting on the most effective way to lay Zeng Jing's charges to rest and to dissipate the wraiths of rumor that still swirl around his rule. Ortai's complex answer suggests that the rebuttal edict has raised at least as many problems as it has settled, and the attempt to present Zeng Jing as an unthinking dupe of Lü Liuliang's posthumous machinations may not have been convincing, either. Perhaps it is not the best strategy merely to belittle Zeng Jing or to trace, step by step, the route that led him to perdition. How much better to have Zeng Jing rebut himself: to win him over to the imperial side and transform him from an uncommon criminal into a willing accomplice and mouthpiece of the throne. Not punishment but education will be the path to Zeng's redemption. And the beginning of education lies in facts.

The emperor formally launches this new program on June 27. On that day, in an edict to the investigators Hangyilu and Hailan relayed through the Grand Secretariat, he instructs them to begin briefing Zeng Jing on the realities of government. Zeng Jing claimed in his various writings and in his oral testimony that his path to treason began with his belief that Yue Zhongqi disliked and distrusted the emperor. The alleged proof of this was that Yue had defied two imperial summonses to audience in Beijing. Accordingly, let the first step on Zeng's road to recovery be the realization that the emperor and Yue Zhongqi trust and admire each other. To this end, the grand secretaries are to hand over to Hangyilu several dozen reports—each with vermilion endorsements in the imperial hand—that the emperor has exchanged with Yue over the past few years. Hangyilu will in turn take these to Zeng Jing's prison cell, so that the conspirator can read through them at his leisure. Once Zeng has read them and written out his thoughts, the materials can be passed on to the messenger Zhang Xi. The emperor adds that since the reports thus made available constitute only a small percentage of the total exchange between himself and Yue, they will give Zeng Jing a still imperfect idea of the range of favors that Yongzheng has showered on this particular official.

As a further gesture of his generosity and compassion, the emperor gives orders that Zeng Jing's elderly mother and Zeng's young son are both to be released from the Beijing jail, where they have been held along with the other conspirators and suspects since they all arrived from Changsha in the spring. The weather in Beijing is scorching, and they might perish if left where they are; some of the other imprisoned conspirators have already suffered so badly that they needed special medical attention.

When he has read through Yue's reports and the imperial endorsements to them, Zeng Jing writes out a reply, as instructed by Hangyilu. After general expressions of remorse for his conduct and awe at what he has learned concerning the emperor's generosity to Yue, Zeng settles down to mustering all the detail that he can on why and how he so totally misunderstood the relationship between General Yue and the emperor. Elaborating on his previous statement that the stories about General Yue came mainly from his neighbors, Zeng now adds that he heard other stories from various people who passed near his home as they were migrating down to Sichuan. These travelers came mainly from Hunan and Guangdong, and they all seemed to have heard that "down on the western frontier there was a certain 'Honorable Yue,' a man who truly loved the common people, and had won the people's hearts. The people on the western frontier all cherished him." But none of the people who passed on these stories knew the rest of Yue's name, or what office he held.

This information fused in his mind, Zeng now tells the emperor, with a series of tales that he heard about a remarkable governor-general of Shaanxi. These tales were recounted to Zeng Jing at the end of 1727, in the winter, by licentiate He Lizhong, who lived nearby. Licentiate He, whose name Zeng had recently passed on to the Beijing interrogators along with the names of the geomancer and the doctor, was a mine of the most detailed information, all of which Zeng seems now to remember. For page after page, Zeng writes out for the emperor everything that the licentiate told him, "in private and in a hushed voice, in Shijian village, nineteenth ward, Yongxing county." At the time, the story appeared a tangled one, full of dramas, hidden fears, conspiracies, all complicated by the fact that the licentiate had no idea what the name of his protagonist was. As He Lizhong summarized it, the emperor summoned this governor-general to the capital again and again, planning thereafter to whittle down the man's military power and to kill him. Suspicious of the emperor's intentions, the governor-general repeatedly refused to go. Only when the emperor sent his most trusted grand secretary, Zhu Shi, an original sponsor of the official in question, to act as the guarantor of safe conduct did the man travel to Beijing. Arriving in the capital, he confronted his emperor bravely, declaiming: "Your Majesty, please do not suspect those whom you employ, and do not employ those whom you suspect." Impressed by the man's courage, the emperor relented somewhat and ordered him to return to his post. Again, the governor-general refused unless some guarantor could be found. No one volunteered to take on the task, and at last Emperor Yongzheng had to pledge his own word. But within four days, receiving a report that the official was forming a secret cabal of followers, the emperor sent a trusted courtier to chase after him and bring him back to the capital. When the governor-general refused to turn back, the courtier—shamed by the failure of his mission—committed suicide by the roadside. Reaching Xi'an safely, the governor-general sent a report back to the court, reproving the emperor for his conduct.

These tales suddenly became mutually reinforcing when Zeng heard Dr. Chen, a resident of the neighboring eighteenth ward of Yongxing county, recounting geomancer Chen Dixi's stories of the courageous report sent to the court by Yue Zhongqi. Realizing suddenly that these stories referred to the same person, Zeng was all the more impressed. Since the Hunan harvests had been bad two years in a row and Zeng had been corrupted by Lü Liuliang's writings on the inferior nature of the barbarians, his own "treacherous and wild thoughts" now had fertile ground in which to grow. "Besides everything that I have recorded in this confession," Zeng Jing concluded, "there was no one else who passed stories on to me. That is the absolute truth."

In the emperor's eyes the experiment of having Zeng read the original documents is proving successful. Accordingly he decides to deepen Zeng Jing's appreciation of the way that the bureaucracy works and how the emperor he conspired against responds to the problems the country faces. In another brief edict, Hangyilu is instructed to assemble from the Beijing files "several hundred" of the provincial reports from a wide array of governors-general, governors, and other senior officials from all over China, so that Zeng Jing can read them and take note of the emperor's personal vermilion comments on a wider range of issues. Such an exercise will not only give perspective on the emperor's work with Yue Zhongqi but also illustrate how Zeng's own case fits into the wider flow of business from around the empire.

As Zeng Jing reports to the emperor once this new batch of reading is done, he has been especially impressed by the examples of the emperor's meticulous attention to detail, of the ways the emperor concentrates so carefully on the documents before him that he would catch miswritten phrases and wrongly calculated figures. Zeng notes that even reports about the most auspicious events, that seem to promise great blessings for the dynasty, are rejected by the emperor if clumsily presented—as in the case of the Anhui educational commissioner's report of the discovery of an especially rare plant that was always taken as an admirable omen, or the report from the direct lineal descendant of Confucius himself that he had seen a mass of auspicious clouds. And even governors-general like Gao Qizhuo of Fujian, who wrote reporting a corruption and impeachment case, might be caught up short by the emperor's noting of their errors. Zeng Jing is especially struck by the secret reports he is shown that deal with the recent case of the Fujian retainer Ma, who spread abroad the story of the imminent threat of killing all the boy children in Fujian. Such a story, Zeng notes, seems to echo the reports he had read about the cruelties of a governor such as Bulantai in Jiangxi province. Zeng Jing feels privileged to read the full reports that explained how this particular rumor grew and spread, he assures the emperor, because this is exactly the kind of thing he would have believed in the past, and would have written down in his own book. Truly things have changed since he left Changsha a few short months ago, writes Zeng. It is only now, with all the evidence before him, that he can see how he has been behaving "like an ant who cannot see the size of the sky."

Without attempting to summarize the contents of each report, or to comment on specific imperial notations, Zeng Jing contents himself with summarizing the cumulative impact the huge volume of paperwork has had on his thinking: "Now that I have humbly read through all these edicts," he writes, "I can see how in all his varied comments and responses my emperor always acts in accordance with correct moral principles. When responding to administrative and judicial problems, he is attentive to virtue and to ritual—he appears always to know the absolute essence of every problem, and always to find the correct way to handle it."

Not only is Emperor Yongzheng in harmony with the activities of the sage emperors of long ago, Zeng writes, he even matches the genius of his own late father, Emperor Kangxi. But if the moral strength the emperor displays is impressive, so is the amount of work that he undertakes, and so uncomplainingly: "From dawn until nightfall every day there is so much to attend to, endless items for the emperor to scrutinize, countless words of the emperor's own comments; senior and junior officials from the capital bureaucracy and from the provinces must be received in audience every day, so he can hear their reports one by one, and admonish them constantly to love and care for the people. There is a constant flow of business and each thing must be taken care of, so that no one feels a trace of rancor over something's not being handled with thoroughness, confidentiality, clarity, and propriety. It is often only around ten at night, sometimes even at midnight, that the emperor at last gets to comment on the confidential reports sent in by the various governors-general and governors, yet even so the emperor does not use any assistants to write out his comments for him. Such is the painstaking attention he devotes to his duties!" Now at last, Zeng Jing concludes, he can understand his own errors, see the folly of the wild rumors that vilified the emperor's character, and begin to plumb the treacherous nature of a man like Lü Liuliang.

Zeng Jing's reference to "judicial problems" meshes neatly with a subsidiary goal Yongzheng has been contemplating for some time: that of demonstrating to Zeng how the law functions, and how clemency is often granted by the emperor even in cases for which capital punishment at first seemed fitting. In anticipation of this, Emperor Yongzheng tells Zeng in yet another special edict relayed by Hangyilu, he has been compiling a list of the more challenging cases that have been sent in for review during the spring and summer of the present year. According to long-standing practice, predating the current dynasty, all cases involving a sentence of capital punishment are forwarded to the emperor, either by the provincial governors-general and governors or by the senior officials in the Ministry of Punishments. The emperor had decided to take the step of sharing a sample of these with Zeng Jing after reading his Hunan confession from earlier that spring. In that document, Zeng specifically stated that he believed the emperor "was fond of killing people, and that the people of Beijing all lived in fear." The only effective way to eradicate such a charge was to present the evidence. Accordingly the emperor was sending to Zeng Jing, via Hangyilu, the transcripts of a dozen legal cases. Cumulatively these showed the range of ways that judicial reviews might be undertaken. Zeng was to read them through carefully and report back his views of the judgments made in each one, particularly whether they supported the view that the emperor took pleasure in killing. Zeng Jing was also to tell the emperor exactly from whom, and where, he had heard the stories of the emperor's cruelty.

The selected cases happen to come from six different provinces: Yunnan in the southwest, Jiangxi and Anhui in central China, Zhejiang and

Guangdong on the southeast coast, and Shanxi in the north. The accused represent a wide range of age groups and occupations, and their crimes span a gamut of criminal activities. The oldest of those found guilty was an eighty-two-year-old widow in Yunnan who along with her three sons had beaten a man to death and tried to dispose of the body by setting it alight on a pile of straw in the middle of the night. The Yunnan officials had sentenced the widow, as the brains behind the murder, to immediate beheading, and her sons to what was considered the far less degrading punishment of strangulation. In amending the decision, the emperor asked whether a woman of her age had the strength to beat someone to death or to gather a large pile of straw—in addition to which, now that her husband was gone, her eldest son should have taken a leadership role in the household and prevented his mother from going through with the plan. In what had obviously been a group homicide, it made no sense at all to punish the elderly lady more harshly than her sons, and hence a review was in order. But, the emperor noted, holding a son responsible in *all* such cases was not sensible either. In a parallel case submitted for review at the same time, the son had been away from home when a fatal beating began and was summoned home by his parents to force him into complicity. In that second case the son had been initially absent and then morally coerced, so clemency was possible.

In certain other cases of battery or homicide shown to Zeng Jing, the emperor explains how mitigating factors led him to revise the original sentences. A dispute in Guangdong over the dividing up of certain lineage lands belonging to the Xie family, which originally had been designated to provide a regular income for sacrificial and religious purposes, had led to one member of the Xie family's seriously beating his uncle. Such a crime against a senior by a junior in the family could bring the death penalty, but there were questions about who held the club and who had been cursing whom before the quarrel flared. And in Jiangxi, a woman's lover had killed her husband, and she was held to be guilty in principle and was sentenced to death by strangulation. But the emperor had a host of problems with the verdict: it was clear that the woman had not known anything about the planned murder; her affair with the lover took place well before the murder; for a considerable time she had been estranged from her husband; and the married couple had an eight-year-old son they still looked after together. Everything suggested that she would have gained nothing by having her husband killed. Or take a case from Anhui province, the one in which a younger brother killed his older brother with a heavy wine jar and was sentenced to be beheaded. Once again, there were several mitigating factors, primarily the fact that the killing was totally unpremeditated. The two brothers had always gotten along harmoniously, until this particular quarrel flared over a quite trifling sum of money. In a rage, the elder brother picked up the wine jar and threw it at his younger brother, but missed. The younger brother picked it up and threw it back, killing his elder sibling. But certainly this should be treated more as an accidental homicide, and the sentence should be reviewed.

A different category of cases was those where the victims were in the wrong in some way or another, and one had to work out how or why. When Cao killed his wife with a piece of wood in Zhejiang, for instance, it was because she had already ignored the proprieties of being a wife: she had refused to give her husband tea when he asked for it, and when he blamed her for that, she not only showed no contrition but tried to hit him with a stone. It was at that point that he seized the piece of wood and beat her to death. The authorities had sentenced the husband to death by strangulation, but the emperor waived the death penalty on the grounds that the wife had violated the "basic bond" of obedience to her husband. It was enough for the husband to be sentenced to wear a heavy wooden cangue around his neck for a period of time, instead. Formed from two wide planks of wood, slotted together around the guilty person's neck, the cangue was so designed that those wearing it could breathe but were quite unable to feed themselves. That would be satisfactory warning to Cao to curb his violence in the future and would serve to remind everyone in his neighborhood of the correct relationships between husband and wife.

The last three cases Zeng is told to study concern those who were proven criminals and yet in some ways might not have understood the laws they broke. There was no doubt that Zha Shengwen in Shanxi province had led a gang of robbers, but it was not something he had really intended to do. He had been talked into it by a blind man named Li, who persuaded him to seize land contracts and burn them, so as to redress old inequities. The emperor commuted Zha's death sentence. There was also the case of three prisoners who escaped from jail: in the eyes of the law such an action must lead to an increase in their sentences, or even to the death penalty. But the emperor was worried that they did not understand the consequences of their act, and ordered their sentences left unchanged. He did however order that in future the laws punishing escape attempts be written out and placed prominently in all state prisons, so all those sentenced to prison terms would be aware of them.

Though it was a very different kind of case, one could use the same type of argument in the case of Zhang Xian, sentenced to decapitation for privately and illegally minting coinage. Zhang, it transpired, had earned his living from making and selling bronze utensils, but had been threatened with financial ruin when a sudden shortage of coinage had led the emperor to promulgate a new law forbidding the manufacture or sale of all objects made of bronze. What Zhang had done, casting coins from his stock of otherwise now unusable metals, was criminal but understandable. His death sentence too should be subject to review.

Summarizing his reactions for Hangyilu, after reading the cases through and adding his own brief commentary on each one, Zeng Jing writes that they have indeed changed his mind about his emperor. He can now begin to see how his ruler invokes the Dao, the way of moral rightness, to inform his judgments. The Dao is flexible, the law is rigid; the Dao adjusts to circumstances, the law is merely imposed. Never again, writes Zeng Jing, will he dare to accuse the emperor of being unfeeling about the lives of others. But on the matter of *how* he had come to hear that the emperor took pleasure in killing, Zeng Jing writes, he regrets that he can be of no help. He is just a man ignorant of true human feelings, who stupidly listened to the random gossip around him.

The emperor realizes that such a vast mass of reports and court transcripts give Zeng a decent insight into the problems of running the country, but they do not necessarily delve into the economic details of everyday life, which had filled so many of Zeng Jing's rebellious thoughts. For such an understanding, one needs to focus on specific problem areas. An excellent example is the minting of coins, which featured prominently in the last of the legal cases shown to Zeng Jing. As it happens, that same summer of 1729 the emperor has been mulling over the ban on bronze implement making and discussing it at court as a good example of the kind of decision rulers have to make in order to achieve a higher and more general good, even though the same decision would be unpopular with some minority. The ban on the making of bronze implements was designed mainly to prevent people from melting down coinage for its copper content and using the copper to make bronze artifacts that would bring in a higher profit than the face value of the coins themselves. The long-range effect of the ban would therefore be a healthier economy for the country as a whole. To the emperor, this example is very similar to his recent ban on the slaughtering of cattle, over which so many Muslims have been protesting. That ban was in no way aimed at the Muslim community's livelihood, as some of them had stridently claimed. It was, rather, an attempt to increase the amount of oxen available for plowing and thus to foster the prosperity of the farmers in general. (High beef prices had led many farmers to slaughter their cattle—and some were still doing it in defiance of the ban— while agricultural productivity shrank in the absence of deep plowing.) A recent ban on gambling had a similar intent. It was not aimed simply at individual gaming houses; its aim was to stop people from ruining themselves in a useless and nonproductive way, one that managed at the same time to destroy the moral strength of the community.

So that same summer, the emperor sends a lengthy comment on this problem to Zeng Jing. He places his arguments in the context of the remarks about the current state of the coinage that Zeng Jing had included in his treasonous book, the *Knowledge of the New*. In that book, notes the emperor, Zeng Jing wrote that the coins made from the accession of Emperor Yongzheng onward were so poorly minted, and the images and writing on them so blurred, that nobody wanted to use them. People even made up a jingle that they sang: "Use Yongzheng's coins—and go broke in six months"! If someone found they had one of the coins, they would throw it in the ditch. In fact, the emperor explains to Zeng Jing, the sharpness or lack of it in the calligraphy and decoration on the face of a coin is a function of the ratio of copper to other base metals used in coinage, such as lead. (Such ratios had veered vastly in the past, from a high of over ninety percent copper in the mid-sixteenth century to a low of thirty percent in the 1620s.) The late emperor, Kangxi, had decreed that his coinage should be minted from a combination that was sixty percent copper and forty percent lead, and the images on those coins were indeed beautiful and sharp. The trouble was that because of the high copper content it was worth people's while to melt them down and use the copper in combination with tin or zinc to make bronze utensils. As the copper coins grew scarcer, the exchange rate of copper coins in relation to silver rose sharply, till by the year 1706 or 1707 an ounce of silver was only "worth" seven or eight hundred small copper coins. It was for that reason, and that alone—not for imperial greed nor for a wild scheme to build a copper palace in the northern reaches of the empire, as some had claimed—that the current emperor had imposed his ban on bronze utensil manufacture, and at the same time had ordered all coins in state mints to be made of half copper and half lead, so it was no longer profitable to melt them down.

The policies worked, Yongzheng points out, and currently the exchange ratios had returned to exactly where they should be, at one thousand copper coins to one ounce of silver. That was far more important than having a sharp image on the coins' face. Naturally the coins might be slow to reach some isolated rural areas, but they were valid specie, and were automatically exchangeable for rice and fuel and convertible into silver at the accepted exchange rates. Who had told Zeng Jing these wild tales? Had Zeng Jing personally ever seen anyone throw the Yongzheng-reign coins into a ditch? If so, where and when? And what were the names of the people who thus threw their money away? Why should Hunan be so different from provinces like Jiangsu and Anhui, where the Yongzheng coins were widely used in business dealings and were even traded well above par for the old Kangxi-reign coins of the same face value?

Unfortunately he can not provide any names of those who spread these stories, replies Zeng; he "had just heard people talking like that," and had written the stories down without making any attempt to check out their veracity. That was doubtless because in his home area, far from any big town, almost no money was in circulation, and the traders who did come to the area usually bartered their goods for grain. When Zeng Jing at last saw some of the Yongzheng coins, he noted how inferior they were to the previous emperor's. This confirmed in his mind the various stories he had heard: that the mint workers could not do any better and so Emperor Yongzheng had killed them, and that the bronze-utensil ban was because the emperor was secretly hoarding all the country's copper to build a metal palace. If there had been officials stationed in the rural areas who could have explained the emperor's copper policies clearly, says Zeng, the misunderstandings would not have arisen. Similarly, if there had been a well-ordered and administered community compact of the kind recommended by various earlier political thinkers, the policies could have easily been explained at the monthly meetings. But as it was, "The rumors spread by one or two irresponsible people ended up being heard and believed by hundreds of thousands." Only now, concludes Zeng Jing, after receiving the emperor's own explanation, does he understand what really happened, and the reasons for it.

The economic dialogue continues all through the summer, as the emperor passes new batches of questions on to Zeng Jing through Hangyilu. Sometimes he is sarcastic: Why has the one province of Hunan suffered so badly when the rest of China experienced only limited hardship? Surely the answer must be that Zeng Jing was living in Hunan, and his intransigent nature led Heaven to scourge his home province with floods. And why has Zeng Jing written so slightingly in his book of the government's relief efforts in those areas hit with natural disasters? Can Zeng Jing not see that transfers of grain between the provinces, or trans-shipments of silver specie in bulk, when ordered by the emperor, were not for private gain or because of greed but were designed to achieve price stabilization and reduce scarcity? But when the emperor challenges him to come up with one example of people "who cried out in bitterness at their plight" and to state where these people lived and what they had to complain about, Zeng responds vigorously. There are indeed such people: they are the farmers in the Dongting Lake region—just north of Changsha—who lost their livelihood in the recent Hunan floods. Those people had nowhere to turn as they cried for help. Though they did receive a little government aid, most of them were forced to emigrate elsewhere, and those who could not do so have been left to fend for themselves.

The details of these written exchanges between emperor and conspirator are known to only a handful of officials, such as Hangyilu and the grand secretaries. But Yongzheng is anxious to keep the wider discussions going as well, and since the bureaucrats have not responded to his requests for their views on the penalties that should be imposed in the Zeng and Lü cases, in late July he tries a different tack. His vehicle for this is a scholar from Guangxi province named Lu Shengnan who had served as both a county magistrate and a section chief in Beijing before being dismissed ignominiously by the emperor for incompetence and arrogance. As the emperor now reminds his officials, he had ordered Lu Shengnan to serve in a military unit on the northern borders so that the condemned man could learn the meaning of discipline and hardship and thus get a more accurate view of the world: "By observing the sincerity of the Manchus' obedience to their own commanders, he would come to understand the meaning of awe and respect; by observing the organization of our military units, he would come to understand the meaning of true discipline; by observing the glories and the noble simplicity of the various Mongol tribes, he would come to understand the meaning of real integrity. Thus would he slough off all selfish and treacherous thoughts and embark on the road to self-renewal." A wider knowledge of the shape of Chinese history would also benefit Lu Shengnan: he would learn that it was the Mongol dynasty of the period before the Ming that first brought order and unity to the peoples beyond China's borders, just as the founding Qin dynasty two thousand years before had brought unity for the first time *within* those borders. Now it had been the turn of the current Qing dynasty both to consolidate those grand achievements of the past and to raise them to a higher stage. Never before, the emperor noted proudly, had China had "the incredible territorial extent that it does under our own dynasty."

Instead of absorbing those central lessons, the emperor now declares Lu Shengnan spent his time amidst the troops writing an elaborate treatise on history in which he praised the decentralized political systems of China before the first consolidating emperors, who ruled two thousand years before, and implicitly found fault with most of the policies of the present age. Lu Shengnan, declares the emperor, was involved with a factional grouping of scholar-bureaucrats from Guangxi who had undermined morale at home and in Beijing; besides which he had been in the group who gravitated to the emperor's hated and now dead eighth brother. In the rebelliousness of his thinking, Lu Shengnan is similar to both Lü Liuliang and to Zeng Jing. But, adds the emperor, as a member of an elite scholarly family, born and raised in privilege and hand-picked for high office, Lu Shengnan is guilty of a far more serious offense than Zeng Jing, who had been raised in rural isolation, knowing nothing about the wider world and with no one to guide him. It is the emperor's recommendation that Lu Shengnan be executed. This time the court officials respond swiftly, reviewing the case and ratifying the death sentence within two days. After a cursory reprieve, allegedly to see if Lu Shengnan expresses remorse—he does not—he is beheaded in front of the troops he was meant to serve.

It is one of the features of Emperor Yongzheng's ruling style—inherited to some extent from his father, Kangxi—that although he is in so many respects an absolute ruler, with no formal institutional constraints on his power, he nevertheless seeks ratification and moral support from his senior bureaucrats when he is making certain types of decision. The Lü Liuliang–Zeng Jing case is one of these, in that the emperor seeks a more public endorsement of the steps he is taking: it is clear that he is tilting toward clemency for Zeng despite his treason and for posthumous punishment of Lü Liuliang, despite the forty-five years that have passed since Lü's death. The officials have shown no trouble at all in swiftly consigning Lu Shengnan to a brutal death; why are they being squeamish about Lü Liuliang? And why do they refuse to see that Zeng Jing is different from these privileged and conceited scholars? But despite all the hints the emperor has dropped, summer turns to autumn, and the October 28 anniversary of the delivery of the treasonous letter to General Yue comes and goes with as yet no sign from the senior officials of what their recommendations might be.

Finally, on November 2, the emperor increases the pressure on the bureaucracy with a toughly worded edict on problems of race, guilt, and government responsibilities. To attain and maintain power, he argues, rulers from the past to the present have all had to combine concern for their subjects' welfare with the ability to earn their subjects' trust and affection. That is the meaning of the phrase that "only the virtuous are able to rule all under Heaven." One's geographical origins were inconsequential here. The emperor approvingly cites the earliest surviving historical text in China, written two millennia before, which contains the lines "Great Heaven has no personal attachments, it helps only the virtuous." Many other passages from the same text show that the essence of good ruling had never been linked to the area whence the ruler came. Why, then, he asks, when the Manchus have successfully brought peace and unity to the country and its border regions, do the Chinese keep using the invidious comparisons of "inner" and "outer," or of Chinese from the heartland as opposed to those they call the "Yi" and "Di" barbarian peoples from the outer lands? Just because the latter wear different clothing, or have different ways in warfare, that means nothing about their skills at government. Some of the greatest rulers of the past, now saluted as "Chinese," were in fact Yi or Di, just as some of the most disastrous ones were Chinese. They destroyed their kingdoms not because of where they came from, but because they ignored the principles of decent governance. Confucius himself wrote about the days of disunion and fragmentation in which he lived that "the Yi and Di tribes have their rulers, unlike our own land where there are none." Boundaries and even language had changed over time: what were now the provinces of Hunan, Hubei, and Shanxi were all once seen as "Yi" territories; insults against a particular ethnic group—"island barbarians"; "chained slaves"—sprang from specific historical moments, and then acquired permanence.

For the rest of his November 2 edict, the emperor elaborates on these various themes. He adduces historical examples of men without conscience or morality who tried to found dynasties, and notes how they had all failed—even if they appeared to triumph for a while, they always burned themselves out in the end. He reflects on the basic sense of moral relationships, which are what separate humans from the birds and the beasts. And he ponders, from different perspectives, the misplaced arrogance and inadequate logic of those Chinese who find fault with outsiders even when those outsiders bring law, propriety, peace, and order back to the land. The Qing have "rescued the Chinese people from the boiling cauldron" in which they were plunged at the end of the Ming. In those terrible days of warfare and death, Ming commanders slaughtered their own people and claimed rewards for their "valor." The emperor estimates that half of China's population perished in those war-riven years; even more died in Sichuan, where the few who survived had lost hands or feet or had their ears and noses sliced off by a rebel leader. Sixty years after those nightmare events, the elderly still wept as they recalled them. Yet false rumors against the Qing kept springing up, and claimants and usurpers still arose invoking the name of the fallen Ming, unlike recluses of the past who simply withdrew to the mountains and lived out their lives in anonymity. Given the persistence of this bitterness, the emperor "does not know where to turn, or what to do in the future."

Herein, continues the emperor, lies the true menace of a traitor like Lü

Liuliang, with his vicious comments such that after the Song dynasty fell to the Mongols, Heaven and earth suffered catastrophic change, so that even in the present era astral portents and other signs not seen since ancient times were once again appearing. Picked up by Lü's disciple Yan Hongkui, the spreading waves finally reached Zeng Jing. In Zeng's mind, "The bizarre and the delusory fanned each other into flame," with the result that he ended up writing such crazy things as that "for over eighty years the heavens and earth have been darkened, and the sun and moon stopped shining."

People such as Lü, Yan, and Zeng Jing, the emperor ended, "incorporate all the negatives of those who resist Heaven, turn their backs on principle, confuse the world, and mislead the common people. And so we must reveal to them the great meaning of the sacred texts of the past, our morality, our correct behavior, and our proper relationships. If we can bring a true awakening to the deeply ignorant and to those who are constantly immersed in a sea of depraved gossip, and can spare them the wrath of Heaven and the punishments devised by men, then we will have acted on behalf of all humanity. So let this edict of mine be transmitted to and distributed in every prefecture, department, and county in the land and to the most distant and isolated villages, so that everyone—from erudite scholars to the poorest people in the hamlets—will know these words." This time the emperor gives no suggestions as to how this distribution should take place, nor does he seek his ministers' advice on the matter.

By November 19, still having received no sign of a response, the emperor once again pushes matters forward. Several months ago, he announces in a short edict, he instructed Hangyilu and Hailan to review all the details of the case against Zeng Jing. Over that whole period the emperor had been sending in his questions, and Zeng Jing returning his replies. It is the emperor's conviction that "the detailed responses that Zeng Jing gave to the questions show that he is full of remorse, and grateful for our kindness." But people in Zeng's situation might well dissemble, or simply be scared of death and hence put on a show of acknowledging their guilt. Therefore the emperor is now instructing his senior officials at court to sift through the evidence again, and question Zeng Jing himself for one last time, "to see if he truly understands the enormity of his crime, and if his shame and remorse truly comes from the heart." That done, they are to report their findings back to the emperor.

In the face of such an order, the officials have no alternative but to act. They take exactly one week to complete the task, reporting back on November 26.

Their report is succinct. Zeng Jing has offered three excuses for his behavior: his rustic and isolated upbringing; the disquieting effects of the rumors spread by the emperor's renegade brothers and their staffs; and the effects on his untutored mind of the works of Lü Liuliang. Thanks to his recent protracted period of study, Zeng now claims that he fully understands and regrets the error of his ways, and sees the wisdom and generosity of the reigning Manchus and the unity they have brought to the troubled land. He acknowledges his guilt and throws himself on the emperor's mercy.

In the opinion of the officials, it is indeed true that Zeng Jing's crimes are completely self-evident: he yielded to the suggestiveness of the wildest rumors, spread crazy ideas to his followers, and wrote a treacherous letter in Hunan with which he tried to suborn the governor-general of Shaanxi province. His intent was to bring chaos to a peaceful land. And how was it possible that after fifty years of secluded life in the countryside he should suddenly decide to lead this reckless conspiracy? In all of Chinese history no rebellious official, no reckless bandit, had ever behaved in such a way. Listening to Zeng's repeat testimony, none of the officials have been able to contain their feelings of anger and disgust.

The law of the land, they write, stipulates that in treason cases of this kind the punishment is a lingering execution by slicing for the traitor himself, with summary execution by beheading or strangulation for all his close male relatives aged sixteen or over, and exile and enslavement for all the women and minor males in the criminal's family. All the traitor's property is forfeit to the state. The officials see no reason whatsoever not to act immediately: "With regard to Zeng Jing, we humbly request the emperor to allow us to implement these punishments promptly and sternly, so as to maintain the clarity of the law of the land, and to gladden the people's hearts."

In every other document connected with the case, the reports have come from individuals, specific bureaus, or the small inner council of advisers to the emperor. But in a highly unusual gesture of solidarity, this one is signed by one hundred and forty-eight officials, each with his name and sonorous titles clearly written out in full. It is an imposing roster: in serried ranks across the pages flow the names of the grand secretaries, who supervise the workings of the capital staff; the presidents and vice-presidents of the six ministries that handle the day-to-day business of the government; the officials of the Censorate, who check on the uprightness and accuracy of their colleagues; the directors of the transmission office, who keep the flow of documents moving across the country; the teachers and scholars of the Hanlin Research Academy in Beijing—masters all of the classical past, from whose ranks the chief and associate examiners are drawn for every national and provincial exam; and the various experts in economic matters, who coordinate the tax and budget reports that stream endlessly toward the throne. Zeng Jing's remorse does not impress them. The law is the law, and clemency is not an issue. Whatever the emperor's views might be to the contrary, on that they speak as one.

Eight

The
Pardon

For months, Emperor Yongzheng has been seeking to build a mood among his officials, one that encourages them to see the essential gullibility of Zeng Jing and to contrast that gullibility—with its tincture of innocence—with the ingrained menace represented by Lü Liuliang. The forceful request by so many senior bureaucrats for Zeng Jing's painful and humiliating death is proof that the imperial strategy has failed. But does their demand for Zeng's death mean also that they reject the emperor's insistence on the guilt of Lü Liuliang? Are they seeking to reverse the emperor's judgment absolutely, and contrast the essential innocence of Lü Liuliang with the ingrained menace of Zeng Jing? Since the emperor's officials still refuse to render any verdict on Lü, despite his vigorous requests, it is hard for him to be sure.

Yongzheng's initial response, delivered on November 27, is conciliatory. Ordering the officials to assemble in the main audience hall of the

Forbidden City, he assures them that he fully understands how the stark nature of the case, and the law of the land, combine to make the death penalty for Zeng and Zhang seem the obvious solution. But he has decided to hold off from ratifying the sentence for two main reasons: First, General Yue, in order to get the messenger Zhang Xi to talk, had sworn a solemn oath not to betray the prisoner and his teacher. In justice to Yue, and the loyalty he showed on that occasion, the seriousness of that oath should be recognized. Second, the sources of many of the vilest rumors had been traced over the last few months to the eunuchs and retainers of the emperor's treacherous brothers, and therefore in a strict interpretation of relative guilt, Zeng and Zhang should be considered the subsidiary parties in the case, rather than the principals.

The key precedent for treating the two men, therefore, should be found in the way that Yongzheng's father, Kangxi, treated those who rebelled along with Wu Sangui back in the 1670s. Once that rebellion was over, Kangxi decreed that those who had simply followed along with Wu should be pardoned, as long as they showed remorse and the promise of truly renewing themselves. That made perfect sense in this case as well. To underline the delicate nature of the whole proceedings, Yongzheng orders that Li Fu, the former governor-general of the northern provinces—currently being held on charges of corruption and factionalism in the same Ministry of Punishments high-security prison as Zeng and Zhang— should be present in the audience hall as the edict is read aloud. All present are aware that Li Fu is also the man who ordered the emperor's ninth brother shackled and deprived of food in the boiling Baoding jail cell three years before, leading directly to the prince's death. The reading of the short edict completed, Yongzheng merely announces that a further edict will be issued later.

News coming in from the provinces has shown that uneasiness over the case is by no means confined to that long list of officials in Beijing. One example is the judicial commissioner of Hubei, Wang Suzheng, whose anger over the attacks on Lü Liuliang is so impassioned that it soon comes to the emperor's ears. Wang has become "so anguished and agitated over the issue," writes Yongzheng, that he has become "temporarily deluded, to the extent of losing all decorum." But the emperor decides not to punish Wang, on the grounds that his intentions were not bad in and of themselves: if Wang did in fact have some malicious purpose in making his remarks, then Heaven would punish him.

A separate report, from the financial commissioner of Guangdong province, describes how the subprefect of Canton—a man named Zhu, renowned locally for his "reclusive nature and eccentric behavior"—regularly and publicly displayed an honorific tablet bearing the name of Lü Liuliang and performed obeisance before it. When Subprefect Zhu learned of the emperor's public diatribe of the summer against Lü Liuliang, he removed the votive tablet from its prominent location and stored it in his own home. But he might have continued indefinitely with his acts of reverence to the scholar so hated by the emperor, had not four alert and loyal government students within his jurisdiction heard of his outrageous behavior and reported him to the higher-level provincial authorities. (Zhu was later harshly beaten and died the following year.)

Yet another report comes from the financial commissioner of Zhejiang province. He alerts the emperor to the fact that in one of the large and prosperous cities of northeastern Zhejiang, on the Grand Canal, a retired subdirector of schools named Zhang not only made a wooden tablet in honor of Lü Liuliang but erected it inside one of the town's leading scholarly academies. This treacherous act was reported to the authorities by another retired official in the same city, and they moved swiftly to arrest Zhang and to burn the tablet. But the case was tangled, noted the financial commissioner, and Zhang seemed genuinely contrite. Nevertheless, he also was condemned to a harsh beating.

Random though they may be, these examples clearly show that in at least three provinces men entrusted with responsible positions, including the administration of justice and the education of the next generation of scholars, are deeply influenced by Lü Liuliang and pay open homage to his memory. As examples they are certainly in the emperor's mind as he seeks to marshal his own thoughts and respond at greater length to the powerful plea for Zeng Jing's death that has come from the one hundred and forty-eight of his officials in Beijing.

Writing with extraordinary speed, Yongzheng has mustered his basic arguments by the next day, November 28. One thing is at once apparent: the emperor's words have now come to resemble a formal plea for the defense of the condemned man rather than being a mere rejection of the officials' views. "The histories of China have more accounts of rebellions, treasons, and uprisings of various kinds than one can number," Yongzheng tells his officials, "but truly from ancient times to the present nothing has ever been seen as weird and extraordinary and as jammed with false and misleading statements as this Zeng Jing case." It is true that the case has agitated and infuriated people, and that the law of the land has been broken, but the purpose of the whole investigation has been to see if there is any scrap of evidence, involving either the emperor himself or his subjects, that would support Zeng Jing's wild charges. Only if it could be proved that "there was no scrap of truth in his words, and no connections with the emperor's person whatsoever, only then could one reject the whole thing as being no more than hearing—on a barren mountainside or in a desolate ravine—the baying of a dog or an owl's hooting."

When he first heard the outlines of the case, the emperor continues, he thought it merely silly, as many of those who heard his words then can testify. But as the volume of Zeng Jing's confessions grew to thousands of words, all carefully written out in Zeng's own hand, the emperor came to believe the conspirator's sincerity and the depth of his remorse. Anyone can see how the ideas on the Manchus' being so different from the Chinese have come from Lü Liuliang. Similarly, Zeng's charges against the emperor clearly sprang from the poisonous gossip spread by the emperor's brothers and their exiled retainers. He has now had a full year to think about the case, the emperor adds, and one thing is totally clear: not one of the major facets of the case can be said to originate with Zeng Jing. Thus, in the emperor's judgment, "There must be points of origin for all the things that Zeng Jing was misled by hearing. There is no way that his guilt should be considered as something for which no pardon is permissible."

To support his contention that all Zeng Jing's wrongful thoughts can be traced to prior sources, the emperor spells out in page after page of detail all the evidence he has been accumulating since his lengthy edict of December a year ago. Additional information has been arriving at the palace regularly, most valuably from the new governor of Hunan, a tough and effective career administrator from the Chinese Bordered Red Banner named Zhao Hongen. Governor Zhao has proved infinitely more resourceful than the previous incumbent governor, Wang, who so often exasperated the emperor with his dilatoriness. This new evidence allows

Yongzheng to explain how Zeng Jing's testimony concerning the geomancer has narrowed the search to four soldiers from a princely household traveling to the south; though the soldiers have not yet been identified, it is now believed they were heading for Guangdong. There is also new information on the eunuchs identified through their arrest records, on their interrogations, and on their transfer to Beijing for further questioning. The locations of the lodging houses where the eunuchs and other exiles spread their poisonous gossip are now all known, along with the names of those they talked to on their journeys, including the womenfolk in certain homes who later spread the tales they heard.

In his late November edict, the emperor also shares with his officials the exact story spread by the eunuchs that purported to describe how his fourteenth brother had been wrongfully denied the throne. The eunuchs alleged that the dying Emperor Kangxi wished his fourteenth son to inherit the throne, and so wrote in his will; but in the palace confusion at the time of the old emperor's death, a confidant of Yongzheng, the emperor's fourth son, managed to alter the number so that "fourteenth" was now read as "fourth." Thus did the fourth son seize the throne for himself. Yongzheng shares with his hearers a host of other tales: of how he was alleged to have given his aging father a "restorative" potion that in fact hastened the old man's death; of how the elderly empress dashed out her brains against an iron pillar when her request to see her imprisoned son was denied; how another imperial consort strangled herself when her son was arrested.

Step by step the emperor shares the rumors that his father had planned to make the fourteenth son his heir and had commissioned the young man to be a general with the Qing armies fighting in Tibet so that he would increase his military experience and prestige and amass an army loyal to him. Step by step the emperor demolishes the same stories, asking how a man as shrewd as his father would ever have sent his favored son and successor to Tibet as his own death neared—the dying man would have known his fourteenth son could not possibly plan for the succession across such a colossal distance; and how could that particular son have led his troops in any kind of coup attempt all the way from Tibet, when the families of all the soldiers loyal to him were living in Beijing, natural hostages to any of his rival claimants?

With equal care, Yongzheng traces to the root every other story that Zeng Jing heard in his apparently isolated Hunan world: rumors of the emperor's lavish pleasure palaces in Hangzhou and other cities, rumors about his avarice, his lusts, his drunkenness, his greed. He turns these stories back onto his bitter brothers and their angered friends, arguing that as each rumor is traced and discredited, the brothers' varied guilts grow ever clearer. He is confident that future generations will understand why he acted as he did, writes the emperor. This brings him a measure of solace, so that even "in the midst of my greatest unhappiness a true joy has emerged. This is not something that could be assured by human strength alone. And in this process Zeng Jing has not been without his helpfulness to me."

What the emperor means is that Zeng Jing's actions provided the first links in a chain of evidence that revealed the full range of multifarious evils concocted by others. For this reason alone one could consider pardoning Zeng's crimes. But the emperor's desire to pardon Zeng Jing "should not be seen as my dissembling way to win a good name for myself," Yongzheng tells his officials. It is, rather, a way of reinforcing the old saying that "pardoning an error is not such a great matter, but executing someone is no small matter." Crimes—and the punishments meted out for them—are all, in their different ways, affected by the ability of the criminal to change his ways and by his capacity for sincere remorse. That is why "a criminal whose crime is great and yet can truly change is superior to one whose crime is slight but who cannot change."

Besides which, continues Yongzheng, there is the fact that "Zeng Jing's crazy charges were directed only at my own person. There really was no substance behind his attempt at rebellion, nor were many others marshaled to help in this plot." Why not then spare Zeng Jing from death, and believe in his apparently earnest repentance, proof of an innate capacity for reform, which shows clearly throughout the many lengthy confessions that Zeng Jing has written out with his own hand over the previous several months? If there are those, the emperor adds, who argue that he wishes to pardon Zeng because he enjoys Zeng's cringing flattery, then such people are themselves producing the same kinds of "dog barks and owl cries" as those with which Zeng Jing first assaulted the imperial ears.

It is his intention, the emperor notes, to continue with the trials of all those other plotters of various kinds who have been circulating the wild rumors all along. He has also been wondering about printing the testimonies and confessions of Zeng Jing and his messenger Zhang Xi, and even their treasonous writings, so that everyone will know the true facts of the case, especially those in Hunan province itself. Those who feel bitter over the proffering of pardons to Zeng and Zhang, or who try to use the situation for their own illicit or covert purposes, will in their turn be strictly punished. No one in the pardoned men's own neighborhoods should think of trying to harm the pardoned men. Nor should any of the emperor's sons or grandsons at any time in the future reopen the case, on the grounds that Zeng Jing had threatened the emperor's own person, and hence should be executed. For the emperor has come to think of Zeng and Zhang as "being covered by a special act of imperial pardon."

The case of Lü Liuliang, however, is completely different, the emperor concludes. The late emperor had never known about Lü's crimes, and therefore had never pardoned them. Thus it is Emperor Yongzheng at the present time who is free to decide on the punishments for Lü's crimes. "Had I received any edict suggesting a pardon from the late emperor, then of course I would have obeyed such an edict, and pardoned Lü's guilt."

It is not an edict designed to encourage further discussion, especially since the emperor follows it up over the next three days with two more edicts that give additional details of his brothers' crimes, as if those have now come to overshadow all the other issues, rendering the pardon of Zeng Jing almost a side issue to these higher-level problems of state and family politics. In these two follow-up edicts the emperor not only elaborates on the crimes of his eighth, ninth, and fourteenth brothers—on whom he has spent so much space already—but on those of his tenth brother too, who is now also imprisoned in the Forbidden City. This tenth brother, the emperor tells the court, aware of the enormity of his crimes and of the disloyalty he has shown, remains in such fear for his life that even while under arrest he practices all kinds of magical arts designed to protect him from harm. Such devices are useless, the emperor points out, since the tenth brother's formerly most trusted eunuch, after being promised total immunity, has turned against his former master. This eunuch offered damning evidence concerning the plots hatched by the other three brothers at the time Emperor Yongzheng was consolidating his hold on the throne, plots in which his own master had eventually gotten involved.

Even now, writing these edicts, the emperor tells his officials, the memories are so vivid that he is often weeping as he writes down the words.

With such a barrage of imperial pressures being brought into play, it is perhaps only because their dissenting voices can shelter under the wing of the emperor's own most trusted confidant that the officials dare to protest one final time. In their November request for Zeng Jing's execution, the one hundred and forty-eight officials issued their findings under the name of the Ministry of Punishments. This final time, on December 5, 1729, they protect their plea with the name of Prince Yi, the emperor's thirteenth brother, head of his innermost circle of advisers, whose watchful messages have gone out on many of the most crucial and delicate moments of the initial investigations into the treason case. If Prince Yi is willing to express his doubts about his older brother's judgment in public, the case might indeed be reopened once again; and if it is, those petitioning along with Prince Yi will surely not be punished, despite the emperor's warnings.

Heading his document "A Request to Execute Zeng Jing," Prince Yi boldly announces the theme that has come to dominate his own and his colleagues' thinking: "The evil of some crimes is such that the waves from them break against the sky," he begins. "These are hard to forgive. Some hatreds reach across the entire land; these are of the utmost urgency." The reason China has clear statutory punishments for certain crimes is so that the law will be respected and the people's hearts be at rest. For the emperor to suggest pardoning Zeng Jing is an act of generosity and compassion unmatched by even the earliest sage rulers of China. But it misses one salient point, which is that of the conspirator's volition. Zeng Jing, living in contented and prosperous times, *chose* to read the treacherous books of Lü Liuliang, he *chose* to listen to the wild rumors spread by the dead or arrested princes' exiled followers. It was he who ordered his own follower Zhang Xi to go from Hunan to the Shaanxi office of Governor-general Yue Zhongqi. It is all very well for the emperor to say that "there really was no substance behind Zeng's attempt at rebellion"; but there could be no doubt at all that Zeng Jing had the intention to launch a rebellion. Similarly, though it might be true that "one whose crime is great and yet can truly change is superior to one whose crime is slight but cannot change," Zeng Jing's crime was that of high treason. This is fixed in the dynasty's legal code as one of the "ten great crimes," for which no clemency is possible. And Zeng Jing's disciple Zhang Xi is guilty of the same crime. "It is therefore our most earnest plea," Prince Yi concludes, "that the emperor grant our request to forward Zeng Jing and Zhang Xi to the requisite department of punishment, so that they can be executed as the statutes require in such cases, by having their bodies cut in fragments and their severed heads exposed to the public. By thus exterminating this rebellious clique, we will maintain clarity for the laws of our dynasty, and assuage the anger felt by the officialdom and by the common people. We are driven to make this plea in all sincerity, and respectfully request the imperial response."

The imperial response to Prince Yi, issued later on that same December day, is short, rhetorically unornamented, and blunt. The emperor makes it abundantly clear that since he has failed to get the endorsement he sought he will now act as his conscience demands, and let posterity be the judge:

"In this matter of pardoning Zeng Jing and others, I do not require the legal views of the princes and the senior officials. Later generations in our country will either consider the pardon correct, or they will find it wrong. This is a matter for me alone, it does not involve the bureaucracy or the wider public. I have thought everything through with the greatest care, and the edicts I have issued on the case have all been absolutely clear. There is no need for any of the princes or the senior officials in the capital to send in any more reports on this. If those stationed out in the provinces, such as governors-general, governors, or senior military commanders, send in reports or petitions concerning my pardon of Zeng Jing, such reports are to be returned to the senders by the bureau for the transmission of documents."

The emperor has spoken. Zeng Jing and his messenger are free.

Strong though they are, these words of the emperor's are not just left to stand alone. For in a highly unusual development, his views are given vigorous support by the statement of a complete unknown, from outside the bureaucracy, which is printed at length in the *Capital Gazette*. The author so singled out is a junior scholar from the flourishing Fujian harbor city of Quanzhou whose name is Zhuge Jisheng. The young man initially wrote out his thoughts in the form of an open letter; apparently someone in the bureaucracy who supported the emperor's position on Zeng and Lü obtained a copy of the letter and decided to enter it into the public record, thus assuring that it would be circulated all across China.

Having read the passages from Lü Liuliang's diaries already quoted in the emperor's edicts, Zhuge writes, he can see how those diaries were specifically designed to slander the present emperor's father. It is obvious, too, that Lü's sons and grandsons deliberately hid Lü's treasonous works, conniving together and refusing to reform their ways. No sensible person can doubt that the Lü family has been seeking to undermine the Qing dynasty. In support of this argument, Zhuge shows how among Lü Liuliang's ancestors, stretching back in time a millennium or more, one can find numerous generals and officials who were similarly infamous for their treasonous ways, several of whom were executed. By contrast, Zhuge Jisheng himself, he points out proudly, is a direct descendant of the justly famous minister Zhuge Liang—a man whose perspicacity and loyalty to his ruler fourteen hundred years ago have been celebrated throughout China ever since—whom the emperor himself has recently added to the roster of worthies whose memorial tablets are placed within the Confucian temples. Since Lü Liuliang is long dead, Zhuge Jisheng concludes, the only fitting punishment must be to dig up Lü's grave and publicly expose his corpse.

By restating his own views at such length, and allowing—or at least acquiescing in—the publication of a young scholar's message of support, the emperor is putting extra pressure on his court officials to accede to his views. Presumably it is with the same intent that on January 24, 1730, the emperor issues an edict publicly praising the four junior scholars in Canton who turned in the subprefect of their own district for venerating a tablet of Lü Liuliang. By their action, the emperor declares, these young men showed they possessed "a profound understanding of true morality. Instead of being deluded by heterodox language, they reported to their superiors according to the facts. They have thoroughly absorbed the meaning of pure behavior and scholarly practice and are to be congratulated." As a reward to the entire community in which the four scholars live, the emperor gives an order to increase the Canton city quota for the higher-level provincial examinations by a total of four slots. The four young men will be permitted to use those extra slots in order to sit for the upcoming provincial examinations; and if successful, and adjudged worthy by the educational commissioner of the region, they will be allowed to proceed to Beijing and sit for the national-level *jinshi* exams to be held in the capital that summer.

Only one week later, on January 31, Yongzheng receives an additional gesture of moral support, which he at once passes on to the court. What he has learned is that just as the huge ridge beams were about to be installed in the temple of Confucius—situated in the grounds of the sage's original home in Qufu, Shandong province, and nearly destroyed by fire in 1724, as Zeng Jing had pointed out in his treasonous writings—astonishing portents were seen in the skies to the north of the site: at noon time, clouds shaped like a phoenix appeared above the temple complex, spinning in a blur of blazing circles around the sun for several hours. The men reporting this auspicious occurrence, namely, the director of the temple restoration project and the young acting governor of Shandong province (who also happens to be the son of General Yue Zhongqi), both state that thousands of people witnessed the amazing sight. Passing on the news, the grand secretaries add that such a proof of imperial virtue has never before been observed on an occasion of this kind. He is delighted at this sign of heavenly approbation, comments the emperor, but he cannot accept the credit for it; if credit is due, it must go to Confucius himself, who has taken this way of acknowledging the loving attention to detail and disregard of cost with which the temple restoration is being undertaken. As proof of his satisfaction, Yongzheng decrees that the number of those to be granted the degree of *jinshi* at that summer's examinations will be 400, as opposed to the 226 awards made in 1727. And the following day Yue Zhongqi's son, who brought the good news, is promoted to full governor's rank from his previous "acting" status.

The emperor cannot resist passing the information along to the newly pardoned Zeng Jing. How is it, he asks, that Zeng Jing in his original treasonous letter cited the burning of the Confucian temple as one of the many proofs of Yongzheng's lack of virtue? What made Zeng Jing so determined to report only negative portents relating to the emperor? Was it not time for Zeng Jing to start recording the good along with the bad? Zeng Jing makes what is clearly the one acceptable reply in the circumstances: these particular clouds can mean only one thing, he answers. They prove that at the present time "the hearts of the emperor, the sage Confucius, and the Heavens all beat as one."

It remains only for Zeng Jing to restate his contrition in polished prose and to spell out for his ruler the steps by which he has emerged from his strange experience like a man from a dream. He does this in the form of a twenty-seven-page essay, written to the best of his ability, which he entitles *My Return to the Good*. Despite its length, the burden of his message is simple: China produced its share of sages over the previous millennia, and in many different regions, but gradually its capacity to do so dried up. It was thus natural that later sages should come from more distant lands, as the rulers of the current Qing dynasty had also done. The swiftness with which the Manchus conquered China, their routing of the domestic rebels, their assumption of imperial power, the excellence of their rule—all testified to the truth of this proposition. Arguments about the Chinese being inherently different from those living in the so-called barbarian regions were without merit. Lü Liuliang was wrong. Those brothers who turned against Emperor Yongzheng were also wrong. Their apparently implacable refusal to halt their criticisms or change their conduct showed the depth of their evil. The current empire of the Qing had led to a rebirth of the virtuous days of the ancient sage rulers Yao and Shun, and a deeper understanding of the teachings of Confucius. Now this was clear to all. It remained only to eradicate the treasonous writings of Lü Liuliang, and all would live in peace in a realm to which correct morality had at last returned.

Almost from the moment the Zeng Jing case came to his attention, Emperor Yongzheng has been talking about publicizing the conspirators' views, along with his own arguments refuting them. He has even made preliminary gestures in that direction, by circulating his initial attack on the treasonous letter, and ordering wide distribution of his edict on race and history. But now, by early February 1730, the emperor has all the materials he can possibly need, and he calls the process of accumulation to a halt. Accordingly, the January 31 edict on the dramatic omens at the Confucian temple, and Zeng Jing's response to the order that he comment on those occurrences, constitute the last items chronologically to be included in the massive book on the whole case that the emperor has decided to publish. It is apt that a discussion of Confucius should mark this moment of transition. Apt, also, that Zeng Jing's own reflections, *My Return to the Good*, should mark a satisfactory conclusion in the emperor's eyes for that protracted process that had led the former conspirator from treachery, through remorse and confession, down to relearning, pardon, and self-renewal. Somewhere around this time, also, the book-in-the-making gets the title by which it will be known: *A Record of How True Virtue Led to an Awakening from Delusion.*

It is up to the emperor and his officials, now, to undertake the laborious task of selecting from the mass of materials at their disposal, editing them into an acceptable sequence, and discussing the procedures for carving the printing blocks and arranging the mechanics of distribution. There is nothing more for Zeng Jing to do in Beijing, and the emperor authorizes his departure. The two fifty-year-old men have still never met face-to-face, and perhaps they never will, but surely they will not forget each other. Yongzheng has already arranged for Zeng Jing to be given a job when he gets home, in the Changsha office of the Hunan supervisor of public morality. And as the departure date nears, a messenger arrives from the palace, bringing a gift for Zeng of clothing, and some other mementoes.

It is time to go. In the third week of February, Zeng Jing leaves Beijing, heading south through the winter countryside.

Nine

The
Solitary
Bell

Zeng Jing's ultimate destination is his home in Yongxing county, to which his mother and his young son, released the previous summer on the emperor's orders, have been permitted to return. But Zeng has not been authorized to return to Yongxing at once, by the direct overland route. Instead, he has been ordered to go first to the cities of Nanjing, Suzhou, and Hangzhou, where the senior officials in charge of the provinces of Jiangsu and Zhejiang have their main offices. Only after he has consulted with them and responded to any further questions they may have will he be free to head for Hunan, where the emperor has ordered him to report to the office of the supervisor of public morality.

Though Zhang Xi is not with him—the former messenger has been told to wait in Beijing, pending further instructions—Zeng Jing is not traveling alone. He is accompanied by Hangyilu, who for a full year was his chief interrogator as well as the conduit for the emperor's constant questions and who has now been promoted to general in the Manchu Bordered Red Banner. Apparently unmoved by Zeng's contrition, Hangyilu—in his capacity as vice-president of the Ministry of Punishments—was a cosigner of the November request to the emperor that Zeng Jing be executed by slicing as the treason laws demanded, but now his task is more prosaic: to convey to the senior southern provincial officials the news of Zeng Jing's pardon, and to pass on to them a brief message from the emperor, that they are to persevere in the attempt "to hunt down and arrest the man who falsely assumed the name of Wang Shu with the goal of spreading false and malicious rumors." Hangyilu also has copies of the painted likeness of the fake Wang Shu, based on the description given by Zeng Jing, which he is to distribute among people in the Yangzi delta region in the hopes that by this means someone will identify the elusive figure.

On February 28, while they are still about one hundred miles north of the Yangzi, near the town of Huaian, Hangyilu and Zeng Jing by chance meet up with the entourage of the recently appointed governor of Jiangsu, Yinjishan. Only thirty-three years old, a Manchu from the Plain Yellow Banner, Yinjishan has had a spectacularly swift career rise since he gained the *jinshi* degree in 1723. He has just been on an inspection tour of the intricate network of locks, sluices, and dikes around Huaian, where a number of west-to-east-flowing rivers and canals intersect the north-to-south flow of the Grand Canal, and is now heading back to his office in Suzhou. Hangyilu seizes the chance to give him the emperor's instructions and the picture and to pass on some new information he has just been given by Zeng Jing. Apparently the fake Wang Shu, when visiting Zeng Jing back in 1723, had mentioned that he once worked as a scribe in the office of a certain Pan Zongluo, when Pan was serving as the educational commissioner in Hunan. Since Pan had held such a senior position, as well as being a Jiangsu native, this is a potentially important lead that Yinjishan will have to check out.

That night, Zeng Jing has a dream about the fake Wang Shu: in this dream, Zeng Jing has returned home to Yongxing county and is talking to one of his distant kinsmen about the case. The kinsman, who appears to know all the principal figures concerned, tells him that the key must lie with a man named Deng, a Hubei native, who once worked as a tutor in Wang Shu's home. Another member of the Zeng clan knows where Deng lives, and all the other details. Zeng Jing recounts the dream to Hangyilu, who in turn passes it on to Yinjishan when they meet up with him again in Suzhou. Though Yinjishan has had no luck with the latest lead to the man called Pan, he nevertheless feels obliged to follow up this lead as well. As he tells the emperor, "With men guilty of as heinous a crime as these, one cannot afford to ignore conversations held in dreams." The reason is that "one can never be sure how heavenly principles will make themselves manifest, and perhaps it is by this route that the truth will appear."

On March 11, Zeng Jing and Hangyilu reach the city of Hangzhou, where Li Wei, the man who so successfully rounded up Lü Liuliang's family and disciples over a year before, is still serving as Zhejiang's governor-general. On meeting Zeng Jing for the first time, after hearing so much about his terrible crimes, Li Wei is astonished at his mediocrity. As he writes to Yongzheng: "When I saw what he looked like, and heard him speak, I realized how base a figure he was, how unimpressive, how totally ordinary." And yet, Li Wei adds (in words somewhat reminiscent of Yinjishan's train of thought), perhaps Zeng Jing spoke in a way for something deeper: it could be "a device of the heavenly, earthly, and ancestral spirits, to use the words uttered by such deluded people to show us the eternal difference between yea and nay, between the treacherous and the true." Li Wei circulates the picture of the fake Wang Shu around the region, and has Zeng Jing meet with various local figures, in case some flash of expression or tone of voice might connect to his earlier memories; but Zeng can make no positive identifications. Nor can anyone else make connections to the man called Deng, whose name appeared to him in a dream.

So, for the time being, Zeng Jing's work is finished. Hangyilu will return to Beijing, while Zeng proceeds overland to Changsha, prior to taking the familiar road south to his Yongxing home and reunion with his mother. To ensure the former conspirator's safe arrival, Li Wei designates a senior Manchu scribe from his staff, along with a small squad of soldiers, to travel with Zeng on the journey west. (Li Wei will cover their expenses from his own provincial funds.) But the fates decree that there will be no joyful family reunion after all: On March 17, just as Zeng is preparing to leave Hangzhou, a message arrives with the news of his mother's death, at the age of seventy-eight. So it is as a mourner that he completes his journey.

As he has in the past, so now, Yongzheng responds promptly and succinctly to the various reports he receives on Zeng Jing. To Yinjishan he writes: "Noted. But how is it that you can treat these dreams by someone in a deep sleep as being the equivalent of reality?" And at the end of Li Wei's report he jots down the words, "Noted. How would you gauge the level of Zeng Jing's remorse?" But well before he scrawls these brief words, Yongzheng's attention has been deflected back from Zeng Jing to Lü Liuliang by the arrival of a secret report from Hubei province which demonstrates all too clearly that Zeng's pardon and release have utterly failed to dissipate the darkening clouds of rumor.

The documents illustrating this reach the emperor's hands in early March, in the form of a memorandum enclosed along with a careful report from Maizhu, the governor-general of Huguang, the region encompassing the two provinces of Hunan and Hubei. Like so many others whom Yongzheng trusts, Maizhu is an able career Manchu bureaucrat from the Plain Blue Banner—level-headed, experienced, and hard-working. The story Maizhu has to tell is unsettling: It concerns a scholar called Tang Sungao, a native of Zhejiang, who has been serving for some years as the private secretary to the magistrate of a sizable town, not far from the Hubei provincial capital of Wuchang. Such posts out in the provinces are the common lot of many able scholars, who have considerable learning and yet have been unable to rise up the examination ladder and attain official positions in the bureaucracy. Often they travel great distances to accompany their employers, for even such unprestigious jobs are coveted for the income they can bring to lower-level gentry families. Such has been the case with Tang Sungao, who has been some years now with his patron, Magistrate Jing.

As Maizhu explains, the case of Secretary Tang is an odd one, in that its basis is an apparently ungovernable rage. The origin of Tang's fury can be found within the pages of a copy of the *Capital Gazette* from January 1730, which came to Tang's attention in mid-February. Every magistrate in China received a copy of the *Gazette* from the special couriers of the Ministry of War, and though its general distribution was limited to official circles, private secretaries naturally had access to the paper, which summarized the recent business of the capital. It had thus been a perfectly routine act for Tang to read the issue of the *Gazette* containing the young scholar Zhuge Jisheng's assault on Lü Liuliang. What was totally unpredictable was Secretary Tang Sungao's reaction. As Magistrate Jing tells the governor-general, who now passes on the information to the emperor, after reading the piece by Zhuge Jisheng, Secretary Tang "suddenly became crazed. He swore terrible oaths, and cried out so loudly that one could hear him everywhere. I repeatedly reproved him for his behavior, and finally issued a stern rebuke, but he would not moderate his language. Then on February 19, with no warning, he told me he wanted to resign." When the magistrate asked him exactly what he intended to do after his resignation, Tang replied, "To visit the senior officials, and hand over a document." When asked what the document was, Tang Sungao handed to Jing a lengthy draft manuscript he had been working on for the past several days. The manuscript consisted of a sustained assault on Zhuge Jisheng's analysis of Lü Liuliang, a bitter critique of the spineless officials who had misled the emperor into misunderstanding Lü, and a passionate statement of Tang's own moral principles.

Zhuge Jisheng, Tang wrote in his draft, "was an example of the worst kind of Chinese, a mean and despicable man, the kind of man who was destroying Chinese culture." Tang knew that he himself was just an ordinary scholar, a man with no official insignia to his name, but at least he knew how to love the good and how to hate evil, and how to speak out in the name of scholars of integrity. By nature, he was a "solitary bell," wrote Tang, one whose ambitions were carved into his heart; he could not stop himself from calling out when he encountered injustice, even at the risk of his own life. What was so terrible about Zhuge Jisheng's attack on Lü Liuliang was that it muddled up the most fundamental principles. Like everyone else on earth, Zhuge Jisheng had been "endowed by Heaven with a measure of goodness, but now it had all vanished. By writing this totally deceptive message, above he beclouded the emperor's intelligence, below he cheated the scholar class. His intention is to induce us to lose our Dao, and to sweep our culture into the mud. In truth, now is the autumn of our existence or nonexistence; since I have made up my mind to die, I can write these words just before death comes, in the hopes that some great official might take a glance at them. Then I can close my eyes in peace."

The current emperor obviously had good intentions, Tang noted; he tried to curb corruption, nurture the people, and bring prosperity to the country. But the Qing dynasty suffered from the flaw that had affected China ever since the first days of centralized empire: in early China, before that fateful strengthening of the center, the bonds between rulers and subjects were enlightened, criticism was encouraged, "there was a mutual cooperation between rulers and subjects, and thus the possibility of governing and transforming people was virtually limitless. Those ancient times have never been surpassed." How different things were at the present time, said Tang, when officials servilely echoed every command of the emperor, and did not offer their own advice or constructive criticisms.

The Lü Liuliang case was a perfect example of what he meant, Tang continued. When discussion began of Lü's books, the emperor was still interested in getting his officials' true views, for his "doubts and beliefs were in the balance." The emperor had asked his officials to read carefully through Lü's philosophical writings and come to an informed judgment on their merits. That at least showed that the emperor had the potential of ruling according to the Dao and would keep an open mind before acting. "How different are his officials in the capital and the provinces, who are all so scared of being blamed for criticizing the emperor that they would far rather issue statements that contradicted their inner feelings. So this one says 'chop up his corpse' and that one says 'scatter his ashes'; this one says 'burn his books,' and that one 'exterminate his whole clan.'" Such unanimity of official voices made it hard for the emperor to reach an independent decision. Naturally the emperor was able to use his power over life and death to spare people when he chose, wrote Tang, as the case of Zeng Jing well showed: "Even when the entire crowd of his officials were clamoring for him to 'kill this man' the emperor prolonged the investigation, and sought among all people to find some way of letting the man live."

In the matter of Lü Liuliang, no one had even asked Zhuge Jisheng for his opinion, and yet he pushed ahead anyway. In Tang's opinion, Zhuge Jisheng had "a heart like a snake or a scorpion, and a nature like a wolf's." That was why Zhuge wrote his diatribe against Lü, "embellishing his deceit in the name of loyalty, and seeking advancement in his own career." It was this that had forced Tang to speak out in his turn, for if a man like Zhuge Jisheng attained his ambitions, what hope could there be for others, what solace even in death?

Zhuge Jisheng's statements were a mass of contradictions, wrote Tang. If Zhuge knew that Lü Liuliang's private works were so treacherous, why on earth had he not said so earlier, instead of waiting for the court to make its pronouncements? And if Lü had been trying to corrupt all his descendants, why did he tuck his deepest thoughts away inside some private diaries, which were themselves but a fraction of his life's output of thousands of pages of scholarly writings? And how could Lü have destroyed the virtue of the whole reigning dynasty when the early Manchus established the basis of their state before Lü was even born, and Lü had died long before the death of the current emperor's father? Similarly specious was Zhuge's trick of digging out the names of long-dead people named "Lü," as if that could throw doubt on Lü Liuliang's own integrity. By the same process, one could choose some virtuous and scholarly people also called "Lü," of whom there were plenty, to prove that Lü Liuliang was a worthy teacher and exemplar for later ages.

Zhuge Jisheng would have better spent his time reading Lü Liuliang's basic philosophical works, especially his celebrated *Commentaries on the Four Confucian Books.* To Tang, "this work exemplifies the subtlest teachings of the sagely way, and all the scholars of China respect it. If the sage [Confucius] himself were to come back among us, he would not change a word." For this reason, one might expect the work to have had more influence in the present age, but alas that was not true: "What a pity it is that the current emperor's daily duties are so heavy that he has no leisure to study this book with care. And his attendant officials don't dare to push the books on the emperor's attention because his rage is not yet spent. So instead they take the private and informal family writings that Lü kept stored away in his home, and make them available to the emperor a day at a time; and as for all the admirable things Lü wrote, which would serve future generations, those are all buried a little deeper each day." The result, Tang felt, was an intellectual climate perfect for sycophants and despicable people like Zhuge Jisheng, who could spread their defamations at will. Their wild barking so filled the air that even those one or two officials who might have something constructive to say, and the nerve to say it, had no way to break through the din and have a reasoned discussion of the issues. So naturally the emperor had come to believe that everyone in the country wanted Lü killed and all his books and printing blocks burned.

Things had reached such a pass that there was talk of exhuming corpses and defiling graves, a practice of the barbarians in former days, and something that "made ghosts howl in the night." Upon hearing that mournful sound, any scholar who read widely and valued true principles felt his heart turn cold; "Confucius and Mencius, in their tombs in Heaven, would surely weep at the sound. How tragic that the inherited attempts of the last eighty years to nourish the country's scholars should finally fall into the hands of this one worthless scoundrel. We have reached a juncture where the senior officials have no idea how to remedy the situation." But there was a remedy at hand for those who felt utterly helpless, Tang added. They could take this current writing of his and show it to the emperor. They could help Tang get to Beijing so that he "could confront Zhuge Jisheng face-to-face, in front of the imperial audience hall." They could try to ensure that even if the books by Lü Liuliang declared treasonous were burned, his other scholarly works were kept. And they could "cut off the head of Zhuge Jisheng and hang it aloft for all to see."

In the last two pages of his manuscript, Tang offered historical justifications for Lü Liuliang's behavior. Obviously Lü had not been without fault. But Lü was a man of talent and a man of his time; he grew up when the coasts were untamed, gangs of bandits roamed the southeast, and Ming loyalists—to whom Lü felt bound by ties of blood—still resisted in isolated pockets. In those troubled times, Lü wrote works of enduring value—not just on the classics and other early texts, but on the administration and the arts of two successive dynasties, the Ming and the Qing: "All his various discussions are clear in meaning and reasoning; one can see the subtleties of the earlier sages and worthies in operation there. All these can be used to enlighten the less-informed people of later ages about his achievements." Tang admitted he did not have the scholarly skills or credentials to talk more about the finer points of Lü's work, and he was not the kind of person who could have any effect on the grander issues of the time. He knew he might be seriously punished for what he was writing, or just become a laughingstock.

Tang wanted his readers, whoever they might be, to know that he supported Lü because of shared principles, not because he happened to have been born in the same province and was raised fairly near Lü's hometown. There were no family ties linking the two men, not even any prior social contact. Tang was speaking out just because he *did* live in prosperous times—and in such times, as Confucius had warned, if people indulge their own private interests then the world will start to decline. Such times as the present, to Tang, "were those in which one really did not know what to do, and yet felt there were certain things one just had to say."

Tang closed his manuscript with a ringing affirmation of his own sense of purpose: "I have written this manifesto knowing there is only a one-in-ten chance that it will touch the emperor's heart, and there is a nine-in-ten chance that I will be caught up in the miseries of the law's net. But even so, why should I want to spend my life in this earthly world with a shameless person such as Zhuge Jisheng, when I could be in the netherworld with such accomplished men of learning as the Lüs, father and son? Alas for us all! There is no one now to act like Zhong Shanfu, and Wei Zheng is dead; there is no one left at court to raise a voice in protest. The weeds are springing up again, and the brute beasts come close behind them. Shall we let those who write our history sneer that our age produced no heroes? No, they will not be able to say that there were none at all. For Tang Sungao was here, and he was not afraid to die."

Magistrate Jing read this document with nervous bewilderment. These were the words of his own longtime personal secretary, and he had not known that personal secretaries wrote such things. Like any educated man of his place and time, Jing recognized the two closing references Tang had made. Zhong Shanfu was a chief minister in the fragmented China of two millennia before, a man whose practicality and courage in offering calm advice to unpredictable rulers were celebrated in the long ode, found in China's earliest surviving anthology of poetry. Schoolchildren would have known Zhong's name, and the poem's most quoted stanza:

> *People have a saying:*
> *"True virtue is light as a whisker,*
> *But few of us can lift it."*
> *I thought this over.*

Only Zhong Shanfu could lift it;
Sadly, no one helped him.
When the robe of state had a hole
Only Zhong Shanfu could mend it.

And for any Chinese student of history, Wei Zheng stood above all other ministers in the early Tang dynasty, fifteen hundred years after the time of Zhong Shanfu, as a rather similar model, a minister famous for rectitude and for bravery in remonstrating with his all-powerful ruler whenever he felt it necessary for the country's good.

Magistrate Jing saw no choice but to put Tang Sungao under arrest. On February 22, 1730, he sent the initial details on Tang's strange behavior, together with a full copy of Tang's long text, to Governor-general Maizhu in the provincial capital, Wuchang. Maizhu received the report and the enclosure three days later and read through the lengthy document at once. By the next day, he had drafted his own secret report to the emperor and sent it off at once by courier. Tang Sungao's crazed words and lawless actions astonished him, wrote Maizhu. How could such people rise up among their fellows in such a glorious age as the present one? Maizhu had already ordered the judicial commissioner of the province to have Tang brought under strict guard to Wuchang, where he would be kept closely confined and would be rigorously questioned until he made a full confession. Along with his report, Maizhu enclosed a copy of Tang's manifesto for the emperor's perusal. He would await the emperor's instructions, and then act accordingly.

In five lines written in swift cursive strokes at the end of Maizhu's report, the emperor who so recently pardoned Zeng Jing gives his verdict on Lü Liuliang's defender: "Be sure not to allow this particular criminal to commit suicide, and thus earn a name for himself as a martyr. Don't let anyone else know about the document he wrote, don't let anyone know about the report you sent to me, and don't let anyone know about this matter in general. You can have him beaten to death, or kill him in some other way, either will be fine. Be sure too that Magistrate Jing does not let anyone know about, or discuss, the manifesto. Magistrate Jing's reports on the investigation must not be shared with anyone else. Pass this message on to him."

Governor-general Maizhu is almost as crisp in his reply: "Secretary Tang Sungao fully showed his refractory nature by writing that crazed manifesto, and there is no way he can escape the stern punishment that he deserves for such vile deeds. But I was afraid that if we had him beaten to death the news would get spread around. Fortuitously, said criminal, while in prison, fell seriously ill and died after a few days. His was indeed the terrible crime of defying Heaven, and could not be forgiven either by Heaven or on earth. As to the copies of the magistrate's detailed report to me and the draft manifesto, kept on file in various offices, I have already sent secret orders to the staffs there to completely destroy them, in accordance with my own intention that nothing about this case leak out."

The decision to eradicate Secretary Tang, along with his disturbing manifesto, seemed to fly in the face of the decision—so recently made—to send Zeng Jing back to his Hunan home and to publish all the details of his case. But the two situations were very different: Zeng Jing had lived and worked on the fringes of society, Secretary Tang held a responsible position in the county government. Zeng Jing based his charges on the vaguest of roadside rumors while Secretary Tang took his target from the pages of the *Capital Gazette*. When arrested, Zeng Jing had wept and shown contrition almost from the start whereas Secretary Tang showed nothing but defiant rage. And one might add another factor: unlike Zeng Jing, whose knowledge of literature was slight, Secretary Tang had a respect for Lü Liuliang that ran deep and pure and was based on discriminating knowledge of Lü's philosophical and literary works. Hence eliminating Tang had a certain logic to the emperor and his governor-general.

Yet despite Yongzheng's confidence that any threat from Secretary Tang has been permanently removed, his satisfaction does not last for long. For on March 28, in a small mountain town called Yuanzhou, on the western Hunan border, an official from the Censorate busy with other matters finds himself reading, in complete astonishment, a copy of Tang's entire manifesto. This official's name is also Tang, though the two are in no way related. Censor Tang is from the wealthy Grand Canal city of Yangzhou, a recent recipient of the *jinshi* degree, assigned to this town in west Hunan as an investigative censor for the Ministry of Public Works. He has absolutely no idea, he tells the emperor in a carefully worded report, how the copy of Secretary Tang's manifesto came to be among his official papers, nor who had put it there. But because of its deeply disturbing content, he feels he has no choice but to send it on to the emperor in Beijing for his perusal.

The receipt of this second copy of the manifesto leaves the emperor deeply uneasy. As he writes in a follow-up note to Governor-general Maizhu, not only have they not managed to suppress the whole unpleasant incident but, even worse, "it seems that everyone in the country has already heard about the shocking nature of this case." The only slight solace is that "the people trying to understand this case interpret it in different ways." That, he might have added, will certainly never be the case with Zeng Jing: for the text of the *Awakening from Delusion* is finished, and soon the copies will cover the country like a cloak. Multiple interpretations will not be possible. Surely, at last, the emperor's views will prevail.

Ten

Coauthors

Through the last days of winter and into the spring of 1730, the emperor's staff pass the manuscripts selected for the *Awakening from Delusion* over to the Palace Printing Office. On April 4, they give their ruler the news that the first sets of printing blocks for the whole volume are ready. The documents Yongzheng has chosen fill 509 pages in all: for practicality's sake, the massive manuscript has been divided into four main sections, each of which is to be bound separately as two paper-bound volumes.

Given the pressures of time and the size of the project, for his own contributions to the *Awakening from Delusion*, Yongzheng relies on existing material, either the various edicts he has issued on the Zeng Jing case over the previous year or the extended questions he passed on during the same period to the conspirator via Hangyilu. To open Section One and serve as a foreword to the book as a whole, Yongzheng chooses the edict that he had originally issued on November 2, 1729. In that November edit he focused on the irrelevance of racial identity to providing morality in government, illustrating the point with detailed expositions on the place of racial concepts in earlier Chinese history; the edict thus provides a convenient way to introduce a central theme of the *Awakening*, that invidious distinctions between Han Chinese and allegedly "barbarian" Manchus were spread abroad by Lü Liuliang and his disciples, and by them passed on to Zeng Jing.

The bulk of Section One of the *Awakening* that follows is devoted to the critique of Zeng Jing's treasonous letter, originally presented by the emperor to his court on December 11, 1728. Obviously, for officials at court or in the provinces, who have read the original version, there are no surprises here; but for the students currently entering the state schools, who are to be its future readers, the tantalizing personal details on the members of the imperial family and the emperor himself and the virulence and personal intimacy of the charges will surely be both exciting and bewildering.

At the close of this second part of Section One, Zeng Jing is permitted his own voice. The book ceases to be an imperial monologue and becomes a protracted series of discussions between the two men, as the emperor poses his questions in writing—thirteen questions by the emperor are printed in the remaining pages of Section One and a further twenty-four questions in Section Two. Zeng Jing answers each one at length, his responses often in the form of extended essays. Though Zeng Jing himself is far away from Beijing by the time of the final compilation—first on the road to Hangzhou and Changsha and then in Yongxing county seeing to his mother's burial—he has left behind in the palace a vast store of words, which the emperor now mines on his behalf. It is true that the relative hierarchical positions of the two authors are dramatically shown by the size of the type in the book: that used to record Zeng Jing's thoughts is half the size of that given to the emperor, and his answers are printed sixteen vertical columns to the page, as opposed to the emperor's eight. It is also true that Zeng Jing, in his responses to the emperor's questions, never uses his own name but always refers to himself, using a derogatory four-character term, as "the man whose crimes reached to Heaven." But the one hundred and seventy-eight pages dedicated to these exchanges in Sections One and Two give Zeng Jing an astonishing opportunity to share his own thoughts with his countrymen at large.

Section Three of the *Awakening from Delusion* follows somewhat the same format, but now the questioner is formally identified as Hangyilu, the vice-president of the Ministry of Punishments, who has headed the interrogations ever since he was sent to Changsha over a year before. It was Hangyilu who passed on to Zeng Jing the documentary materials that Yongzheng had selected as being most effective in illuminating his own sense of compassion and in exploring the complexities of governing the country: the sample legal cases, the reports of General Yue, the hundreds of provincial reports from different officials, and the specific material on the economy and the currency.

As if to prove that Zeng Jing's lengthy responses to these materials have fully shown his contrition, Section Three switches direction after fifty-two pages, the remainder of the space being devoted to the series of reports and counteredicts in which the emperor and his senior officials debated the punishments that would best fit Zeng's crimes. Again, though well known to those at the senior levels in the bureaucracy, these examples of tense give-and-take between Yongzheng and his ministers will make strange reading to students in county schools, who can have little idea of the pressures that lie behind specific imperial decisions. As is the case in Section One, many of the edicts in Section Three reveal astonishing details about the machinations at the court among Emperor Yongzheng's brothers—or at least the way the emperor chooses to present those struggles. And the emperor's ultimate rejection of his officials' pleas for harsh and exemplary punishment—first by the one hundred and forty-eight officials, and then by the bureaucracy under the protective shield of Prince Yi—is presented without any more justification than the emperor gave at the time.

The fourth and last section of the *Awakening from Delusion* changes direction and chronology once again, to focus on the treasonous materials that can be found in the writings of Lü Liuliang and his disciple Yan. Here the main bulk of the documentation consists of the emperor's prior edicts of denunciation against the two men in July 1729. The insulting and inflammatory passages from the two men's writings are now being made available to the country as a whole, through the device of selective quotation, even though the senior officials in Beijing have still not rendered any definite verdict on the guilt of either Lü or Yan. But Zeng Jing's appended commentaries on the ways he learned to reject the false messages of Lü Liuliang clearly show the direction that the emperor intends later arguments to take.

The *Awakening from Delusion* closes, appropriately enough, with the carefully rendered statement of contrition by Zeng Jing himself, the twenty-seven-page essay entitled *My Return to the Good.* In a brief preface introducing Zeng's essay, the emperor comments on the conspirator's past sins and on his present change of heart. The moral transformation that Zeng has achieved, the emperor writes, shows the wisdom of the ancient texts that suggest that any person, however evil, is capable of change. Zeng Jing has shaken off his evil ways and understood the meaning of virtue at last. Thus it is fitting that Zeng's own essay should bring the book to a close.

As for Zeng Jing, his own rebirth is symbolized by his reclaiming of his own name. In the third-to-last line of his essay, on the last page of the book, for the first time in the entire text of the *Awakening from Delusion*, he refers to himself by his given name, "Jing," rather than by the self-deprecating term "the man whose crimes reached to Heaven," which he uses in every other passage. It is thus as one newly reborn that he writes the closing words: "Now correct morality has made its permanent return. People all rejoice, persuaded by the sincerity of the emperor's love and protection. Everywhere people will hold fast to their proper roles as filial sons and obedient subjects. Each will accord importance to human relations, in order to realize the great goodness of Heavenly principle. Once more I shall reclaim my basic inner nature. People will take these examples of Jing's total ignorance, unworthiness, gullibility, and delusions, as a warning. All within the four seas will be transformed, the nine continents united in one virtue, and all will possess the Dao of Heaven and enjoy a boundless happiness. We will not waste our chance of living in a glorious age, but will feel the joy of living in such times. This is my testament."

The *Awakening from Delusion* was the first time Zeng Jing's views had all been drawn together in one place so that someone could read through them in a reflective way. It was presumably obvious to any general reader that the concluding essay, *My Return to the Good,* was written the way it was because of Zeng Jing's need to win the emperor's approval and justify his clemency. But this essay was only a fragment of a much larger whole, and for those who sought some fuller message, the body of the book allowed a very different Zeng Jing to make his presence felt.

The mood for this sense of earnest rectitude was nicely set by a passage Yongzheng chose to go at the end of the November 2 edict, which now found service as the book's foreword. This was an extended reflection on the concept of "glibness" among Chinese scholars. The emperor drew his passage on glibness from the *Analects* of Confucius, as he knew the students in their schools would see at once. The passage that he cited described how a former student of Confucius named Zilu, shortly after being made an administrator, ordered a young man in his jurisdiction to withdraw from his studies so he could be posted to control an unruly local tribe. When Confucius rebuked Zilu for ruining the young man's future career by cutting short his education, Zilu replied tartly that a practical education was what one needed in this world: "Why must one read books before one is considered a learned man?" he asked. To which Confucius responded, "Remarks like that make me hate you glib-tongued people." Such glibness, the emperor noted in his own commentary on the passage, was all too prevalent in the current age; it enabled crafty and mean-natured people to twist concepts of morality by quoting them out of context, thus destroying their inner significance. By identifying such glibness, the emperor noted, and preventing its recurrence, one could perform a service for all humanity. An inference many of his readers might draw, if they had followed Yongzheng's public pronouncements with any care, was that he was here recalling the ways in which the various Zhejiang scholars he had come to hate and despise abused their education by playing elaborate word games with the past and muddling the moral values of the present.

Some of the new material from Zeng Jing in the *Awakening* was presented in the form of autobiographical passages. The emperor's detailed questions about statements in Zeng Jing's earlier writings—or some of the things he had written in his Hunan confession, for instance—allowed Zeng Jing to respond at length in terms that illuminated his own moral ideals. Thus, when the emperor asked him about his in-laws, the Chens, and why Zeng had quoted them as declaring that Zeng Jing "had the virtue to benefit the world, and the magnanimity of a prime minister," Zeng replied that the remarks in fact had no political implications whatsoever.

The Chens were not expressing the hope that he would become the minister in some new dynasty. They had used the phrase because in a turbulent family crisis one of Zeng's female relatives had been forcibly remarried to a neighbor of the Chens, on the ground that she got along so badly with her first husband. Zeng Jing had resisted this forced remarriage for moral reasons; he argued vigorously with her first husband in opposition to it and spoke kindly to the woman, trying to help her in her predicament. It was for this reason, because they considered Zeng to be "serious, honest and kind, without being frivolous or impudent," that the older Chen in-laws had uttered their words of praise.

Equally apolitical in intent had been his uncle-in-law Chen Meiding's expressed nostalgia for "the clothing and customs of the previous dynasty," wrote Zeng. The remark had nothing at all to do with Lü Liuliang. It was just that Chen Meiding was over seventy when the conversation took place, back around 1700, and naturally remembered the days of his childhood and youth, when things had been different. Besides which, Zeng added, "Chen Meiding was essentially a countryman from a farming family, who did not read books or study cultural matters. How could he make allusive remarks?" And Zeng Jing himself never knew that Lü Liuliang had written down a rather similar thought until Zhang Xi came back from Zhejiang with some of Lü's poems in 1727.

Such details helped to create a sense of Zeng Jing as a person, or at least his sense of how he wished to present his own person, and made it easier to understand some of his more openly stated political beliefs. As many passages in the *Awakening from Delusion* illustrated, Zeng Jing had his own firm opinions on the need for change in China. His was a nostalgic view, but it was one that had been shared by many Chinese thinkers across two millennia and one that had indeed been shared also by Lü Liuliang: in one of his responses to the emperor printed in the volume, Zeng Jing specified that the key period of Lü's influence on his own thinking had come between the last months of 1727 and the spring of 1728. His view then was that an individual's virtue was the main criterion of the right to rule, and that when true virtue was present, Heaven would be in sympathy and the people obedient. The country known as China was defined by being a land that contained the elements necessary for ordered, moral governance—from such elements sprang wisdom, virtue, correct rituals, and trust. That there was an imbalance of these elements in the present age was proved by many factors, wrote Zeng Jing, not least the growing inequalities of wealth and status in China. In olden days the land had been equitably divided, but now, as the poor grew poorer they were forced to sell their land or else were evicted by force. They lost their livelihood as the rich acquired ever greater holdings. In such a situation peace and stability were not enough.

The emperor argued back that Zeng's was an oversimplified view: the poor were able to improve their economic situation through hard work and good management of their resources, just as the rich could lose their wealth through idleness or inefficiency. In this exchange, as in many others, Zeng Jing had no effective counter arguments to make to the emperor's probing—the goal of the *Awakening from Delusion* was, after all, to show that Zeng Jing had been deluded by negative influences and, under the benevolent aegis of the emperor, had at last come to see the error of his ways.

On matters of governance, however, Zeng Jing held surprisingly firm. As he wrote in response to a question from the emperor, he had been drawn to the system of equitable land distribution ever since he was a youngster and first read the philosopher Mencius' description of the "well-field" system. Under that system, landholdings of equal size were grouped around a central block of land worked and owned in common, the produce of which made up the food and revenue required by the state. The fact that he later discovered that Lü Liuliang admired the same system and even believed it could be put once more into practice increased his admiration for Lü Liuliang, but was not the source for his holding that belief. It had occurred to Zeng that if the well-field system could indeed be revived, then perhaps his own family would have no need to migrate to Sichuan in search of a better life, as they had decided they might have to. This encouragement drawn from Mencius and substantiated by Lü Liuliang found further reinforcement in the posters announcing the favorable stellar conjunctions that he had seen in Changsha.

In other passages of *Awakening from Delusion* Zeng wrote that he had long since come to believe from his reading that the best path for China was decentralization, to allow many independent rulers the freedom to exercise control over their own local areas, even if somewhere above them there was one coordinating or supervisory power. That had been the way China was governed during what was known as the "Spring and Autumn" period of its history, before the country was unified under a single all-powerful emperor. Zeng was confident that the organizational system prevailing in those earlier days—Chinese philosophers called it the *fengjian,* or "divided enfeoffment," system—had great potential benefits for the China of his own day, both for internal government and for frontier defense.

Zeng explained his reasoning: "The vastness of the world is such that one person's eyes or mind cannot grasp it all, and the seas extend so far there are always areas one will never be able to reach. And Heaven apportions our talents unevenly—some are great sages, some are worthies; and among the worthies some are more talented than others. But all of them once had responsibilities for ruling over the people. The sage presided over the worthies, as the most important matters took precedence over the lesser. Thus, a balance was reached: day-to-day business was managed by the worthies, but there was still one person who decided on overall policy. Such was the system of 'divided enfeoffment' set up by the rulers in ancient days. Though the Son of Heaven presided over the rituals and the music and the waging of war, the job of nurturing the people and the responsibility for governing them devolved on the enfeoffed rulers of each smaller region." How different that was from the later system of the bureaucratically unified empire, Zeng argued (in reference to the system first imposed on China in 221 B.C.E.) whereby the entire country was divided up into administrative units such as prefectures and counties, and officials came and went, never staying long enough in one area to bring constructive changes and blaming each other for the things left undone. Seeing the people as an undifferentiated mass, they never grew close to them.

The emperor's comments on this passage showed that he was not convinced. Things had changed since those far-off days, he pointed out; history had taken a different course, and such fragmented government in the present age would only mean chaos at home and weakness on the country's borders. But Zeng Jing was ready with more specific arguments, which could address the problems of local order. The answer, he believed, lay in the "community covenant" system, as devised and first described by a scholar from Shaanxi in the eleventh century and amplified and praised by Zhu Xi—the most celebrated of all the later commentators on Confucius—at the end of the twelfth. Zeng Jing had read the documents on these original covenants with care, he wrote, and had come to believe that through such local covenants one could instill morality into any community, form strong social ties, care for the distressed, and mediate disputes without recourse to law. What was ideal for the present age was that the covenants "were modeled after the past and modified to suit the present."

Each community forming such a covenant would choose an older man of experience and integrity to be its leader and would select twelve younger men who were conscientious and wrote well to be his assistants, each for one month in turn, and to keep the books and records. These were of three main kinds: one book recorded the names and attendance details of all the members of the group; one recorded the merits of those in the community who had earned praise in the given month; and the third noted the failings and criticisms that were raised against individuals in the community. Meetings were to be held at least once each month, in a convenient location so that all the members could attend. Wine would circulate, the rituals would be performed, the covenant's rules would be read aloud, and lively discussion would follow: "Everyone in the meeting could raise questions that troubled them, argue over moral issues, discuss any problems of family livelihood, analyze literature, and practice archery." At sunset, the group would disperse.

It was his hope, Zeng Jing added, that the emperor would take the lead in fostering the idea of such community covenants, using his intelligence to modify them, and in distributing copies of the most successful ones all around the country; the emperor should instruct his governors-general and governors to establish such community groups in even the most inaccessible areas of each county and to ensure that membership was open to all—scholars and farmers, craftsmen and merchants. Setting up such a system of covenants would not be hard, since the government already sponsored meetings on the first and middle day of every month, at which local scholars gave readings of the sixteen moral maxims that had been written out for community guidance by the late Emperor Kangxi and amplified by Emperor Yongzheng. Why not build on those by adding discussion of the local covenant's main principles and of its specific programs? Such occasions would also offer an opportunity to explain current government policies and to improve the public morality of every rural area.

Since the current system was limited mainly to towns, Zeng emphasized, "Locals do not know the emperor's moral teachings. They live in the countryside most of the time, and seldom go to town; also, they are illiterate, and cannot understand the emperor's intentions." Thus the meetings to discuss the emperor's moral maxims were generally ineffectual: "The meetings often do not take place as scheduled, and the officials treat them as mere routine. The ordinary people, if they listen at all, do so in the most casual way, and many don't even bother to come. Far more people live in the countryside than in towns, in distant areas where they have no supervision. Even if there were to be a public lecture, how would they hear it? Take my own case as an example: living as I did, so far from the county town, I had never attended a single discussion of the community covenants or their rules and regulations. And as to the [sixteen] moral imperial maxims, with the emperor's commentary, not only had I never seen them before, but I had never even heard of them!" If the covenant ideas were spread effectively, Zeng Jing concluded, so that they reached into all the many subcommunities that together made up the larger administrative units, then there would be no one in the country who was ignorant of imperial policy. "Not only would we end all the problems that are caused when subordinates fail to carry out the orders of their superiors, but the ruler and his people would be as one, and there would be no impediment to their perfect communication."

From the way that many of these debates were presented in the *Awakening from Delusion* it is clear that the emperor was especially interested when Zeng Jing gave a classical origin for a particular idea, for then he could challenge the conspirator textually, demonstrating at the same time how a Manchu emperor was able to absorb the finer details of the Chinese philosophical tradition. The case of Guan Zhong's views on race was a good example. Zeng Jing had written about this man at some length in his earlier, treasonous book, *Knowledge of the New*, stating there that the example of Guan Zhong proved clearly that "the distinctions between Chinese and barbarians transcended any consideration of the bonds between ruler and minister." In passing this judgment, Zeng had clearly been influenced by Lü Liuliang's own commentaries on Guan Zhong. Not surprisingly, the emperor demanded clarification, and in doing just that Zeng Jing was able to elaborate on his own previous and briefer statement.

He did not have to repeat the whole story of Guan Zhong, which was an integral part of any student's reading, and well known both to Zeng and to his emperor. Guan Zhong was a historical figure from the seventh century B.C.E., about two hundred years before the time of Confucius. He had served successively as the chief minister to two able but ruthless brothers who ruled a vast domain. When the second brother killed the first so as to seize the domain for himself, he asked Guan Zhong to continue in his post as chief minister, and Guan Zhong agreed.

For this failure of loyalty to his first master, Confucius' contemporaries criticized Guan Zhong, but Confucius himself took a complex and contrary position of his own on the case, as was recorded in his book the *Analects.* Like many important passages in the *Analects,* this one was presented in the form of a debate between Confucius and his students. The students were described as having criticized Guan Zhong on two grounds: first, that he refused to commit suicide when his master was killed, although his own closest colleague did take his own life to prove his loyalty to his murdered lord; and second, that Guan Zhong not only took office under the murderer, but performed his duties as first minister with such exemplary skill that he raised his new master's domain to a pinnacle of power that enabled it to dominate its neighbors.

Those two criticisms by Confucius' students could be seen as supporting the moral beliefs of many Ming loyalists in the period just after the Manchu conquest—among them Lü Liuliang. Confucius' response also supported the Ming loyalist position, albeit from a very different perspective. As Confucius put it: "Guan Zhong served Duke Huan as chief minister, made him paramount among the princes, and both unified and brought order to the land. Down to our own time we benefit from his contributions. Had it not been for Guan Zhong, our hair would hang wild, and our clothes be fastened on the wrong side." Chinese students of Zeng Jing's time would all have known that having the hair hang unbound was a characteristic of the eastern barbarians, while fastening clothes on the wrong (or left) side, was natural to the barbarian tribes in general. It had been Zeng Jing's interpretation, in the *Knowledge of the New,* that

Confucius' strong praise for Guan Zhong was because the minister had saved the Chinese people from being like the barbarians who surrounded them on all sides. The clothes and hair were thus symbols—though not of course the only ones—for the values of civilization as a whole. From this, Zeng Jing had drawn his conclusion that in Confucius' mind the ability to support the values of Chinese civilization against encroaching barbarian peoples obviously had a higher priority than the obligations for a minister to serve his lord with unquestioning loyalty.

The emperor's reply to Zeng Jing's arguments on these controversial themes was firm. He emphasized that the relationship of a ruler to his ministers was the paramount one within the hierarchy of five relationships that were central to Chinese life, the other four being those between father and son, husband and wife, brother and brother, and friend and friend. It was the ruler-minister relationship that defined the meaning of Chinese moral behavior: "There is simply no way that one can abandon this fundamental relationship, and still claim to be a fully formed human being." When Zeng was writing those words that in the relations between Chinese and barbarians there could be no ruler-subject distinctions, whom then did he believe to be his emperor? And at the present time, was Zeng Jing still convinced that ruler-subject distinctions were irrelevant when one was discussing the various types of "barbarians"? Did Zeng Jing still insist, after all that had happened, that in relations with barbarians there were no ruler-subject distinctions? It was not a debate that could continue further, and Zeng Jing backed away with humility, pointing to his reading of Lü Liuliang on the Guan Zhong passage as having led to his undoing. Now, he observed, having pondered the emperor's remarks on the changing size of China as new areas were incorporated and on the shifting definitions of exactly which people should be considered Chinese, he could see the error of his ways.

In a somewhat different use of a classical passage for the purpose of debate, the emperor also challenged Zeng Jing to consider the contradictions in his *Knowledge of the New* on the topic of the human family as a whole and on the relations between the Chinese and those living on the periphery. In his book, Zeng Jing had stated specifically that China was surrounded by barbarian territories and that only within the barbarian territories close to the heartland of China could one find a certain amount of truly human elements. The farther away from that heartland one traveled, the more like the birds and beasts the barbarians became. How on earth could that be true? asked the emperor. The *Doctrine of the Mean* (a basic part of the Confucian canon, drawn from a text on rituals of great antiquity) had expressed it perfectly clearly: "Let the states of equilibrium and harmony exist in perfection, and a happy order will prevail throughout Heaven and earth, and all things will be nourished and will flourish." But, the emperor continued, the world, with its nine continents and four oceans, was vast, and China—however large it appeared to those living in it—occupied only a one-hundredth part of the whole. In every part one found the same principles of being, and the same material essences, so how could there somehow be one Heaven and earth for the people of China and another one for the barbarian tribes? "All things will be nourished and will flourish," wrote the sage. Did Zeng Jing really think barbarian peoples were somehow excluded from "all things"? Could they receive none of that nourishing?

To pursue his own argument further, the emperor could have chosen any one of scores of textual reference points, but the one he chose to concentrate on was the sixty-first hexagram from the most ancient text in the so-called Five Classics of the Confucian canon, the work known as *The Book of Changes*. The sixty-first hexagram was entitled "inner trust," and its opening image was presented in these words: "Inner trust is such that even fish and swine have good fortune. It is fitting to cross the great river, and fitting to practice constancy. Firm, but also attaining what is appropriate: that is how you transform the state." It was clear from this opening to the hexagram, the emperor pointed out to Zeng Jing, that "the sage intended to inspire and morally transform even the fish and swine. So how can one still say that those who are far from China are no different from the birds and beasts?" In such a context, a person like Zeng Jing, with his treacherous inner feelings, had surely been below the birds and the beasts. Though now they had reached the current stage of their discussions, the emperor added, was there a chance that Zeng Jing "might be inspired and transformed as the pigs and fish could be, or was that impossible? Let him give me a true reply."

Zeng Jing replied that he had read *The Book of Changes*, but he was only a child at the time; he thus stupidly missed the significance of the reference to the idea that trust could reach even to pigs and fish. So he embarked on his own reckless pattern of writing without recalling that particular passage and using it to correct his own mistaken views. From now on he would always remember "how the swine and the fish also have their inspiration and moral transformation: how much more must that be true for a human nature that had not yet been completely destroyed, and still has the ability to respond intellectually."

If Zeng Jing might appear to have been more convincing than his emperor with his use of the Guan Zhong analogy, in the case of the sixty-first hexagram the emperor had the better of his former prisoner. The emperor had also selected this topic artfully, since a number of traditional commentaries on that same hexagram introduced other themes that had particular relevance to Zeng Jing's recent plight. Central to many of these was the conviction that the shape of the sixty-first hexagram—two straight lines at the top, two broken lines in the middle, and two straight lines at the bottom—could be seen as being like a hollowed-out boat, whose buoyancy was a feature of the hollowed-out nature of the object. Buoyancy implied flexibility and lightness: just as pigs and fish, both of them ignorant and stubborn forms of life, could be reached by trust, so could the people of all the land be reached by the ruler's compassion.

The commentators noted too that this particular hexagram of inner trust followed in a natural sequence after the sixtieth hexagram, which signified "control." Thus, a function of calling up the sixty-first hexagram in divination was that if restraint came right after control, then people would have faith in their ruler: "Above the lake there is wind," as one of these earlier scholars wrote. "This constitutes the image of inner trust. In the same way, the noble man evaluates criminal punishments and mitigates the death penalty." For when the trust was generated internally, "even one who makes mistakes can find exoneration." The result could be a society in which "none will engage in artful competition, and actions based on honesty and substance will be the rule." Just as the hollow center of the hexagram could suggest the buoyancy of a boat, so could it suggest the fullness of mercy, for "the yielding lines in the center of the hexagram create an empty space." Emptiness of heart and humility could attract what was good, while "central firmness and strength" could "ensure an essential trustworthiness."

The possibilities here had raised a commentator of the seventh century to lyrical heights of rhetoric: "In a world governed by inner trust, it is certain that no deliberate crime would occur, and wrongdoing as such would be but the product of error, something that could be forgiven. Thus the noble man here should evaluate criminal cases that involved such error, and mitigate those that ordinarily require the death penalty." Or, as a twelfth-century commentator had written on the same hexagram, even if the ruler felt the death penalty might be merited, he would still "do nothing less than push his sense of compassion to the limit." The relevance of these arguments to the case and pardon of Zeng Jing is clear enough.

On April 4, 1730, as soon as the emperor gets the news that all the wooden printing blocks for the *Awakening from Delusion* are ready, he instructs his grand secretaries to come up with a feasible plan for the countrywide distribution of the volume, one that will meet the demands for wide-level accessibility that he has stipulated. Six days later they have formulated a general plan, which the emperor accepts immediately: an initial run of five hundred copies will be printed in the Beijing palace workshops from the newly carved blocks and distributed at once to the senior officials in the capital bureaucracy and their staffs. A second run will provide enough further copies to ensure that every senior provincial official receives one for his own personal use.

In addition, governors-general and governors will be sent a second copy, which they are instructed to pass on to their own provincial printing offices. These will serve as the matrices from which each local printing office will make a new set of the blocks of the entire work; each of these provincial printing offices is initially to run off one hundred copies, and as soon as those are ready they will be distributed to the lower-ranking local officials, down to the level of the county magistrates—most provinces have around sixty counties—and the educational supervisors in the county and subcounty government schools. These junior local officials, in their turn, will be responsible for making an estimate of the number of market towns and villages in each of their jurisdictions, along with the number of officially registered students in their schools, and for drawing up figures for the number of copies they would be needing. (These numbers were sizable. In his own earlier confession, Zeng Jing told his interrogators that there were around two thousand licentiates in Yongxing county alone, and as many as twenty-four hundred licensed students sitting for each of the qualifying examinations.) Where possible, the costs of these extra print runs, or of new blocks as needed, are to be born by the local scholars and wealthier landlords in each area. These locally made copies would be distributed throughout each county, so they could be discussed at the bimonthly meetings at which it was mandatory to recite and discuss the emperor's sixteen moral maxims—the very meetings that Zeng Jing had discussed as forming possible linkages to the community covenants.

The Beijing printers and binders work with extraordinary speed to get the book ready for distribution across the country. Within two weeks of the emperor's initial discussion of the distribution plan with his grand secretaries, staff members from their Beijing offices, aided by the personnel from the Documents Transmission Office and couriers from the Ministry of War, begin to fan out across the country with their stacks of volumes of the *Awakening from Delusion.* The first recorded recipient is a military garrison commander stationed just outside Beijing, who reports back in a memo to the Grand Secretariat that his copy reached him on April 27. General Yue Zhongqi, deeply involved in the preparations for a new military campaign ordered by the emperor in the northwest, receives his two copies in Xi'an on May 5 and passes one on immediately for reprinting, as he has been instructed. The military commander in Guangdong, in the far southeast, reports that his set arrived on June 4. The Hunan governor in Changsha, however, does not get his copies till the end of June, because of the disastrous weather conditions in the province. Relentless driving rainstorms have led to the copies directed to the judicial commissioner and the supervisor of public morality being ruined in transit, arriving as a blurred and wrinkled mass. But now the printing of clear new copies can begin, and to make up for the delay the governor orders no less than three sets of blocks to be carved in the local print shops. Clearly, the delay in Hunan is only temporary. By midsummer, local scholars in even the most poverty-stricken and isolated counties east of Yongxing have read their copies of the *Awakening from Delusion,* and have absorbed its message.

On the matter of reading the text carefully, the emperor has left the students and officials little choice. As he writes at the end of the foreword to the book: "One copy is to be deposited in every local school, so that all future scholars embarking on the road of learning can read it and absorb it. Should I later discover that there is anyone who has not read this book, and not heeded my instructions, then the full weight of punishment will fall on the educational commissioners of the provinces concerned, and on the educational supervisors in the counties affected."

So steadily, province by province, garrison by garrison, township by township—as Zeng Jing proceeds with the hundred days of mourning rituals for his mother—the officials continue to report receipt of their copies, and their plans for making the thousands of extra ones they will need if they are to reach all the registered students and community groups in the towns and villages under their jurisdiction. By late November 1730, even the officials in far-away Taiwan, the latest addition to the expanding Qing empire, have received their copies. Despite the fact that much of the island has not yet been settled by Chinese emigrants and that schools are still at a fairly primitive level, Taiwan officials estimate that they will have to make a further 1,230 copies if they are to comply with their emperor's orders.

For years, Zeng Jing has been seeking an audience for his words. Now he has found one, and on a scale that could never have occurred to him, even in his maddest dreams.

Eleven

The Source

Well before April 12, the day Zeng Jing reaches Changsha, the senior officials in Hunan have been alerted to his imminent return. They obtain this news in a confidential message from Hangyilu, which relays the emperor's exact instructions: "Zeng Jing is to be sent under escort from Hangzhou to the office of the Hunan governor. He is to be permitted to return home to take care of his family affairs. Once he is finished, he is to make his own way back, deliver himself up to the office of the supervisor of public morality, Li Hui, and await assignment. If he wants to travel around, there is no need to stop him doing so." But the death of Zeng Jing's mother has added a new dimension to these instructions: for while the emperor's orders give no hint as to the amount of time Zeng Jing should be allowed to spend at home, the basic rituals of mourning for one's mother require a period of one hundred days, and so fate has taken the decision out of the governor's hands. Zeng Jing sets off the following day, and on April 25 is back once more in the home where he was arrested sixteen months before.

The duties involved in preparing his mother's resting place turn out not to be too onerous after all. By mid-May he has finished with the basic tasks of readying his mother's body for burial, obtaining a coffin, and moving it to a temporary grave in the hills where it will remain until Zeng Jing can obtain a final and permanent burial site. That leaves him time for other things.

As Zeng explains later, in a memorandum to the governor and morality supervisor, his homecoming in these sad circumstances was a curious one. Without exception, those he met during the funeral preparations—relatives, friends, neighbors, casual acquaintances—were astonished to see him there, and were awed to hear of his adventures in Beijing and of the role the emperor had played in his release. They were fascinated, too, to be allowed to look at the clothes and other presents that the emperor had given him on his departure from Beijing. And they dutifully expressed their disgust over that scoundrel, the fake *jinshi* claiming the name Wang Shu, who had spread his hateful rumors in the community and caused so much trouble and unrest.

Zeng Jing had been granted one hundred days of mourning leave, and after doing what had to be done he still had almost two months left. By his account, the way he chose to use that time was a deliberate act, a decision to balance off the filial duty he owed to his mother with the parallel loyalty he owed his emperor. He would continue, for the rest of the hundred days, to grieve for his mother as the rituals and his own heart decreed; but at the same time he would seek to requite the emperor's generosity by seeing if he could not track those initial ugly rumors to their source. To do that, he would endeavor to find out where the fake Wang Shu had gone, seven years before, after he had visited Zeng's schoolhouse, stayed two days, and vanished, leaving only his web of tales behind.

For a few days, Zeng Jing's questions elicit no useful answers, but in the third week of May he makes a breakthrough. One of his neighbors tells Zeng that he has heard a story from someone called Cao, which might be of help. Some years before, Cao, a Yongxing native, had obtained his licentiate's degree. But despite his degree, Cao had been unable to find a job in Yongxing, and therefore accepted a post as a schoolteacher in the county town of Guidong, about sixty miles away, deep in the mountains on the eastern border, where Hunan meets Jiangxi. Cao's story concerned an unusual visitor who came to Guidong in the autumn of 1723: this traveler was originally from Beijing, a "person of distinction and great cultural refinement," Cao recalled, who "not only seemed to know everything about the goings-on in the capital but loved to talk about literature and scholarly matters as well. Everything he said seemed solidly grounded in verifiable fact." Cao had heard that the stranger died sometime in late 1723, near the Guidong county border.

Zeng Jing is eager to follow up this important lead, but (as he also mentions in his memorandum) his recent notoriety sometimes works against him. Potentially important witnesses tended "to close their mouths and turn their faces away" when they heard who he was; for these were people "who read books, were law-abiding, anxious to avoid suspicion, and scared of getting involved in public matters. I was afraid that they might have something to say but would not dare speak up or tell the truth, and so though there might be leads they would not get followed up." So Zeng Jing decides to recruit a companion to accompany him and share the questioning. Both would use assumed names, in case their own were recognized. Zeng's choice of companion falls on Zhang Zhao, the elder brother of his disciple and messenger Zhang Xi. (Why Zhang Zhao agreed to help him is not explained; perhaps Zhang Zhao had been in the conspiracy all along and had thrown the interrogators off the scent by his bluff remark that he was only a farmer who knew nothing of his brother's goings-on; perhaps Zhang had been telling the truth about disliking Zeng Jing, but was lured by Zeng's promise that if they found the rumor's source they would be amply rewarded.) On May 26, the two men reach an agreement and begin the rugged overland walk from Anren county, Zhang Zhao's home, southeast though the mountains to Guidong, which they reach on June 5.

In Guidong they are unable to find the licentiate named Cao, but they do meet another local scholar, Zhong Sanji, who responds helpfully to the questions that they put to him. It was in the late summer or early autumn of 1723, Zhong recalls, that he met an unusual man, a man who "kept his head and face covered, had long nails on all his fingers, and a wispy beard. He told me his family name was Wang, his given name was Shu, and that he wanted to spend a bit of time in the library here." Later, Zhong had heard that the stranger drifted around neighboring counties as well, dropping in on various scholars and examining their libraries but never staying anywhere more than a day or two. Some time later the stranger had returned to Guidong and died at a teahouse in a place called Daling Mountain, in the fourth ward of the county. A kinsman of Zhong's, named Zhong Xiang, who had initially found this "Wang Shu" to be a good conversationalist but later grew skeptical of his scholarship, put up the money for a decent wooden coffin for Wang and for a burial site on Daling Mountain, so the wanderer could finally rest in peace.

Once Zhong has shared this information with Zeng Jing and his companion, others in the Guidong area follow suit: some are degree holders, some are commoners, some are wealthy and some are of modest means, but all recall some rather similar experience with this stranger with a wispy beard and long nails, back in 1723, as he visited their libraries if they had them, dined at their tables when they asked him, and spun his intriguing tales of Beijing life. Most had noticed, as had the Zhongs, that the stranger, despite his professed love for scholarship and literature, and indeed the fluency with which he talked about scholarly texts, never seemed to write out any Chinese words with his own hand. Any writing he had to do was done for him by an amanuensis who traveled with him.

In the middle of June 1730, Zeng Jing makes another major discovery. He learns that on May 20, 1723, this stranger claiming to be Wang Shu had been traveling down the road that ran south from Leiyang county to Yongxing, when he stopped for the night at a small Buddhist temple, called "Shrine of the Holy Offerings," on the border of the two counties. The man telling Zeng this has also heard that the stranger left behind some scraps of writing in the temple, where they are still preserved. The date fits perfectly, since it was only eleven days after that, on May 31, that a man calling himself Wang Shu came to visit Zeng Jing in his roadside schoolhouse. Zeng recognizes the name of the temple and even knows the man who tends it, a Buddhist priest named Mizeng. But the two have never been close friends, and Mizeng is reputed to be a man who values his privacy and keeps away from worldly matters. So rather than scare the priest off right away, Zeng Jing asks a third person, a distant relative, to act as his intermediary, both to enquire after the stored scraps of writing and to assure the priest that nothing untoward would happen to him if he shows them the writing and tells them about the visitor. The priest is won over and agrees to show them his small trove. Thus it is that Zeng Jing comes to hold in his hands the first concrete evidence—apart from countless anecdotes and his own fleeting memories—for the existence of the fake Wang Shu.

There are five bits of paper in all. One is a promissory note in the amount of fifty ounces of silver, made over to the priest Mizeng, so that he might buy a sizable plot of land, the income from which could support his little temple in perpetuity. The note, dated "summer 1723," is endorsed with the name of the magistrate of Leiyang county. Its guarantor is stated to be the financial commissioner of Hunan province, and it is signed with the name "Prince Yinyou," younger brother of the emperor Yongzheng and the seventh son of the late emperor Kangxi. Across the prince's name and the last two lines of the note is a sprawling seal and a crude outline of a kind of monogram, which, Zeng Jing learns, was used by the fake Wang Shu in lieu of a signature.

The second document is on a long thin sheet of red paper and contains a mere twenty-one words of calligraphy. It is a pass entitling the bearer to enter the outer area of the Beijing Forbidden City through the Zhengyang Gate and visit the palace of "Yintang." The two characters "Yin" and "tang" are exact homophones for the personal name of the late emperor's ninth son, a wealthy prince known to have opposed his brother Yongzheng's accession to the throne. This pass is also signed with the name of the emperor's seventh brother, Yinyou, and bears the same simple scrawl in "Wang Shu's" hand that appeared on the promissory note. The priest explains that the stranger dictated the contents of this pass to his calligrapher-assistant and made a gift of it, in case the priest ever came to Beijing on a visit. Though, "Wang Shu" added, he knew it was unlikely the priest would ever make the long journey to Beijing, given his retiring nature and his saintly ways. This stranger, the priest recalls, had always been chattering about the imperial family and about his earlier military experiences out beyond the northern borders of Shaanxi province. The stranger had been especially vocal in his praise for the late emperor's fourteenth son, Yinti. The two men, "Wang Shu" told the priest, prince and devoted follower, shared the same ambitions and the same destiny—between them they would accomplish a "great enterprise"; without them, peace would never come to the current dynasty.

The remaining three documents appear to be fragments. One of them consists of a few lines from a poem on the beauties of nature; it is written on celebratory red paper in a meter of seven stresses to the line, and signed with the same homophone for the name of the emperor's ninth brother that appears on the palace pass. The other two are short passages written out on ornamental paper, perhaps for display at the shrine: "Smile, and stroll, like the drifting clouds" runs one; "Those who have suffered come to understand joy," says the other. "Those who have been always busy come to love leisure." On July 7, aware now that this story and the strange cache of documents can no longer be safely hidden away, Zeng Jing pays a visit to the magistrate of Leiyang county and makes a secret deposition about his discoveries, to be entered into the official record. Two days later the magistrate arrests the calligrapher who had written the documents for the fake Wang Shu and orders him held for questioning. Zeng Jing arranges for his own relative—the one who had first approached the priest Mizeng with a request to view the documents—to bring the priest along to the magistrate for questioning.

Zeng Jing's mourning leave is now over, and he has to hurry back to Changsha. He arrives in the city on July 14 and spends the next day fasting and taking a ritual bath at the Buddhist temple near West Lake Bridge. On July 16, cleansed and refreshed, he reports for work at the office of the supervisor of public morality for the province of Hunan, as the emperor had commanded. His duties have not been defined with great precision by the emperor—he is to "assist in the office with specific cases under investigation"—and Zeng Jing both plays it safe and takes the instructions literally. He spends his first days in the office writing out in careful, rather cramped but legible strokes the entire sequence of events that led him down the trail after the fake Wang Shu, and what he has managed to discover so far. When it is done, he submits the lengthy memorandum to his two superiors.

There is no doubt that Zeng Jing has performed an exceptional service in starting to crack the case of the fake Wang Shu, but once his memorandum is completed and handed in, he is put to other work. Now it is the governor of Hunan himself, Zhao Hongen, who takes charge of the investigation. When he is too busy with other things, he passes certain aspects of the Wang Shu case over to his judicial commissioner. Between the two of them, they summon to Changsha and interrogate all those whose testimonies have been recorded by Zeng Jing, whether in Leiyang, Guidong, or elsewhere, probing their stories, tracking loose ends, and occasionally trapping them in contradictions. Steadily, their questioning widens the circle of those who can be shown to have known the fake Wang Shu. By late August they feel they have a good enough grasp of the case as a whole to share their findings with the emperor. Along with their own detailed report, they enclose the original copy of Zeng Jing's initial memorandum.

All through that summer of 1730 the emperor has been in an agony of grief over the sudden death on June 6 of his thirteenth brother, Prince Yi, his closest adviser ever since he came to the throne and the man he trusted the most profoundly during the faction-filled early years of his reign. The records of the time are filled with Yongzheng's anguished edicts expressing his sense of loss and detailing the solace and support this brother had been to him. The emperor was further concerned that Prince Yi's death might seriously imperil the success of the northwestern campaigns, the planning and financing of which had been largely the prince's preserve. Nevertheless, as with every earlier detail of the case, the emperor finds time to read the Hunan governor's lengthy report as well as the appended memorandum of Zeng Jing, and to relay his own comments and reflections back to Hunan in the form of a lengthy court letter. It is his goal, he tells the governor, to get all the facts totally straight, so that the Hunan investigators can finally eradicate "every one of these areas in which some doubt arises." To ensure that is done, the emperor queries every point in their and Zeng Jing's reports about which he feels uneasy, whether on logical or practical grounds. And he demands that each of the problem areas he highlights be investigated afresh.

The first man Governor Zhao cross-examines with care is Zeng Shengren, who in 1723 so obligingly wrote the calligraphy for the elusive stranger. The calligrapher—who was not related to Zeng Jing, though they had the same family name—states that he became involved with the fake Wang Shu totally by accident. In 1723 he had been working as a private tutor at the home of a family in Leiyang county when the man calling himself Wang Shu suddenly dropped by for a visit. "Wang Shu" told his hosts

184 — Treason by the Book

that he was looking for a man called Zeng Jing, but did not know the way
to Zeng Jing's home. Zeng Shengren knew the way and offered to take him
there. The two set off together, and it was on the way to Zeng Jing's that
they stopped off at Mizeng's temple by the side of the road. The priest was
welcoming, and they stayed there a couple of days. Zeng Shengren wrote
out the five pieces, from Wang Shu's dictation, as a present for the priest.
The only thing that Wang Shu wrote with his own brush was the oddly
shaped monogram.

The man who formerly employed Zeng Shengren as his family tutor is
tracked down, and he corroborates the story. The emperor, however, is intensely skeptical as soon as he reads this. Why on earth, he asks, should
this man who had been apparently busily working as a tutor in Leiyang
county suddenly drop everything and agree to escort a man he had only
just met for such a long distance? The story makes no sense. Thus challenged by the emperor, the governor returns to the charge. Now the calligrapher tells a different story: the reason he decided to go with the
unknown stranger was because his own wife was seriously ill, and he was
anxious to consult with a certain doctor Yue, whose house lay on the route
to Zeng Jing's home. Ridiculous, responds the governor. If the calligrapher
had been seeking medicines for his desperately sick wife, why had he continued in the direction of Zeng Jing's home after getting the medicine, instead of hurrying home to his wife and treating her?

The calligrapher's third answer is more convincing. He had gone
when "Wang Shu" beckoned, he said, because he hated his job "teaching
those three- and two-penny books." The man called Wang Shu had promised him riches and glory and a fine career, so of course he went along.
Why did he believe this Wang? Because Wang talked without ceasing of
his grand contacts, his close friendships with the late emperor's eighth and
ninth sons, the secret assignments he was currently engaged in, and his
military service in the far west with Yinti, the emperor's fourteenth
brother. When both the priest and the calligrapher himself voiced their
skepticism over the names on the promissory note and the other writings,
Wang had begged them not to betray his plans, not to ruin this great venture so near fruition. Nothing less than the future of the imperial family itself was at stake.

It was only just recently, after listening to one of the public discussions of the *Awakening from Delusion,* that the calligrapher had realized how completely absurd were all the stories he had once believed. Yes, he had asked why Wang Shu had no luggage with him. Wang had replied that on such a special mission he could not afford to bring all his baggage for fear of arousing suspicion. His baggage carriers were, in fact, all waiting for him on his boat, which was moored on the river in Leiyang county. The calligrapher traveled around with Wang Shu for a while after the visit to Zeng Jing's home, but then one day Wang Shu just took his leave: "He told me he had to go to Anren county, and said that I had better get home. After a little time he would come back for me. But he never did come back for me. I went to the river in Leiyang county to look for the moored boat, but I couldn't find his boat there. So I lost those particular hopes, and everything drifted away. As to what his inner nature was, that I cannot say."

The emperor is puzzled, too, about jumps and gaps in the story told by the priest Mizeng. Why didn't Mizeng ask more questions when Wang Shu gave him the letter of credit? Did he just accept that such a document should bear the name of a prince of the imperial family and be endorsed as debited to the financial commissioner of Hunan province? Didn't the priest think it odd that such a man traveled with no retainers? Hadn't he been puzzled by Wang Shu's clothes and appearance?

In his preliminary affidavit, the priest had said he never really believed this man Wang Shu, because though Wang talked so much about his life in Beijing, his accent was markedly from the Yangzi delta region, and he was obviously not a northerner as he claimed. For that reason he never tried to collect on the promissory note, or to make a down payment on the land he had been promised. Informed of the emperor's doubts about his testimony, the priest admits he did not dismiss the stranger's stories, as he formerly claimed. In fact he came to believe them, especially those about Wang's friendships with the princes, his military service with Yinti, and his boatload of baggage moored on the river. To Mizeng, these stories coalesced in a coherent whole. The priest does indeed remember the odd mixture of garments that the fake Wang Shu was wearing during those days they were together: a short purple underjacket, with a blue cotton robe worn over it, on his head a black felt hat, and on his feet satin shoes with socks. At the time, they all seemed to go with the stories Wang was telling.

As to Wang's face and body type, the picture shown for identification by the governor is an astonishingly good likeness.

When interrogated by the governor, most of the scholars who encountered the fake Wang Shu in those last months of 1723 pretty much corroborate what they have already told Zeng Jing, with one important exception. That is the scholar in Guidong county called Zhong Xiang, the man who eventually arranged for the burial of the stranger on Daling Mountain. Zhong is the holder of a higher-level literary degree than the other local scholars, and apparently remembers details they have forgotten. As he explains, he first encountered this Wang Shu in the summer of 1723, and his clothes were as the priest described them, except that Wang Shu was wearing a wide-brimmed bamboo rain hat on his head. Wang's face was long, his complexion purplish, his beard wispy—he looked around thirty years old. He had no luggage, not even a bedding roll. Wang claimed to be a provincial-level graduate of 1705 (not a *jinshi*) and sang his own praises as a man of talent. To prove his point, Wang began to recite what he claimed was one of his own literary compositions—but after a few lines Zhong recognized the composition as being one by a scholar he himself knew in the nearby city of Hengzhou. But he had let the stranger stay the night and saw him off down the main road the following morning with a present of a hundred copper coins. (The portrait of "Wang Shu" is useless, Zhong adds. It looks nothing at all like the stranger he met.)

Early in the spring of 1724, Zhong continues, shortly after the time of the annual festival for sweeping the graves, Zhong heard from a passerby that a stranger named Wang Shu had died on Daling Mountain, some six or seven miles from Zhong's own home. Unable to bear the thought of the body lying exposed to the weather, Zhong got together a small group to pay for a coffin for Wang. Zhong did not attend the funeral ceremony, nor had he visited the grave mound—but it can be seen there, by the side of the road. Had the two been better friends, says Zhong, he would have let Wang die in his home, rather than sending him off to die on the road.

Reinterrogated by the governor, Zhong follows the pattern of several previous witnesses in admitting that much of his earlier account was not true. The reason he lied was because he feared getting into trouble with the authorities and losing his cherished degree status. In his revised testimony, Zhong gives an intimate picture of the ties of friendship and marriage that bonded the small community of licentiates and other scholars in Guidong county, of their visits and their conversations. It was thus that he met the fake Wang Shu, while on a social and family visit to the home of a scholarly friend who had married one of Zhong's female relatives. Zhong speaks too of the importance of the local family libraries, and of the insecurities that the younger holders of purchased literary degrees—like him—feel when in the presence of real scholars. Initially, this made him a gullible target for the fake Wang Shu.

Zhong admits now that Wang had spoken to him at length about his close connections to the emperor's eighth, ninth, and fourteenth brothers, references that Zhong only came to see through completely after he had read the *Awakening from Delusion*. Wang was the kind of man who constantly switched subjects, at one moment saying that all he wanted was a quiet job, and the next that he was embarked on some great and mysterious project. Zhong had seen much more of Wang Shu than he initially admitted, and Wang Shu had in fact paid a second visit to Zhong's house, in April 1724. This time Wang, who appeared desperately ill, was accompanied by an attendant. Despite Wang's illness, Zhong at last turned him away, giving him another small present. He put up the money for Wang's burial after the attendant returned one day to tell him that his master had died.

Interested in this new angle, Governor Zhao orders an all-out search for this man who served as an attendant to the fake Wang Shu in 1724. He also orders the local authorities to locate the teahouse in Daling Mountain where Wang allegedly died, to find out where the coffin is buried and have the corpse exhumed. A crowd of officials descends on the Daling area, a dozen miles from the county seat of Guidong, in the fourth ward. Assembling a group of locals, they slowly narrow down the list of teahouses and small pavilions that are both near the main road and have grave mounds nearby. Checking them methodically, they locate the one they are seeking.

Buried in the grave they find a coffin of white wood made of planks one and a half inches thick, around five and a half feet in length, and a foot or so wide and deep. Inside the coffin lies a body about five feet tall: there is nothing left of the skin or flesh, but the skeleton is intact. And though the desiccated bones give no clue as to what the body once looked like or its age, the bones are wrapped in a long blue cotton robe and the remnants of a once purple-colored short jacket. (These however could not be kept as evidence, for shortly after the coffin was opened the colors faded, the fabric disintegrated, and only a blackish-yellow dust remained, among which one could see the fastening tags of polished ox-horn.) The skull is pillowed on a pair of cotton socks, and the feet, pressed against the end of the coffin, are encased in what seem to be the remains of a pair of satin shoes. The heads of the local village security organization, chided for not reporting this death to the county authorities as the law prescribes, are unrepentant: "A desperately ill man died. There was no doubt about the cause of death. So we saw no need to report it."

It takes time to find the man who served as the fake Wang Shu's attendant. The only clues offered by those who saw him are that the man was "slightly bearded, neither tall nor short, and spoke with a Jiangxi accent." But the man is believed to have stayed on in Guidong county after Wang Shu's death, and the magistrate's staff are able to track him down.

His name is Luo Yikui, he tells the governor, and he is indeed a Jiangxi man, from Xinfeng county, not far from the Hunan border. Luo used to make his living by peddling salt in the small towns and villages of western Jiangxi. Luo knows exactly when he first set eyes on the man who called himself Wang Shu: it is one of those dates made to be remembered—the second day of the second month of the second year of the current emperor's reign. Luo happened to be doing business that day in Longquan county, right on the Hunan border. He entered the general store in a village named after the nearby Gaohui Temple just as it began to snow, and that was when he saw Wang Shu: "As I came in, I saw there was another man in the same store, taking off the stockings from his feet and trading them to get money for food from the storekeeper," Luo tells the interrogators. "I could see that he appeared to be an educated man, so I asked him the reason for this. He said that his name was Wang Shu and that he was a Jiangnan native, trying to get to Hunan. He had just run out of money for his travel expenses, so he had no choice but to trade his stockings for food. I saw that it was starting to snow and could not bear the thought of him getting frozen with cold. So I let him have twenty-six coins I had with me." As the two men talked, Wang told Luo of his great plans. Learning that Luo was an itinerant trader, Wang invited him to come along as an attendant and baggage carrier, until such time as the great plans came to fruition. Wang, of course, would repay the money later, and in the meantime would allow Luo's wages to accrue in the amount of thirty coppers per day.

So began the two men's brief life together, walking by day through the little villages on the edge of the Jinggang mountain range, till they crossed over into Hunan, stopping along the way at any hut where they could find shelter. Wang Shu was spitting blood and had grown very weak. On the edge of Ling county, crossing back into Guidong, they met up with a convivial group of students returning home from the local examinations. Some of these students, moved by Wang's plight, gave him several coins to help him with his travel expenses, though others refused to contribute anything. Luo himself still had an ounce of silver and a few coins; Wang borrowed some of it, saying he would repay the loan when they got to Hengzhou. But that was far away, and in the meantime Wang was getting too weak to walk. With some of his remaining money, Luo hired a sedan chair for Wang so they could make a return visit to Zhong Xiang's house in Guidong. They got there in early April 1724, just at the time of the Qingming festival, dedicated to tending to the graves of the departed. Zhong put them up for the night and gave them a meal, but next day told them to be on their way, giving Wang a pair of cloth shoes as a parting gesture. They were traveling on foot again, despite Wang's weakness, and they found shelter for a while in a shop on the edge of the road, owned by a man named Li. The shopkeeper let them stay for several days, but he was scared Wang's illness might spread to his own family, and so he too sent them on their way.

Thus it was that they came to the pass at Daling Mountain. There they happened upon an open pavilion, next to a Buddhist shrine and teahouse, in which they found a modicum of shelter for a few more days. But when a heavy rain began to fall, they moved into the shelter of the teahouse itself. Wang told Luo to go back to Zhong Xiang's house and beg for more money for their journey. Luo did so, and Zhong gave him a one-peck sack of rice, which Luo carried back to the teahouse. Luo used some of the rice to make his companion a hot meal, but it was to be Wang's last. Wang started to vomit up greater and greater quantities of blood, and on April 13 he died. The teahouse owner would not let Luo leave his friend's body inside, so he went back one last time to Zhong, who gave him the money for a coffin and a small gravesite. Luo had no choice but to bury Wang in the clothes in which he had died. He had also placed in the coffin one last pair of satin shoes that Wang had never worn. Wang had also owned a black felt hat and a purple cotton bed coverlet, but neither could be found. They must have been taken by the keeper of the temple teahouse in partial payment for what they owed. Even at the end, Luo adds, Wang still looked no more than thirty years old, and conveyed the impression that he was a cultured man.

If Wang was such a cultured man, the interrogators ask, what books or papers did he carry with him? None at all, replies Luo, Wang had nothing with him but a purple floral bed coverlet. So how could a salt peddler just drop everything, they ask him, and follow such a man—a man dressed so shabbily, with no retainers, no luggage, who even borrowed his own attendant's money? Because he seemed so cultured, answers Luo, and shared such stories of his great plans, and talked of his friends the princes, and of how he would repay everything at a later time, if he could just recover from this illness. And thus it was "that one day simply led to another."

But who *was* this man who called himself Wang Shu, the interrogators ask, and where was he from? "When he was near death," says Luo, "I asked him, 'Where is your home? Do you have children there, or relatives? Or is there no one at all?' Tears flowed from his eyes, but he made no answer. And so he died."

Twelve

—

Sounds of Discord

It is on September 22, 1730, that the officials in Hunan first see the anonymous poster. Prominently displayed in the city of Changsha, it calls on the people of the city to assemble on a specified day the following week, and to proceed at once "to seize Zeng Jing and drown him." In reporting this new development to the emperor, the governor and the supervisor of public morality send along a copy of the poster and note that they have, of course, expressly forbidden any such mob action, and have taken steps to ensure that Zeng Jing is protected. But they do not mention that they have made any particular effort to find out who wrote the poster, nor do they report that anyone has been arrested. Instead, they point out that the imperial policy of forgiveness for Zeng Jing seems to be turning back on itself: "In our opinion, when Zeng Jing came back to Hunan, the basic purpose was that he should spread abroad the evidence of the emperor's benevolence to all the ignorant local people. But now, according to everything we have heard from our subordinates, a sense of injustice is building up in the minds of the locals; the people are deriving no benefit, and we are laying the groundwork for future trouble." The emperor's response is equally muted: "Noted. I have issued a separate edict on this."

There is a good reason for the emperor's cautious reply. The report on the desire of unnamed Hunanese to drown Zeng Jing literally crosses in the courier system with a court letter sent south to the Hunan governor via Grand Secretary Marsai, a veteran Manchu administrator who has now taken over many of the confidential duties formerly exercised by the emperor's thirteenth brother. In this court letter the emperor instructs the governor to give to Zeng Jing as "a reward for his recent services" the sum of one thousand ounces of silver. The money is to be drawn from the provincial funds in Hunan and made available to Zeng Jing so that he can "put his household affairs in good order." One can see, in the emperor's mind, the logic of this gift: only that summer, Zeng Jing has been able to show that the fake Wang Shu had given the priest Mizeng a forged letter of credit for fifty ounces of silver, under a false signature, with a fabricated guarantee from the provincial authorities. (This document, along with Zeng's memorandum, was sent to the emperor for his perusal.) In return, Zeng Jing is now being given one thousand ounces of silver in hard currency, with an imperial order mandating the payment of the funds by the provincial authorities. The fake Wang Shu had estimated that his gift would be enough to buy ten *mu* of land, or around two acres, to endow the priest's little temple, but it had turned out to be a futile promise. On the other hand the emperor's gift to Zeng Jing is a true fortune by any standards of the time: it will enable him to buy at least one hundred *mu* of farmland, as well as a permanent burial site for his mother and whatever other local appurtenances of gentry life he chooses to acquire. There could be no clearer proof of the difference between wishful thinking and reality.

The governor passes on this astonishing news to Zeng Jing at the end of October, and a few days later Zeng writes a fulsome letter of thanks to the emperor, saying that the officials are already making arrangements to withdraw the full amount from provincial funds and to transfer the money in to the county treasury of Yongxing. In their own confidential acknowledgment of the immense gift, the governor and the morality supervisor are far less effusive. In a province where many people want to drown Zeng

Jing, they observe, Zeng Jing could hardly "return home with this huge sum tucked under his arm." Instead, the governor would assemble the money carefully from various local funds and then secretly transfer it via the grain intendant to the county treasury of Zeng's hometown, to be doled out to Zeng at suitable intervals. In the meantime, they would keep a close watch over Zeng Jing and restrict his movements to the city of Changsha. It is clear that they do not share the emperor's enthusiasms for the reprieved conspirator. As they have already reported to the emperor, Zeng Jing's own letters and reports are sometimes so full of obsequious flattery and improper language that they have felt constrained to correct him: they certainly never expected Zeng Jing to call the supervisor of public morality his "ruler-father" while referring to himself as the supervisor's "subject-son." Such usage violates the most basic principle of China, that "as our sky does not have two suns, so the people never have two masters."

It is clear that others share their uneasiness. All through the summer and autumn of 1730 the copies of the *Awakening from Delusion* have been spreading deeper and deeper into Chinese society, first from Beijing to the cities, then down into the counties, and at last to the individual students in the local school districts, where the emperor believes their maximum effect will be felt. Already in the testimonies from those caught up in the new round of investigations into Wang Shu, one could see the impact of the book: the man lured to do the calligraphy for the fake Wang Shu had told his interrogators that it was only after listening to a public discussion of the *Awakening* that he had realized the full absurdity of Wang Shu's stories of the various princes; and Zhong Xiang, provider of the coffin and burial plot for the fake Wang Shu, had similarly stated that it was only after perusing a copy of the same book that his own eyes had been fully opened.

Others find in the book a ruder awakening, even elements of danger and public humiliation, and they respond with shock and outrage when they first read through the lengthy text. Prominent among these angry men is the one at whose office the whole case started, the Shaanxi-Sichuan governor-general, Yue Zhongqi. As Yue tells the emperor in a formal report that makes no attempt to hide his anger, he duly received his two copies of the *Awakening from Delusion* on May 5, 1730, and read through

194 — Treason by the Book

the book as soon as he could in the midst of his other duties. It was thus, with no warning at all, that he came upon the pages in Section Three which printed the messenger Zhang Xi's own version of the two men's meeting in Xi'an on the fateful October day in 1728. Needless to say, there was little similarity between Zhang Xi's version—which would now be read all over the empire, and discussed by every student—and the one that the general himself so carefully conveyed to the emperor at the time.

In Zhang Xi's version, General Yue appeared more as an ineffective and insincere bumbler than as the worthy descendant of the great warrior Yue Fei, whose name he bore. As Zhang Xi phrased it in words now printed for all to read: "In the autumn of the year 1728, my teacher suddenly ordered me to take a letter to the Shaanxi governor-general Yue Zhongqi. Because I was ignorant and had only a student's status, I wrongly heeded my teacher's command and rashly set off on the journey. After I had handed over the letter, Yue began a harsh interrogation. My teacher Zeng Jing had told me that I should feel free to participate in general discussion, but must never reveal people's real names or where they lived. Again, in my ignorance, I followed these orders from my teacher and stubbornly carried out this responsibility for him. Believing in the existence of heavenly principles and natural justice, I thought that by giving up my life I could in the end attain the moral way. So it was that I never wavered, and tranquilly endured the torture from the three forms of presses, until I fainted.

"Yue Zhongqi knew that I would never testify, even unto death, and that he could not change my mind. So he loosened the presses, conceding that I was a fine fellow indeed; he comforted me, thanked me, and even treated me like an honored guest. As to the contents and arguments in my 'treasonous letter,' he praised everything in it as true. Not only that, but he told me that in his home he had a copy of the collected works of Qu Dajun, and that the arguments in that book were in complete accord with those of my letter. Seeing that I had no intention of giving him my teacher's name, he called on Heaven to proclaim his honesty, and said that he himself was in great personal danger. He went so far as to weep, to show me his sincerity. Besides which he drafted a letter and drew up a list of presents [for Zeng Jing], saying that he was waiting the opportune time to invite Zeng Jing to come and assist him. He told his own nephew to get all packed up for the journey, and wanted me to go along on the trip too.

"Besides which, he got Magistrate Li of Changan to pretend to be his trusted retainer 'Grandpa Wang,' and to spend every moment of his time with me. Yet still I refused to yield up any details whatsoever of my secrets. That was because I still clung to my teacher's instructions and never wavered even in the face of death. At last, they managed to convince me to divulge everything. And at that point they sent their report to the emperor."

What made General Yue so particularly agitated at this account was the statement that he had been keeping stored in his own home a copy of "the collected works of Qu Dajun." It had been one thing for general Yue to try to force Zhang Xi to yield up his treasonous associations with Ming loyalist figures like Lü Liuliang, or turncoats against the Qing regime such as Wu Sangui. Now Zhang Xi had neatly reversed the process. For there was no doubt that Qu Dajun, distinguished writer though he was, had proved his rebellious nature again and again. Qu had pledged his allegiance to a fugitive Ming regime at the time of the Manchu conquest in the 1640s, and after the Ming defeat was final had shaved his head and become a religious eremite in his own self-styled "Retreat of the Dead." Later, giving up the religious life of withdrawal, he married the daughter of a Ming general who had been killed by Manchu troops. When she died, he once again took up the fight, this time with the rebel troops of Wu Sangui in the 1670s. Despite this remarkable history of opposition to the state, his scholarly writings had won him the support and protection of prominent scholars, and he had died peacefully in 1696, revered as one of "the three great scholars of the southeast."

General Yue could not convincingly deny that he had talked about Qu with the messenger, even though he had not mentioned the exchange in any of his earlier reports to the throne. All he can do, now the facts are in the open, is to try and explain it away as innocently as possible. He has carefully read the passage in the *Awakening from Delusion*, he tells the emperor, in which Zhang Xi talks about the Qu episode. Now he wishes to set the matter straight. Contrary to Zhang's printed testimony, what the messenger had in fact said was that "he had heard Qu's literary works—

both essays and poems—were especially fine, and that Qu refused to take office under the Qing," although the messenger himself had never had a chance to read them. "It was at just that moment," General Yue explains, "that I was trying to lead him on to talk, so I went along with him and said that the main ideas in Qu's works seemed very like the ideas in the work of both Lü Liuliang and Zeng Jing. In actual fact," continues Yue, "I had not the faintest idea what sort of person Qu Dajun was, nor did I know anything about his writings. Nor had I ever heard anyone talk about them before. I simply had no idea whether Qu's works contained heterodox passages or not. The only reason I randomly said all those things at the time was because I was trying to probe the truth out of the traitor, and make him believe absolutely in my sincerity, so as to induce him to speak frankly and hide nothing from me."

Yongzheng makes no attempt to placate his general, but responds dismissively, as he often does with officials who have said too much: "If you hadn't raised this matter yourself, I would have paid it no attention. And none of the officials at court have made anything of it." Though there were other reasons as well, connected to Yue's mounting record of failures in the western campaigns, it is from this time that one can date the steady disintegration of the hitherto spectacularly successful career of General Yue, who was now aged forty-four. Later that summer, Hangyilu was dispatched to Yue's military camp in the west, from which Yue was supervising the campaign against the Zungars, and ordered the general to return to Beijing for talks with the emperor. Over the next two years, the Qing troops suffered a series of setbacks, and intense rivalries surfaced among the various area commanders. Yue was blamed for the army's failures and for errors in planning and was dismissed from his various official posts. His property was confiscated by the state, and he was sentenced to death—though the sentence was reprieved, perhaps partially in memory of that earlier day when his loyal and apparently totally honest report had first alerted his emperor to the existence of Zeng Jing's conspiracy.

The shock of reading about oneself in the *Awakening from Delusion* was even harsher for Qu Minghong, eldest surviving son of the Ming loyalist Qu Dajun. Qu Minghong had managed to flourish under the Qing dynasty, despite his father's attitudes, and had risen to be the educational supervisor of the government school in Huilai, a coastal town in Guangdong province. As the school supervisor, he now had the duty to study and give lectures on the *Awakening from Delusion*, and it was in preparing conscientiously for this task that he found himself reading the debate between Zhang Xi and General Yue about his own father. Not surprisingly, other officials in Guangdong had noticed his father's name there, and Qu was brought in for questioning by the governor. The governor was not initially impressed with Qu's argument that, as he had been only a young child when his father died in 1696, he had never realized that his father's poems and essays might contain passages considered treasonous. Rather, the officials suspected that Qu Minghong had deliberately kept his father's literary works hidden away in his own home, intending to transport them to other areas of China and to sell them. But they grew convinced that his surprise at his own discovery was genuine and that he was innocent of any wrongful intent. Nevertheless, the coincidence was damaging: Qu lost his job and along with his family was sent into exile in Fujian province. The descendants of the other two "great scholars of the southeast" were also subjected to interrogation and to searches through their family libraries, though they themselves were not punished. There is no knowing how many other families suffered similar pressures or unwelcome disclosures. The *Awakening from Delusion* was awash with names, and clearly, at the time of its compilation no one had worried about the consequences to those whose names appeared at different points in the rambling but often devastating text.

The complexity of the responses from those mentioned in the book was matched by those of ordinary people who were influenced in other ways. Strangest of these were the people who, as a result of hearing rumors about the Zeng Jing case, or hearing it read aloud at the monthly meetings, came to identify in some way with the protagonists. Such, reported the Zhejiang governor-general, Li Wei, to the emperor in July 1730, was the case with a young man named Chen Quan from Hangzhou. Chen had purchased a scholarly title, but spent much of his time consorting with a rough crowd of hoodlums, including a crooked fortune-teller he had met in a local book shop, who took him on as an informal assistant in his scams at a salary of three taels a month. This semischolar had frequently bragged that he had been befriended by Zhang Xi when the messenger visited Zhejiang on his trip to buy books by Lü Liuliang; later he elaborated the story, seeking to boost his scholarly credentials by saying he had been a close disciple of Lü's own former student Yan Hongkui, with whom he had often discussed the finer points of literature. It was only thanks to his own cleverness, Chen told his friends, that he had managed to avoid getting caught up in the toils of the law. Arrested and interrogated for his boasting, Chen not only did not retract the stories but embroidered them even further, claiming now that he was befriended by Zeng Jing as well, when Zeng made a previously unknown visit to Hangzhou.

Despite the fact that there was no shred of evidence for this final assertion, such extraordinary stories demanded special countermeasures: Chen was known to have been an eccentric and a wanderer for years, and he must not be allowed to spread his contagion further. Accordingly, the governor-general stripped Chen of his degree and condemned him to wear the heavy wooden cangue. Chen was remanded to the care of his father and forbidden ever to leave his home again. As to Chen's motives, Li Wei suggested to the emperor that Chen "enjoyed making completely groundless fabrications, which he spread around so as to make trouble, deceiving the gullible local people into thinking he was a truly crazy man."

The flamboyantly obvious bragging of Chen had made it essential to silence him, and the task had not been difficult. But others protested more quietly, or else merely aroused suspicions through their antisocial attitudes. In such cases, it was no protection to be from a famous family. It would be hard to have more famous forebears than Xu Jun, son of one of the three celebrated Xu brothers, who during the previous reign, of Emperor Kangxi, had all been listed in the top three places in the *jinshi* examinations, a feat unparalleled in Chinese history. Xu Jun and his four brothers all in their turn attained the same coveted degree, even if not all at the same stellar level. Xu Jun himself passed number eight in the second class in the exams of 1713. He was at once appointed to a research position in the Confucian Hanlin Academy in the capital, only to be sent home after a few years because he had grown "careless" in his studies. Thereafter, in the words of the Jiangsu governor, who pulled him in for questioning in that same July of 1730, Xu Jun became "a wild kind of person, contrary by nature, a man who often left home to go drifting around in the Dongting Mountains, and suchlike areas, swaggering along, singing and whistling, lighthearted about family responsibilities and uncaring about the future."

Such behavior, in the governor's mind, was quite enough to justify an official search through Xu Jun's library in pursuit of family correspondence with Lü Liuliang and to keep Xu Jun under arrest while the search was being conducted. Though the search turned up no correspondence with Lü or his family, it did reveal passages within Xu Jun's own poetry that were considered both reckless and treasonous. When these samples were shown to the emperor, he agreed to the sentence of immediate beheading for Xu and to the burning of all Xu's books and manuscripts. Other prominent families in Jiangsu were subject to the same searches, with the promise of sharing Xu's fate.

The emperor's hatred of the Lü family was perhaps not untinged with fear. Li Wei, the long-serving governor-general of Zhejiang, was under permanent instructions to keep up the hunt for all members of Lü Liuliang's family who might have escaped the earlier searches, and in August 1730 Li received a special imperial order to see if he could find any traces of an alleged "Lü family orphan" about whom dramatic rumors were spreading. "If there should be any descendants of Lü Liuliang who have concealed themselves in any hideouts and thus escaped legal prosecution, it would be a matter of great consequence," the emperor wrote to Li Wei. "These rebellious renegades have indeed sinned against Heaven; and this incident has occurred unexpectedly, in conflict with normal human principles. Their iniquities cannot be removed even by having their bodies sawn in pieces." By September, when he answered the emperor's message, Li Wei had located an additional eighteen male descendants from Lü Liuliang's family whose existence had not been known when the preliminary sweep was made. Some of these were Lü's great-grandchildren. (In the meantime, too, one of Lü's grandchildren arrested in the initial sweep back in 1728 had died.) Li Wei also itemized for the emperor a list of women from at least twenty-four separate lineages who had married male members of the Lü family, as either primary wives or secondary consorts. And these numbers did not include those who had left the clan home for some reason as children and had gone to live elsewhere. He was not sure about any specific "Lü family orphan," wrote Li Wei, but he had come up with an unusual case of someone who had eluded their net for a long time. This was Lü Liuliang's daughter-in-law, a woman called Cao, who had been the second wife of Lü's eldest son, Lü Baozhong. When her husband died so suddenly in 1708 she had shaved her head and entered a Buddhist convent as a nun, and it was in a convent that they found her, now aged sixty-eight. It was because of this withdrawal to a religious community that her name was not entered in the family's genealogical records.

Such a woman did not sound as if she were a threat, but the emperor had grown nervous about those possessing special religious or other powers and was anxious to have them on his side. That same summer and autumn of 1730 the emperor was seriously ill, and he reached around desperately to locate any experts in the arts of prolonging human life who could be found—regardless of their philosophical or religious schools of allegiance. All such practitioners would be treated well, he told his officials, and given "a generous monetary allowance, so that they may have the means to support their families"; officials were not to worry whether or not the healers really had the skills they claimed to have. As the emperor remarked, "Even if you should have recommended the wrong persons, I will not blame you for it. I have my own ways of testing them."

Knowing of this interest, Li Wei had already brought in an expert in martial arts and breath-control techniques, luring the man to his office with a request to teach archery and other martial skills to Li Wei's son. During the questioning of the tricked man, Li Wei had gained ample evidence that the man "could endure physical tortures unharmed, regardless of the kinds of devices used." The emperor made some astonishing promotions of men with special medical skills who were already serving in the palace or elsewhere in the bureaucracy: one was promoted to the position of vice-president of the Censorate, and another to vice-president of the Ministry of Finance. In addition, the emperor endured gross indignities at the hands of some of these men who turned out to be ignorant charlatans, and one—he screamed out wild chants and spells and pummeled the emperor's body unmercifully—was ultimately executed by the enraged ruler.

Few officials had been as cautious in their recommendations as General Yue Zhongqi. Instructed to track down a certain Daoist hermit "versed in supernatural abilities" who lived in Xi'an, where he was known as the "Deer-Skin Immortal," General Yue did just that, but he informed the emperor that the so-called magus was no more than "a mentally deranged Daoist monk" and a "dispirited homeless bum." Undeterred, the following year the emperor called on various senior officials to seek out others with special powers, including those who could see great distances, those who could see in the dark, and those who could cover several hundred miles in a day.

While the emperor was making these excursions into the occult, the more prosaic attempt to provide some solution to the Lü Liuliang case continued. But it was not until January 1731 that the emperor at last received from his bureaucracy the judgment on Lü Liuliang that he had demanded eighteen months before. Whatever resistance there once had been among the senior bureaucrats had now been stilled, and their ruling was stern—as stern, indeed, as the one hundred and forty-eight officials had once been to Zeng Jing, until overruled by the emperor himself. Lü Liuliang's corpse was to be disinterred, said the officials, and exposed to the public gaze; his property was all to be forfeit to the state. Exposure and humiliation of the corpse was the sentence too on Lü's brilliant eldest son, Lü Baozhong, the second-highest *jinshi* candidate of 1706, who had died only two years after his examination triumph. The other surviving members of Lü's family were to be executed or enslaved according to the closeness of their relationships to the principal offenders, in accordance with the current laws on the settling of high treason cases. All those in the entire country possessing any published works by Lü Liuliang, or any of his diaries or manuscripts, should be told that they would have a one-year grace period, at the end of which they must hand them over to the authorities for burning.

Surprisingly, the emperor did not endorse his officials' finding, even though he seemed to have been pushing for just such a verdict. The experience of compiling and circulating the *Awakening from Delusion* had apparently convinced him of the value of bringing into the deliberative process of the court not only the hundreds of thousands of scholars scattered across the face of China, but even the millions more who were aspirants for the degree status. So instead of merely endorsing the ministries' request for harsh punishment, the emperor added a curious gloss: "I have been reflecting on the fact that though the nature of Lü Liuliang's crimes has been made absolutely clear in our prior discussions, and there are no grounds for pardoning him either according to Heavenly principles or under human law, yet our country is vast, and we have masses of scholars. It may very well be that among these millions of people there are still those who say that Lü Liuliang's crimes were not so excessively grave. I am extremely cautious about doling out punishments, and even in eradicating traitors or weeding out dissidence one must act in accordance with people's feelings about fairness." In the case of Lü Liuliang, the emperor continued, this meant reconsidering the ministries' request to destroy all Lü's works: if the order to destroy was not fully carried out, then it would be useless; if it was carried out completely, then later generations would never know what all the fuss had been about, and would feel the emperor and his bureaucracy had overreacted.

Similarly, in the case of Lü's vilification of the late emperor, hateful though it was, there was no exact precedent for what the correct penalty should be. Therefore, Yongzheng argued, instead of sending orders to the local officials to implement the destruction of all Lü's works after the one-year grace period and having Lü's corpse disinterred immediately, a somewhat different set of orders should be sent to the educational commissioners in every province. They should be told to ensure that every student in the local academies was questioned on his view of the appropriate punishments for the various members of the Lü family and on the efficacy of ordering the destruction of all Lü's works, whether published or unpublished. The commissioners were to "act impartially and according to the facts, and to move swiftly in obtaining the students' and degree holders' conclusions and to report on them. Those who have private views that they want to make known should submit their own separate reports. The commissioners must send all these in together, and not impede them or hide anything. After all these reports have come in, I will issue a separate edict."

Given the emperor's experience of the various ways that pressure could be applied and people's true feelings could be concealed, one can only conjecture as to whether he believed that he would hear every dissenting voice. But certainly the bureaucracy was able effectively to hide things from the emperor, as a thirty-three-year-old scholar named Qi Zhouhua learned to his cost. Qi was born in Zhejiang province to a well-established scholarly family and had successfully obtained the licentiate's degree. He was working in the government school to prepare for the next level of the examinations when—along with all the other registered students—he received his copy of the *Awakening from Delusion* and there read both the criticisms of Lü Liuliang by the emperor and Zeng Jing's apologia, *My Return to the Good.* Though Qi did not know any members of Lü's family, he admired Lü's work, especially his commentaries on the Four Books. In the essay that Qi wrote in response to Emperor Yongzheng's invitation to speak out, he emphasized that Lü's studies of the Confucian classics should be separated out from his other works and given the praise they deserved. And if someone as guilty as Zeng Jing could be pardoned despite his extraordinary crimes, on the grounds that he seriously repented, why not extend such compassion to the surviving members of Lü's family? And surely such compassion could also be extended to Lü's disciples Yan and Shen.

Qi was not convinced, he wrote, that Zeng Jing was as unaware of the details of the Manchu conquest as he had pretended to be in the confessions printed in the *Awakening from Delusion*—for instance, Zeng said he did not even know the Ming dynasty had been overthrown by peasant rebels until he learned it from his inquisitors. Such claims to ignorance should be scrutinized more carefully, Qi felt, given Zeng's apparent familiarity with history and with classical texts. Also, wrote Qi, the people of Zhejiang province were certainly not as disloyal and ignorant of basic moral principles as the natives of Hunan: "No one from Zhejiang took a treasonous letter all the way to Shaanxi and handed it to the governor-general!" If the emperor so wished, Qi himself would act as a guarantor for the good behavior of the younger members of Lü Liuliang's family, to help expunge from their minds any lingering antidynastic thoughts they might have, and to make them loyal subjects of the Qing.

Since the exact procedure for delivering such letters to the emperor had never been spelled out, Qi took his letter first to the supervisor of schools in his own hometown of Tiantai. When that official refused to forward it, Qi traveled to the provincial capital of Hangzhou and petitioned the circuit intendant—who was senior enough in rank to have the right to send reports directly to the throne—to pass it on for him. The intendant also refused. Pawning some of his possessions for travel money, Qi made his way to Beijing, where he tried to hand in his letter to the Ministry of Punishments. The officials there were not sympathetic. The temporary president of the ministry, recently appointed, was Li Wei, former governor-general of Zhejiang and the force behind the initial and ongoing hunts for treasonous works in the possession of the Lü family; his vice-president was Wang Guodong, at one time the morality supervisor of Zhejiang and later governor of Hunan during the roundup of Zeng Jing and his followers. Nobody in the ministry would accept Qi's letter. They told him, instead, to return to Zhejiang and hand the letter over to the commissioner of education for the province, as the emperor had suggested in his edict, so that it could then be processed through the proper channels. Dutifully Qi returned home and tried again. The education officials rejected the letter and arrested the writer. Qi remained in jail for the rest of Emperor Yongzheng's reign, his only solace being a certain fame that accrued to him among other students and scholars for his tenacity and courage. There is no knowing how many others may have gone through similar travails in trying to make their discordant views known to their ruler.

It is unlikely that the emperor ever heard of Qi's frustrated quest, but he certainly knew all about another and more public one that was reported to him on March 17, 1731, by the governor of Shanxi. The incident in question occurred on March 11, in the county town of Xia, tucked among the mountains in the far south of Shanxi province, just north of the Yellow River, and almost three hundred miles from the provincial capital of Taiyuan. Early that morning, just after the students had finished paying their ritual homage to Confucius, the attendant at the district school noticed that his charges had not gone to their accustomed study hall, but were gathering excitedly outside the gate in the west corner of the school compound. The focus of their excitement seemed to be a sheet of writing posted up on the wall, which the attendant himself did not know how to read. The attendant hurried back to tell the teacher—a man called Gao, serving as a stand-in for the regular educational supervisor—and the two returned to the West Gate together.

There were in fact two intersecting messages, teacher Gao saw at once, one in prose and one in verse. The prose message—almost a miniature essay—referred directly to the recent posthumous condemnation of Lü Liuliang and to the earlier pardoning of Zeng Jing: "Zeng Jing, who deserved to be killed, was not killed. Lü Liuliang, who was innocent, was found guilty. This is indeed one of the saddest things that has ever happened; it has upset me so much that I coughed up blood. In this, my heart is as one with the sage rulers whose nature was to love justice. Please spread the poem appended here across the whole world; if any of those who hear about it report it to our Heavenly ruler at his court, then he might reverse his judgment. If it were Zeng's severed head that were hung up in public, and Lü's descendants who were spared, everyone would accept the wisdom of the judgment. Such are my deepest wishes, even though I know there is little hope of their being realized."

The poem referred to in the message was in the classical style, four lines long with seven words to the line:

> *The running dog is crazy and deluded, yet we don't see him boiling in the pot;*
> *The auspicious unicorn, by contrast, is bubbling in the pan.*
> *Such is the chaotic state things have reached in this world of ours—*
> *Our hair bristles with anger under our caps, our swords are yearning to sing.*

The idea of hair bristling with rage under caps and of swords singing as they sliced through the air had been staples of Chinese revenge literature for two millennia or more, and the identifying mark of any loyalist assassins seeking to destroy unworthy rulers.

The rebellious message was pasted firmly to the wall, but the attendant and the teacher—as if experienced in such matters—knew how to strip it from the wall while still preserving it. First, they sprayed vinegar from their mouths onto the face of the paper, until the paste softened; then the teacher gently peeled the offending words off the wall, damaging only two of the written characters that had adhered more stubbornly than the others and so got torn in half. Those two the teacher faithfully copied and mounted back onto the original poster. The document, with an account of the incident, was hurried at once to the governor in the provincial capital.

Nobody seemed to know who had written the poster, the Shanxi governor reported to the emperor. But he was intensifying the search and had ordered his own staff to aid the local officials in tracking down the guilty party; in particular, they had been told to ascertain whether it had been written by one person working alone or by some group. The emperor's comment was laconic: "If the magistrate and the teacher are really willing to go after the truth, it should not be too hard to find who did this. You should all apply yourselves to the utmost to catch them. Don't let traitors like this wriggle out of your net."

The emperor was correct. By the beginning of April that same spring, after an exhaustive check of the degree candidates in Xia county and the nearby districts, the identity of the man who had written the poem and the commentary was discovered. It was none other than the schoolteacher Gao, who had first reported the whole incident and had so carefully replaced the two characters that got torn as he removed the poster from the wall. As far as the governor could ascertain, Gao had acted alone. At one level, however, Gao's strategy had been totally successful. Even if he himself was to be killed for it, his feelings and advice on the relative guilt of Zeng Jing and Lü Liuliang had indeed been forwarded to the emperor, not suppressed as the student Qi's had been. The poster and the poem had been Gao's own private attempt to subvert the public readings and discussion of the *Awakening from Delusion* that Gao—like teachers all across China—had been mandated for a year now to share with his own students.

In March 1731 yet another case was brought to the emperor's attention, that of a twenty-three-year-old ex-student named Fan, who had been raised in the mountains of southwestern Fujian province. Since the young man had proved unable to pass the qualifying tests that would entitle him to sit for the formal licentiate's examinations, his uncle had found him a job as a secretary in one of the local government offices. While working there and reading the various available materials on the Zeng Jing case, Fan had developed his own ideological mix: this was part diatribe against the evils of Zeng Jing and part speculation about the talents of Emperor Yongzheng's three elder brothers and the reasons for the current emperor's accession to the throne. In Fan's mind these reflections were designed to be flattering to the emperor, and the supervisor of public morality for the province of Fujian—whom Fan waylaid one day, and persuaded to read the essay—apparently agreed, gracing the young man's encomium with six characters in his own calligraphy, "You are to be congratulated for your loyal and loving heart."

Perhaps having heard of the emperor's edict on the procedures for submitting thoughts on the Lü Liuliang case, Fan polished the essay, larded it with classical quotations, identified himself as a local stipendiary scholar—which he was not—and accosted the educational commissioner with a copy when that worthy was in town to supervise the local examinations. Fan was arrested and questioned, but no plot was uncovered and no one else appeared to be involved. As the investigating officials reported to Yongzheng, it seemed to them clear that Fan had acted as he did out of a desperate search for preferment. The punishment they decreed for Fan was that he must make no more attempts to attract attention, must never again wander from home, and twice each month must recite in public apposite selections from the *Awakening from Delusion.*

By the late spring of 1731, the emperor has overwhelming evidence that his ambitious attempt to clear the air by publishing the *Awakening from Delusion* and asking for the students' views has not induced unanimity at all. It may be true that—with the exception of the four men with a military bearing heading toward Guangdong—virtually every lead generated by the original Zeng Jing case had now been tracked down in one way or another. Even the fake Wang Shu was known to be safely dead. But the events of the last year have shown how vibrant are the sounds of discord in provinces as distant as Shanxi and Fujian. Despite Yongzheng's urgings, the people have not learned to respect Zeng Jing, nor have they been persuaded to hate Lü Liuliang as the emperor thinks Lü should be hated. To convince the skeptics, it is becoming clear, the assault will have to be spread to the farthest border regions and conducted at a higher intellectual level than that which the emperor—let alone Zeng Jing himself—is able to provide. The scholars will have to be won over by their peers.

Thirteen

*Spreading
the Word*

Ever since the linked treason cases of Zeng Jing and Lü Liuliang first came to his attention, the emperor has never formally sought assistance from the most potent intellectual force in his arsenal: the two to three hundred men who, every three years, are awarded the highest of all the country's literary degrees, the *jinshi*. Finally, in the late spring of 1731, for the first time he openly calls on these examination winners for assistance, focusing mainly on those who have passed the examinations most recently. He does so by assembling two separate task forces: one, containing around forty scholars, is appointed to spread the word in the far northwest of the empire; the other, of four men, is instructed to launch a systematic and line-by-line assault on the classical writings of Lü Liuliang.

The announcement of the creation of a scholarly force to go to the northwest is made first, on April 26, 1731. The idea has been growing for some time in the emperor's mind, perhaps ever since the court audiences with Yue Zhongqi back in November of the previous year. In public pro-nouncements at that time there had been only praise for General Yue, es-pecially for his achievement in persuading the Muslim leader in the oasis city of Turfan, along with all his followers, to declare his allegiance to the Qing. Yue's detailed recommendations of ways to transform the recently pacified border areas of Shaanxi province into new prefectures were also approved by the emperor without comment. Such prefectures could form the staging areas for the armies being massed on Yongzheng's orders, with the long-range goal of expanding the Chinese empire westward. But Yue's return to the western front in mid-January 1731 was not accompanied by any of the special marks of imperial favor often granted to senior officials who had performed meritoriously; and not long after Yue's departure the emperor instructed his grand secretaries to order the former chief inter-rogator, Hangyilu, currently on assignment in the far west, to return to Beijing for consultations. At the end of March, the emperor issued a stern rebuke to General Yue for the muddled and incompetent nature of his suggestions for handling problems with the Muslims and nomads in the Zungar-dominated border areas of the far west: previously, noted the em-peror, it was General Yue who had been most emphatically against an ag-gressive forward policy into the Zungar regions; but now, because Zungar raiders had taken horses and camels from some of Yue's detachments, and Yue was humiliated and angry, the general was suddenly calling for a large-scale surprise attack deep into their territory. What guarantee of vic-tory could there possibly be in that? "Not a single one of the recommen-dations in General Yue Zhongqi's sixteen-point report is worthy of adoption. I am deeply disappointed and frustrated."

For several months, in a delicate balancing act, the emperor has also been expressing his special concern for the troops stationed in Shaanxi and for the farmers living in the military staging areas. After a massive earth-quake struck the Beijing region, the emperor sent urgent messages to the commanding generals in the far west to reassure the banner troops serving in Shaanxi and other border areas that casualties were minimal even if property damage was considerable; if their families were in the Beijing re-gion, they should be reassured that almost no lives had been lost—not more than "one or two in ten million"—and that cash awards were being made to all those whose homes had been destroyed or badly damaged.

Early in 1731 the one thousand Shaanxi troops stationed in Tibet were rotated out of service there, so they could return home to their own families.

In another edict, in late March of the same year, the emperor addressed the problems of military supply and procurement for Shaanxi and Gansu provinces, areas that lay under General Yue's jurisdiction, and the key staging areas for the anti-Zungar campaigns. The troubled situation in the region, declared the emperor, was compounded by the behavior of the local officials, who veered erratically between the two extremes of procrastination and impatience; the senior administrators in the west must understand that if they relaxed their rigors by a certain fraction, then the officials under their jurisdiction would loosen up to a similar extent. But if they behaved with unjustified harshness, the local officials would again imitate them. And the unfair procurement policies currently in operation must be abandoned: fair current market prices must be paid for all goods and services provided, the local people must not be forced to provide goods at artificially reduced rates. Yet so delicate was the situation in Shaanxi that these instructions must be kept secret from the local officials, to prevent their charging the central government too much for the goods they were able to acquire.

The emperor's edict to the grand secretaries of April 26, 1731, introducing the idea of the task force, is brief: "It is my wish to select a few dozen people from among the official personnel serving in Beijing who are both mature and clear-headed, to go to the prefectures and counties deep inside Shaanxi province, to take charge of spreading the word about the emperor's plans for guiding and transforming the people." The members of this task force, the emperor indicates, are to be drawn from three sources: the recently successful *jinshi* winners serving in the Hanlin Academy—these were generally those who had scored the highest in the final examinations; the apprentice officials who, after passing their exams, were being trained for service in the various sub-bureaus of the six ministries; and the stipendiary students who had been selected for advanced study in the Imperial College at Beijing because of their excellent scholarly records. As to exact numbers, the emperor is somewhat vague, contenting himself with a general indication of his wishes. There should be "several" from the Hanlin Academy, "around ten or twenty" from among the ministry trainees, and "twenty or thirty" from the Imperial College. The selection is to be made by the grand secretaries acting in concert with the younger scholars' teachers or supervisors, and the men they choose are all to be brought to the emperor for an audience, so that he can inspect them in person.

By May 13, 1731, the members of the task force have been selected, and the emperor announces the names of the three men who will lead them to their new work area and supervise them while they are there. One is Hangyilu, the original interrogator of the Hunan conspirators, recently recalled to Beijing and simultaneously serving as both vice-president of the Ministry of Punishments and as an army general. The second is the forty-nine-year-old Shi Yizhi, a highly successful career official and *jinshi* degree holder from the year 1700 who is currently serving as both president of the Censorate and acting governor-general of the Yangzi delta provinces. An able scholar from an eminent family, Shi was both the classmate and one of the chief investigators of the powerful Nian Gengyao, whose fall he helped to engineer. He thus knows the intricacies of court politics and the demands of administration in the far west; in his own work in the Yangzi delta, moreover, he has shown himself an expert in the details of military garrisons and supply logistics. The third supervisor, Zheng Chanbao, is from a different area of the bureaucracy, that of the Imperial Household, where he serves as acting director in charge of palace financing and supply. Before that appointment, he was in charge of the salt monopoly in north China and proved himself an expert not only in the technical problems of salt manufacture and distribution but also in tax collection and shifting price ratios between silver and copper.

Although the names and examination records of only two of the forty or so scholars chosen to accompany the three commissioners have come down to us, the differing backgrounds of these two indicate that the emperor was interested in drawing on a range of types for his task force. Though both were winners of the *jinshi* degree in the very latest round of examinations, that of 1730, one was a Chinese born in Zhejiang, from almost the top of the listings (men from Zhejiang had been permitted to sit in the 1730 examination, and he passed fifth in the second class), whereas the other was a Manchu from the Plain Yellow Banner who just squeaked by—he was ranked number 269 out of the 296 in the third class. Both men had been selected for admission to the Hanlin Academy, one clearly on the grounds of academic excellence, the other almost certainly because it was very rare for any Manchus to master the Chinese philosophical and textual traditions, and those who could do so were favored by a quota system and given special recognition.

In a long edict accompanying the news of the selection of the task force's leaders, the emperor spells out more of the reasons why he has taken this step. Some of the rationale is historical—he gives an elaborate and detailed summary of the long-standing problems with the Zungars since the time of the Mongol Yuan dynasty four hundred and fifty years before, and explains how the fluctuating fortunes of China's relations with the Zungar tribes have been of central importance both to the Mongol tribes of the region and to the politics of Chinese involvement in Tibet. He also details the problems, mainly economic but also in terms of the personal hardships of military service, that the recurrent military crises have brought to the inhabitants of Shaanxi. But most troubling to him personally, the emperor emphasizes, is the fact that these perfectly explainable phenomena of history and economics have been so distorted by the spread of hateful rumors that they have led to vicious slanders directed against the emperor himself that seem almost impossible to suppress.

In the emperor's edict, the origin of these slanders is made transparently clear: the hateful rumors and lies have spread because the west was for many years the base of Nian Gengyao, as well as of the emperor's eighth and fourteenth brothers, all of whom made no attempt to hide their hatred for their ruler. These men in turn had a host of degenerate and unworthy followers—private retainers, secret confidants, alleged Daoists with special powers, and women claiming to be priestesses of their own subcults. No wonder the far west was awash with vileness. The purpose of the current venture, therefore, is to have the group of scholars "travel to the two provinces of Shaanxi and Gansu to enlighten the people there about the emperor's instructions and to awaken them from their own false assumptions. If the people in those two provinces can sincerely respect their ruler, feel close to their own superiors, and get rid of their old accumulated grudges, then they would live in harmony and feel at peace. For this, I am also asking Heaven to give us its blessing." Though in this particular edict Yongzheng does not mention Zeng Jing or Lü Liuliang by name, the echoes of their treason cases reverberate behind his words, and in his personal instructions to the three supervisors of the task force he emphasizes the need to spread the message of the *Awakening from Delusion* and orders copies made available to the supervisors and to those who will be accompanying them.

On June 8, while the final preparations are being made for the mission, the emperor summons the three supervisors he has just named to attend a special audience. Refining the instructions for their journey, he adds that he has decided they should take Zhang Xi along with them. (Zhang Xi, though formally pardoned at the same time as his former teacher, Zeng Jing, had not returned home to Hunan; he had stayed on in Beijing, though whether in or out of detention is not clear.) Yongzheng has already instructed Zhang Xi to prepare for the journey and to aid the task force in any way requested of him. Such a journey to the west, including a return to the city of Xi'an, where Zhang first offered the fateful message to General Yue, would enable the three supervisors to assess the extent of Zhang Xi's contrition for the events he set in motion two and a half years before. A trusted retainer of the supervisor Shi Yizhi is secretly instructed to serve as Zhang Xi's traveling companion, to stay with him at all times and to keep private notes on Zhang's conversation and behavior during the journey.

The members of this unusual cortege set off from Beijing in late June 1731. Given the vastness of the territory they have been instructed to cover, the three supervisors—endowed now with the title "special imperial commissioners"—divide the provinces of Shaanxi and Gansu into three blocks, each subdivided into five zones, and draw lots as to who should be assigned to which one. Much of this area is either almost unpeopled and eroded mountain land or else desert, so the distances between the major towns are large, and the traveling hard. It takes almost a month for the three groups to reach their initial destinations. In one of his reports back to Beijing, Commissioner Zheng Chanbao describes to the emperor the particular block that he has drawn: it covers five massive prefectures, spread across both Gansu and Shaanxi and extending down to Xining. Each of these prefectures is several hundred square miles in extent, and the five together embrace a total of fifty-four separate departments and townships. It sometimes takes weeks to get from one zone to the next, and each commissioner will have to spend around a month in each one of his five zones in order to complete his duties there.

Since the three commissioners have been instructed to get the emperor's message down to the local market and village level, and even to the clusters of houses straggling along the edges of the rough country roads, they divide the scholars assigned to them into batches, sending a small group down to a different subregion of each prefecture. In this way, a surprisingly large number of the local people receive the melange of messages from Beijing: exhortations on the need for honesty and a sense of service in the marshaling of supplies and transporting of troops for the war in the west, a concentrated lesson in the history of the relations of China with the Zungar border tribes against whom the fighting is directed, and a series of focused readings and discussions from the *Awakening from Delusion*, designed to show how the factional battles at court in the past affected news and rumors reaching the west and how imperial compassion and an individual's contrition could form a seamless whole.

Some areas through which these scholars travel are so isolated, mountainous, and filled with bandits that the commissioners fear for their safety as they spread out into the countryside in small clusters. Nevertheless, wherever they go they make their presence known by erecting temporary "Dragon Pavilions," in which auspicious setting they read aloud the imperial instructions and deliver their lectures on the *Awakening from Delusion*. At intervals, the three commissioners meet at prearranged points—once in the city of Xi'an itself, once in Fengxiang prefecture in southwestern Shaanxi—to share recent messages received from the emperor or the ministries in Beijing and to coordinate operations among themselves. Because of the distance and the difficult terrain, messages from Beijing can take at least three weeks to reach them, and often far longer.

The imperial household director, Zheng Chanbao, one of the three commissioners, reaches Lanzhou, the capital of Gansu, in late October and sends a description of his experiences to the emperor. Each day during his two-week journey from the Shaanxi border to Lanzhou, he writes, in every town and village through which he and his task force passed, wending their way through the long columns of mules and wagons hauling military supplies up toward the distant battle zone, curious crowds lined the road to welcome them. (The governor of Gansu had been alerted to their coming in a special message from the Ministry of Rituals, sent some weeks before.) But these informal local assemblages have not prepared him for the scale of the reception in Lanzhou on October 22, where, he estimates, at least ten thousand people—civil and military officials, students, soldiers, commoners—assemble to hear the commissioner and his accompanying *jinshi* degree holders read from the emperor's edicts and the *Awakening from Delusion*.

A month later Zheng is in Jiuquan prefecture, four hundred miles northwest of Lanzhou. Though this is the very edge of the settled Chinese territories and at the end of the Great Wall, the crowds who come to goggle at and listen to the now-standard group of texts are so large that he has to hold two sessions: one, for around ten thousand people, on November 23 in the younger students' school compound, and two days later a second one at the senior-level school's compound, where an estimated twenty thousand come to listen. On these two occasions the spectacle is made even grander by the presence in Jiuquan of the acting governor-general of the region and two senior officials from the Censorate, who come to observe the proceedings. The readings are held in front of the "Dragon Pavilions," where the smoke from burning incense rises into the balmy late-November air: it is "as if springtime has come in the winter season," one of the watching officials reports to his distant emperor. The two *jinshi* scholars from the Hanlin Academy who have accompanied the commissioner on this leg of his journey dwell in their presentations with extra care on the dangerous threat of the Zungar tribes massed to the west and elaborate on the accumulated grudges and the harmful actions of the emperor's brothers and their witting accomplice, Nian Gengyao. Once the formal lectures are over, these same two scholars travel even farther west to check on the flow of military supplies and to explicate the now-familiar texts; in these distant regions, their audience consists not only of Chinese settlers and soldiers but also of tribesmen from Hami and other oasis towns along the Silk Road. On January 14, 1732, Zheng's entire task force reassembles in Lanzhou to begin the preparations for the long journey home to Beijing.

In Xi'an, orders from the emperor are waiting for all three commissioners: Hangyilu is to stay in the west and supervise the flow of military supplies to the front; Shi Yizhi, promoted to president of the Ministry of

War, is also to stay and temporarily assume the duties of governor of Shaanxi province. Since there is no special need for Zheng Chanbao, as a director of the Imperial Household, to stay out west, he is to return to Beijing, along with all the *jinshi* degree holders whose work he considers done. But there are no instructions about what to do with Zhang Xi, who, with his specially assigned companion, had stayed with Shi Yizhi and his various task forces of scholars for the whole of the extended journey. What did the emperor want him to do with the former conspirator, asks Shi? Should they send Zhang to Beijing? Keep him in Shaanxi, or specifically in Xi'an, where Shi would now be serving as acting governor? Or ship him home to Hunan?

In the original instructions given by the emperor back in June, Shi reminds his ruler, he had been asked to monitor Zhang's behavior on the trip and to assess whether or not Zhang seemed sincerely contrite for his past treasonous actions. It is Shi's opinion that Zhang Xi has passed this test satisfactorily. When Shi questioned the former conspirator about that earlier visit to Xi'an in 1728, and asked him whether at that time he had made any subversive contacts that he had been concealing from his interrogators ever since, Zhang Xi gave what seemed to be a heartfelt response: "When I made that earlier trip to Shaanxi, I had only been there around ten days when I was arrested and imprisoned for handing in that treasonous letter. I never had a chance to get to know anyone there. And if I *had* gotten to know any criminals at that time, after receiving such profound favor from the emperor, even though I may be a dog or swine, I still have a conscience, so how would I have dared not to confess?" Zhang Xi added that he now considered his relationship with Zeng Jing terminated: "In the past, because Zeng Jing stupidly listened to wild tales, I stupidly listened to Zeng Jing, with the result that I committed this terrible crime so abhorrent to Heaven. But apart from us there were no other people in the conspiracy. There was just Zeng Jing, who misled me into being immoral, and caused me to put my whole family in risk of death because of my crimes. I am now fully aware of the emperor's great mercy, and mindful of the fact that I have elderly relatives back at home. I deeply regret that Zeng Jing misled me, and consider that the moral bonds of my teacher-disciple relationship with Zeng Jing are now severed." Commissioner Shi adds that Zhang Xi has been seriously weakened by the long and arduous trip; he is often sick, and the medicines that they give him never seem to work for long before the sickness returns.

This report on Zhang Xi's answers and his physical weakness reaches the emperor at the end of March 1732, and he responds concisely and clearly: "Let Zhang Xi go back home. But he is not to be allowed to travel far away from there. If I have some way to make use of him, as soon as an edict of mine to that effect arrives, then he should come [to Beijing]. It is best he stay at home to await such an edict. You can pass this message on to Governor Zhao Hongen, so that after Zhang Xi has been delivered the governor will make sure that he gets back home."

Zhang Xi and the small escort assigned to him reach Changsha in early May 1732, having retraced the route from Xi'an to the Hunan capital that he last traveled three years before, at the end of his lengthy interrogations by General Yue. Now it is General Yue whose entire career, even his very life, is in jeopardy, whereas Zhang Xi is respectfully treated. As the Hunan governor, Zhao, duly reports to the emperor, as soon as Zhang Xi arrived in Changsha the governor assigned one of his private legal secretaries the task of escorting the former traitor back to his home village in Anren county. The secretary was given a protective escort and an ample allowance to cover all his and Zhang Xi's travel expenses. Once they reached Anren, late in June, the local magistrate was issued clear instructions to keep a close watch on Zhang Xi's whereabouts, in case the emperor sent fresh instructions on how Zhang Xi was to be employed. But apart from this restriction on his freedom to travel, the former messenger was able once again to take up the semblance of a normal life and to convalesce from his illness.

The initial announcement of the formation of the scholarly task force to carry the emperor's words and the *Awakening from Delusion* to the far west of China had been made on April 26, 1731. Only five days later, on May 1, the second initiative was announced: the formation of a four-scholar group to launch a systematic refutation of Lü Liuliang's scholarly writings. Yongzheng credited a young scholar in the Hanlin Academy, Gu Chengtian, with initiating the idea. Whether Gu had gotten the idea after hearing about the appointment of a task force for the west is not known, but in his own remarks suggesting the new initiative Gu invoked his sense of moral obligation to the dynasty as a whole and also underlined his conviction—which he knew the emperor shared—that Lü Liuliang's scholarship was not especially fine. Gu suggested that the rebuttal team of scholars should concentrate on the most widely read of all Lü's works, the two variant editions of *The Lü Liuliang Commentaries on the Four Books,* which had been compiled from Lü's notes by friends of his just after his death in 1683. The Four Books—Confucius' sayings, known as the *Analects;* sayings of his disciple Mencius; and two shorter volumes of philosophical commentary on ritual and morality as arranged and edited by the great Song scholar Zhu Xi—were a staple in all schools and the basic building blocks for any successful advance into the world of serious Confucian scholarship. Lü's editions were widely used as primers for the examinations by countless young scholars, because of their careful organization and precise marshaling of major arguments. It was also these commentaries, though Gu did not mention this, along with Lü's collections of successful *jinshi* essays, that had initially attracted Zeng Jing to Lü Liuliang. To most scholars, Lü had appeared a pillar of examination orthodoxy, which had made the discovery of his hidden caches of anti-Manchu writings so unsettling to those—again, such as Zeng Jing—who unexpectedly encountered them.

Whereas the members of the far west task force included both a bannerman and a scholar from Zhejiang, the four scholars named by the emperor to the Lü Liuliang rebuttal group had all been raised and educated in the traditional scholarly heartland of China, the immensely rich areas of farms and commerce in southern Jiangsu province, reaching from Nanjing on the Yangzi River down to Suzhou on the Grand Canal, where the finest schools and academies were located. Two of the four seem to have been comparatively conventional scholars who had passed their *jinshi* exams with excellent results (one in 1724, one in 1730) and had been rewarded with positions as compilers in the Hanlin Academy. But the other two had highly unusual scholarly backgrounds, suggesting that Emperor Yongzheng made a special effort to include scholars who had some experience of the problems of intellectual dissidence.

Gu Chengtian himself, the third member of the group, had come to the emperor's attention the previous year in a curious way. An official search through the literary works of a member of the imperial clan court suspected of disloyalty had turned up a poem by Gu that seemed to have many of the elements of nostalgia for the past and a sense of desolation in the present that had been typical of Lü Liuliang himself and other Zhejiang scholars, like Zha Siting, who had so angered the emperor. But when the rest of Gu Chengtian's writings were scrutinized, the investigators found a batch of six poems written in homage to the previous emperor, Kangxi, just after the announcement of his death. These poems praised the late emperor in the highest terms, likening his achievements to those of the greatest semimythical sage rulers of China's ancient past. Stating that this proof of a younger scholar's loyalty (Gu had passed his intermediate examinations in 1717) had moved him to tears, in the spring of 1730 Yongzheng ordered the governor of Jiangsu to send Gu to Beijing, so that the emperor could receive him in audience. There Gu so impressed the emperor with his scholarship that though the preliminary sessions of the *jinshi* examinations were over, Gu was instructed to sit for the final palace examination, along with the other candidates. In the finals, he was placed eleventh from the top in the second class, a performance good enough to have him sent at once to the Hanlin Academy. (Another student similarly favored in that same exam was one of the whistle-blowers from Canton, who the year before had turned in his own superior for erecting a tablet in honor of Lü Liuliang.) It was from his new position as a Hanlin compiler that Gu had launched his suggestion.

The fourth member of the study group, Fang Bao, also had a most unusual history. He was considerably older than the others in the group, having been born in 1668. In the year 1706 Fang had successfully made it through all the preliminary examinations for the *jinshi* degree, and was just getting ready to sit for the final palace exam, when he learned that his mother had died. To follow the correct rituals of mourning he at once abandoned the exams and returned home. In the following years, Fang built up an imposing reputation as a thinker and a scholar, until his involvement in a complex literary persecution case in the year 1713 led to his being condemned to death, a sentence subsequently commuted to exile in the far north of Manchuria. After his release from exile, Fang was given a post in the Imperial Study in the Forbidden City and was also named a director of the Palace Printing Office—in which post he might well have helped to work on the *Awakening from Delusion.* Fang's name had also surfaced briefly in Li Wei's early investigations into the Lü Liuliang case, since it was at Fang's house that the Che brothers first met the tutor called Sun, whom they hired to educate their children. The addition of Fang Bao to the group gave it an unusual intellectual edge and brought in a second person who had an intimate knowledge of the political dangers of literary exposition. Two senior administrators, one a grand secretary and tutor to the emperor's favorite son, one the vice-president of the Ministry of Rituals, were named to direct the project.

The four scholars plunged into their work with energy and had finished a preliminary draft by January 1732, long before the far west task force had returned to Beijing. Their job was a curious once, since Lü Liuliang had, in most of his published writings, been an apparently orthodox scholar, and even where he had made some extreme comments in his classical commentaries, these were dropped by the various editors who organized these voluminous commentaries after his death. It was only in a few places that the scholarly team found their work intensely delicate, for instance in the case of Confucius' commentary on Guan Zhong serving two masters. Though Lü Liuliang (or his posthumous editors) had not directly cited the exact few words in which Confucius said that without Guan Zhong the Chinese would be wearing the clothes and adopting the hair styles of the barbarian tribes, Lü Liuliang's commentary on that section of the *Analects* made it quite clear that Confucius was pointing to the fact that there was a more fundamental loyalty than that of subjects to their rulers, namely the overall moral imperatives of the country as a whole. Without getting into intensely troubled waters, all the rebuttal team could do with such a passage was to cite a truncated version of Lü's own analysis and then to overwhelm the reader with historical data about the various admirable examples of true loyalty that one could find in different dynasties across the ages. They left unaddressed the fundamental question of the nature of the deeper obligations binding members of the same race that might transcend such historically valued patterns of obedience.

The rebuttal group had an equally difficult time with those lengthy sections of commentary on the book of Mencius, in which Lü Liuliang spoke up for the values of a multiplicity of smaller political units in China and for the feasibility of reinstituting something like the old equal-field system of land distribution. The group appointed by Yongzheng knew that this was an idea passionately supported by Zeng Jing and a number of other contemporary scholars, and as passionately rejected by the emperor. Their procedure, once again, was to summarize Lü's own views with selective quotations before proceeding to reiterate, with a barrage of historical data, their own judgment that such archaic systems were no longer applicable to China and that therefore reimposing them would be anachronistic and harmful to the good ordering of society as a whole. Thus the paradoxical effect of the group's intensive labors in producing a rebuttal volume, in eight sections totaling 354 pages, was that their book probably served more to introduce curious readers to the wide spectrum of Lü's thought than to constitute an effective demolition of those thoughts themselves.

On receiving the draft of the rebuttal volumes in January 1732, the emperor expressed complete satisfaction with the four scholars he had selected. Their work showed, he wrote, that Lü Liuliang was indeed "the kind of despicable person who is always talking about the virtues of the sages but is incapable of matching his words to his actions." But at the same time, the emperor argued that this scholarly exercise underscored his own stated opinion on the value of not destroying all Lü's works: "Even by destroying his written work, we won't completely eradicate his influence; and if we *were* to destroy all his works so that none of them were left on earth, how would later generations get any sense of the roots of the problem, or be able to judge for themselves the truth or the falsity of his teachings?"

The emperor observed that the scholar Gu Chengtian, in his original request to write a rebuttal of Lü's works, had stated that he found those works to be crude and unoriginal, and that other scholars should not be taken in by them. Now the ministers at court were asking the emperor to publish the entire rebuttal and have it distributed to all the schools in the country. He had decided to accede to that request: "The offenses of this traitor are covered by the laws of our dynasty, whereas the sentence-by-sentence rebuttal of his work is a matter to be decided by the scholarship of the officials. My role is to carry out the laws in accordance with impartial justice. But on such matters as whether the books [Lü] wrote were wholesome or diseased, or whether this rebuttal of his works is true or false—there I will listen to the broad span of opinion from the entire country, and to the impartial assessments of later generations. I won't pursue those questions any further."

The printing of the *Rebuttal* was not conducted with the same breathless haste as the *Awakening from Delusion*. The carving of the type was somewhat finer, and doubtless there was careful collating and proofreading as the philosophical and political points being made were checked for accuracy and persuasiveness. It was essential to keep mistakes in the quotations to an absolute minimum, for this rebuttal was designed for "the literate of future ages," and the context of all quotations could be checked by any interested reader with access to Lü's already widely disseminated published works. Furthermore, the eight-volume *Rebuttal* was printed and bound in the court printing offices—officials were not expected to bear the costs of recopying the blocks and manufacturing hundreds more copies. This procedure would prevent the kinds of errors that were already beginning to surface in the case of the *Awakening from Delusion,* where overhasty carving and copying had led to variant texts that often differed quite considerably from the original. The *Rebuttal* was for deposit in government schools, not for distribution to every individual scholar in China. The main thing the two texts had in common was that both were initially distributed through the civil and military branches of the state transmission network to the senior provincial officials, who then distributed individual copies throughout their own areas of jurisdiction.

The first recorded recipient of the rebuttal volumes was the garrison general of the area of Shandong province around Confucius' old hometown of Qufu, who reported that he received his eight-volume set in September 1733. His copy was brought to him by the financial commissioner of Shandong, the third-ranking official in the provincial hierarchy. By coincidence, this happened to be the former imperial household director, Zheng Chanbao, one of the three commissioners in charge of the western task force, who had been appointed to this new position after his return to Beijing the previous year. The receipt of the volumes and the renewed reflection on the treasons of Lü Liuliang prompted the general to reflect that the influence of Lü Liuliang was still pervasive in his province. Was there any chance, he asked the emperor, that the governor-general and governor of Shandong could be instructed to print more copies on their own, so that one could be given to every single student and scholar in the province?

Apparently uneasy at this request, the emperor urged the general not to open a debate on this topic, but to be content with the copy he had. Doubtless any other recipients making such a request received a similar answer.

Had it not been for Zeng Jing's rebellious visions, none of this outpouring of energy by the members of the two task forces would have been necessary. But Zeng Jing himself played no part in either project, neither by lecturing in the far west nor by trying to marshal any more intellectual evidence against himself. Ever since the threats against his life the previous year, Zeng Jing had been living under a kind of house arrest in Changsha, allegedly for his own protection. His work with the supervisor of public morality was focused locally, in and around Changsha, and his main duties were to attend the bimonthly readings at which the local scholars discussed the designated imperial texts, which now included the *Awakening from Delusion.*

The restrictions irked Zeng Jing. What he wanted most was the chance to spend the one thousand taels of silver that the emperor had granted him in the autumn of 1730. In the summer of 1731 he began to beg the senior officials of Hunan to request for him a one year leave of absence, so that, in his words, he could "see to his mother's burial, and acquire property." At first they ignored him, but on July 1, 1731, the governor relented and relayed Zeng's message to the emperor. On August 22 Zeng received the emperor's answer: he was granted one year's leave of absence for the reasons requested; but at the completion of that year he was to report back to the supervisor of morality in Changsha and resume his duties. It took only a few days to put his affairs in order, and by September 22 he was home again in Yongxing county.

Certainly Zeng Jing had the money now to buy a family burial site and to put his mother to her final rest. He had the money to care for his sons, one an adult who long ago had been the one sent on the mission to persuade Zhang Xi to travel to Xi'an, the other still a child, who had been imprisoned along with his grandmother in the heat of Beijing. And after those duties were taken care of, he still had ample resources with which to buy land and the respect that comes with the ownership of land.

No record tells us what he bought, or when, but one can still see, in northern Yongxing county near the Anren border, how the spacious, airy houses once owned by the wealthy Qing landowners stand out sharply from the cramped dark quarters of their neighbors that crowd in close upon them. Their curved stone gables arch against the sky; their lofty wooden doors and massive gray walls are clearly visible across the narrow valleys. In front of these wealthy homes, beyond the open expanse of the village threshing floor, narrow paths stretch out across the landscape, poised high above the flooded paddy fields. These paths, the age-old markers between different plots of land, are topped with stone slabs, long embedded firmly in the earth, so that one can walk dry-footed to the well or to inspect one's property. So must the fake Wang Shu and his calligrapher have seen them as they trudged through the hills from Leiyang, after leaving Mizeng the priest with his worthless letter of credit; so must geomancer Chen and the doctor, as they made their rounds.

Did Zeng Jing now stand in the doorway of such a house, bought with the emperor's money, the painted eaves rising high above his head, the threshing floor stretching clear and flat before him? Did he turn back from the waves of light, past the elaborate wooden lattice with its tiny delicate carvings sheathing the windows to either side, into the cool recesses of the ancestral hall that stretched into the darkness of the massive house itself, where the coffins are placed in the rafters to welcome those whose turn is next to come?

Zeng Jing has a year in Yongxing county, from one September to the next. For the last three months of this leave period, in the summer and early fall of 1732, Zhang Xi is home as well, in Anren, just across the Yongxing county line. The last time they saw each other as free men had been in the summer of 1728, when Zeng Jing handed his messenger the manuscript copies of the *Knowledge of the New* and the *Record of Hidden Things*. But we do not know whether either man dared or chose to set out from his house and walk the familiar paths through the wooded hills, above the fields of ripening rice, to call upon his former friend.

Of only one thing can we be sure: in late September, when his leave is up, Zeng Jing turns his back on Yongxing county and makes his way once more to the provincial capital. The supervisor of public morality is waiting for him, and he cannot afford to be late.

Fourteen

*Transfor-
mations*

On January 27, 1733, when Zeng Jing has been back at work in Changsha for a little over three months, the emperor finally issues his long-awaited judgment on the case of Lü Liuliang. Referring back to the discussions held two years before, Yongzheng reminds his senior officials that they had wanted him to punish Lü and his family with the full rigor of the law and to destroy all Lü's books and unpublished writings. But at the time, it was his stated opinion that in such a situation the scholars of China should all have a chance to speak as individuals, and he had issued orders accordingly. Now, after two years in which to read the charges against Lü in the *Awakening from Delusion* and to peruse Lü's own works, the scholars and students—down to those at the licentiate's level—have all had the opportunity to record their views with the provincial educational commissioners, who in turn have reported severally to Beijing. The result, according to the emperor, is that "not one single person disagrees with the verdict" that Lü and his family have been guilty of the vilest crimes.

In the face of such unanimity between the judgments of Heaven and earth, says Yongzheng, pardon for the leading figures is out of the question. Lü Liuliang's corpse and that of his long-dead eldest son, Lü Baozhong, are both to be disinterred and their heads severed and exposed. Lü's last surviving son, his youngest and ninth, Lü Yizhong (now close to seventy), is to be beheaded. (Yizhong's crime is that he helped to orchestrate Zhang Xi's visits in Zhejiang and gave the messenger several of his father's antidynastic writings.) Lü Liuliang's fourth son, who had denied all knowledge of the case or anything but a nodding acquaintance with Zhang Xi, has died in confinement, and no further punishment is decreed for him. Though by law the grandsons over sixteen should all be executed, the emperor commutes their sentences to a life of enslavement and exile in the northern Manchu military garrison camps at Ninguta. Lü Liuliang's published books and writings will not all be destroyed, but all Lü family properties are to be confiscated and sold, the proceeds to be used for the implementation of needed public works in Zhejiang province.

Five days later the emperor pronounces sentence on all the other main figures implicated in the case. Yan Hongkui, Lü's last surviving disciple, who wrote such treasonous thoughts in his diaries and also shared his and his teacher's antidynastic works with Zhang Xi, had also died in prison, at the age of seventy-six. His corpse is to be disinterred and publicly exposed. Yan's pupil Shen is to be beheaded. The two Che brothers and their tutor, Sun, are also sentenced to death, but with the possibility of reprieve should the review procedure seem to justify it. Almost all the others believed to be implicated in the case in some way or other are to be exiled to various regions or given beatings, as seems appropriate to their crimes. But four men who appear to have been erroneously caught up in the case are acquitted unconditionally.

Zeng Jing would have read of these sentences in mid-February, when the copies of the latest *Capital Gazette* arrived in Changsha. He has, indeed, a great deal of leisure for reading, since his duties, already light, seem to be getting lighter all the time. Nobody in Hunan has any new instructions for him, and even the emperor has run out of ideas. The year before, when granting the one-year furlough to Zeng Jing, the emperor had ordered the Hunan officials to tell him when Zeng Jing came back to Changsha, so that he could issue new instructions. But when informed by the governor and the morality supervisor in a joint report of late October 1732 that Zeng has duly returned, the emperor offers no fresh suggestions, merely scribbling "Noted" across the end of their message.

In the meantime, as things have transpired, the supervisor of public morality himself, Li Hui, is clearly in the gravest trouble. The cause of this lies in a completely unrelated case that occurred in Pingjiang county, fifty miles northeast of Changsha, that same October. A Buddhist priest was found lying dead in the road, and after a cursory examination the Pingjiang magistrate declared it to be a case of suicide. But closer examination by others revealed that there were at least five wounds in the priest's body. In reviewing the case, first the prefect in whose jurisdiction Pingjiang county lay and then the judicial commissioner of the province declared that the death came after some kind of fight or struggle, and was obviously a homicide. The magistrate's findings were altered to reflect this new conclusion. It was at this point that the supervisor of public morality, Li Hui, intervened, perhaps becase the case involved a priest, perhaps because he was a friend of the Pingjiang magistrate's. Li announced firmly that in his opinion the case was clearly a suicide, and that the prefect who first questioned that assumption should be impeached.

Zeng Jing now stood by as his employer became ever more entangled. The judicial commissioner reiterated that a careful examination had revealed five separate wounds, and thus a finding of suicide could not be sustained—though it was true, the commissioner added, that the prefect had not been as thorough in his own analysis as the commissioner would have liked. These remarks so enraged Li Hui that he began a campaign of abuse against the judicial commissioner, who reacted with anger. The governor, preoccupied by his duties supervising the triennial provincial examinations of Hunan, in which thousands of students participated, tried to calm the tension by instructing the judicial commissioner to restrain himself. But now Li Hui responded by launching ever wilder charges of irresponsibility and recklessness against the commissioner and the prefect; as a climax, he submitted a formal written indictment against both men to the governor. By taking a careful look at the various dates mentioned in the indictment, the governor could see at once that Li Hui had jumped to his own negative conclusions and filed his formal indictment *before* he could possibly have had a chance to review all the evidence on the priest's death. But now the governor's hands were tied. Such a formal indictment became a matter of bureaucratic record and could not be simply expunged on the grounds of its inadequate basis in fact.

In sharing this news with the emperor in a secret report, the governor, Zhao Hongen, explains that though he has entertained doubts about the morality supervisor's abilities for some time, he kept these thoughts to himself: there was no single act of incompetence by Li that seemed to justify troubling the emperor, who, naturally, was occupied with more serious national affairs. But now things have come to a head: "I know that by nature Li Hui is really inept, and he has no skill at conducting practical business. But because he had not lost all his innate decency, during the three years that he and I have worked together I've tried to overcome his weaknesses, develop his strengths, and tactfully transform him. Whenever he insults those who work with him, I tell them to try and be patient and courteous. I've struggled with this over and over again, as I think everybody here knows." It is only because Li Hui has finally vented his private angers for all to see that Zhao has decided to share his worries with the emperor.

The emperor answers the governor's reflections with some of his own. Next to governor Zhao's four-character phrase that Li Hui "had not lost all his innate decency," the emperor writes, "Of this man, I too would use these same four words. But apart from that, I can't see any other strong points of his that I can use." And he promises to send Zhao more detailed instructions as soon as he decides how to proceed.

There have been problems with other supervisors of public morality before, as the emperor knows full well. It was in the heat of his own anger over what he saw as the treacherous nature of the people of Zhejiang province that back in November 1726 he had first instructed his senior ministers to advise him how to reform the region. Their researches had uncovered a seventh-century Tang dynasty precedent, in which the emperor Tang Taizong had established a special office to "observe customs and regulate morality." Yongzheng endorsed the idea of reviving this earlier office, making some slight changes in nomenclature, and establishing it in those provinces where it was most needed. But none of the incumbents had turned out very well. Wang Guodong, a *jinshi* degree holder from a Chinese banner family and the first man appointed to the new office in Zhejiang, had seemed a perfect choice. But Wang had never done much to justify the praise the emperor had lavished on him nor to repay the gifts with which he had initially been showered—hats and coats of sable, a portable hand warmer, rare medicinal herbs. Nor had he justified his subsequent promotion to governor of Hunan, and had been recalled to Beijing in the middle of the Zeng Jing investigations. Wang's successor had also been appointed with high hopes, but had achieved very little, and in December 1730 the emperor had dismissed him as incompetent and since then had left the Zhejiang morality post unfilled. Similarly the elderly career official appointed as the morality supervisor for Fujian in the year 1729, though famous in his younger days for bold moral stances, generated little excitement and made no innovative suggestions for reforming that province; after he retired on the grounds of illness, no successor to the Fujian post was named. Now Li Hui, after the most promising beginnings—he had been the top-ranking student in the Shanxi intermediate-level exams and won his *jinshi* in 1723—has clearly proved to be more of a liability than an asset in Hunan, the place where all the trouble began. It takes the emperor months of cogitation, but finally he acts: on August 12, 1733, Li Hui is summarily dismissed as morality supervisor on the grounds of his "outspokenness." The Hunan position, like the others, is left unfilled.

In confirming the news of Li Hui's dismissal in a confidential court letter to Governor Zhao, the emperor especially mentions that Zeng Jing is henceforth to be the governor's responsibility, though he still does not specify what Zeng Jing's duties are to be. Responding in early September, Zhao tells the emperor that he had shared this news with Zeng Jing, who prostrated himself in gratitude at the emperor's gesture. Clearly remembering the earlier threat that had been made to drown Zeng Jing, Governor Zhao instructs the prefect of Changsha "to keep a really close watch over Zeng Jing, and to prevent any mobs from wounding or killing him." As for Zeng's work, the governor adds, "When I give the public readings of the emperor's sacred instructions at the beginning and middle of every month, I tell him to come along with me. If I can think of some other assignments for him later, then I will assign that work to him." Zeng Jing must have spent most of the emperor's munificent gift during his year's furlough in Yongxing county, for the governor has noticed that the pardoned conspirator is struggling to make ends meet. As Governor Zhao informs the emperor, he has given Zeng Jing some more cash, "to cover his living expenses and prevent his being in straitened circumstances." The emperor endorses this news with his customary "Noted."

Zeng Jing's already light duties must have dwindled to virtually nothing within a month or two of this report, as two decisive changes affected Governor's Zhao's life: his mother died, and the emperor promoted him to be governor-general of the Yangzi delta provinces, one of the most important posts in China. This meant that Governor Zhao had simultaneously to take charge of the intense and harrowing details of the funeral and burial arrangements, and to prepare his Hunan office for the arrival of a new incumbent. Zhao's father had died in 1726, and he had only recently finished that round of mourning rituals. It was because of her recent widowhood that he had brought his seventy-one-year-old mother to live with him in Changsha, Zhao tells the emperor. She seemed at peace in the city, following the same austere regimen of Buddhist abstinence she had first begun twenty years before, and directing her prayers constantly to the bodhisatva Guanyin. Zhao had felt no worries on her behalf, which was why her sudden death on November 8, as he was in the very middle of the preparations for the transfer to Nanjing and his new post, came as such a shock.

Over the past few years, the emperor has experienced a number of profound conflicts with several of his most senior officials, owing to his insistence that they continue with their full roster of official duties during the mourning periods for their deceased parents, or at least that their mourning periods be shortened so that they could return more swiftly to their work. But these attempts to modify traditional patterns of mourning have sparked such hostility that Yongzheng has had to modify his stance. Zeng Jing himself was a beneficiary in this regard. And now Governor Zhao, as well, is treated with special consideration. In a message expressing his regret at the death of Zhao's mother, Yongzheng authorizes the governor to stay in Changsha as long as he likes, until he has a chance to complete all the funeral arrangements. Only then need he proceed to Nanjing to take up his new duties. To make things more bearable, the emperor orders Zhao's younger brother, an army officer, to travel at once to Changsha, and escort their mother's body back to the Chinese banner burial grounds in north China. The newly named governor of Hunan, Zhao's replacement, will be arriving shortly too, to reduce the work load further. He is a Manchu career official named Zhongbao, who like Zhao himself was noted for his filial piety as a young man—Zhao had once offered to take upon his own head a punishment decreed for his father—and could be expected to respect the demands of the mourning rituals on Zhao's mind and time.

The transfer of power in Hunan proceeds smoothly. Zhongbao seems a good man, Zhao reports to the emperor: "As soon as Acting Governor Zhongbao arrived, I gave him detailed briefings on the local customs of the whole of Hunan, the people's state of mind, and the problems of the Miao indigenous territories. I let him know that on taking up a post as a senior provincial official the highest priority is to maintain the region's fundamental spirit. If one goes after every petty irritation, that is bound to trouble all the people. It appears to me that Zhongbao is a man of integrity and also harmonious; he will also be unprejudiced when he makes his enquiries." The emperor, in his handwritten notation at the end of Zhao's report, concedes that Zhongbao is indeed good at financial matters, conscientious, and a man of probity. The problem might be that he is one of those who "care so much about their integrity that they do not apply themselves." Governor-general Zhao should look his successor over carefully, and let the emperor know what he finds.

During the following months, streams of documents flow from both Zhao and Zhongbao to Beijing, as they each take up the complex tasks of administration in their new posts. But in all their many reports—on the weather, the rice harvest prospects, coastal and internal trade, curbing robbers and taxing overland merchants, the grain storage system, the Miao peoples, the courier systems, and salt distribution—neither man makes any mention whatever of Zeng Jing, nor does the emperor remind either of them of the need to watch over the former conspirator. In the minds of these busy men, Zeng Jing—who had taken up so much of their time for so long—is beginning to recede into the background as other more important matters clamor for attention. It is as if Zeng Jing, from being everybody's business, could almost now be classified as one of those "petty irritations" that Zhao had told Zhongbao not to worry his head about.

But this indifference within Changsha does not mean that in the country as a whole Zeng Jing and his book have been forgotten. In April 1734 the commanding general in one of the mountainous Miao regions of western Hunan is regularly reading sections of the *Awakening from Delusion* at the scheduled bimonthly meetings to massed crowds in the garrison city. As he tells the emperor, the experience makes him wonder if it might not be possible to combine such readings with an additional body of materials drawn from the penal code of China. The local people are stupefied by the complexities of Chinese law, currently subdivided into 1,226 sections, he writes, and as a result make no attempt to master it at all. But if they were to be introduced in a simple way to the clauses of the code dealing with the central areas of public order—the general emphasizes the sections on the practicing of magical arts, hiding away prohibited books, and secretly concealing weapons—they would gain a sharper view of what was and was not permitted in daily life.

For the newly appointed acting governor of Hubei, as well, there is real value in the distributed text. Based as he is across the river from the vibrant commercial city of Hankou, he tells Yongzheng, on a busy river route with its thousands of merchants, its leaven of criminals, and people traveling in all directions, the readings of the sixteen-clause sacred edict of the previous emperor alongside the *Awakening from Delusion* seems to have a calming effect on the populace. The governor is convinced that his delivery of these moral messages—he likes to travel in person from Wuchang across the Yangzi River to Hankou to supervise the lectures—reaches people "in every street and cross street, in every market and alley," and leads to their "transformation." He intends to continue conducting such readings in person every spring and autumn.

When viewed from below, however, the effects of the text are far more unpredictable than these officials acknowledge. Li Wei, former chief interrogator of the Lü Liuliang family and now promoted from Zhejiang to be the governor-general of the northern metropolitan province of Zhili, has learned this at first hand. And the way he gained his knowledge has some curious similarities to the way General Yue was sucked into the Zeng Jing case in the first place. In the late summer of 1734, Li tells the emperor, as he was returning to his office after supervising some official examinations, a man who had been waiting by the roadside hurried forward and knelt before him with a petition. Li Wei sized up the man as being a plaintiff seeking some kind of legal redress and sent him to the military garrison office for questioning. Though the man's first responses to his interrogators seemed to them deranged, after a time he began to make more sense. His name was Meng, he told the officials, and he was from the far western province of Shaanxi. There he worked as a traveling peddler, to support himself and his widowed mother. How he got to Zhili was not entirely clear—he had wandered around in the west for years, traveling as far as Gansu province—and had handed in other letters, for which he had been arrested at various times.

In reporting this incident to Yongzheng, Li Wei did not give details on Meng's petition, except to say that his words were "wild and crazed," and that Meng himself "was truly desperate and without resources." But the way Meng traveled around, and the kinds of things he wrote in his letter, reminded Li Wei irresistibly of the former conspirator from Hunan. As he wrote to the emperor: "The way [Meng] went to a place to hand in his letter was in direct emulation of Zeng Jing's personal crime—the guilt for which reaches to Heaven—and he was always cadging for his livelihood, for warm clothing, and a full belly. That's what I think of as a direct imitation. What [Meng] has done may not equal Zeng Jing's extremes of wild rebelliousness, yet the noisy emptiness of his words, and his slanderous and disordered discussion of our military planning, constitute a monstrous crime, and one not to be forgiven."

It is clear from Li's report that Meng might have gotten his ideas after hearing the readings of the *Awakening from Delusion,* perhaps at the time of the western task force's journey through Shaanxi and Gansu, but in his reply Yongzheng does not comment on the imitative nature of Meng's crime. He merely remarks that the case should be handled by the officials in Meng's own native region, to which he should be returned, and under more efficient restraints this time. (Once in the past, Li Wei reported, Meng had escaped from his guards in the west by getting them drunk.)

Another case some months later, in September 1734, also has strange echoes of the Zeng Jing case and the events that led up to it. This time the site was Kunming, in the far southwestern province of Yunnan. The offender was a thirty-nine-year-old fortune-teller and seller of medicines named Huang. He had moved to Yunnan not long before, from the far northern region of Ningxia, where his father had served in the army. Though none of Huang's relatives or friends had seen any evidence of criminal behavior by him in the past, they agreed he had been acting strangely for some time.

Huang came to official attention when he began circulating around Kunming a document, in three brief sections, that he had composed. Huang's message seemed expressly designed to infuriate the emperor, for it concentrated on praising those for whom the emperor had most publicly expressed his scorn, and in denigrating Zeng Jing. The first section was an encomium in honor of the emperor's previous favorite, Nian Gengyao, who had risen so high so fast, only to be charged with treason and corruption and ordered to commit suicide in 1726. Huang focused especially on Nian's achievements in Qinghai, the barren region on the northern frontiers of Tibet: "Nian Gengyao served with merit in Qinghai," wrote Huang, "yet was suddenly found guilty. Obviously, his skills should be praised, his condemnation should be rescinded. Our emperor instructs all his officials to act justly and speak out plainly, and yet the officials have never spoken one word candidly on this case." From this beginning, Huang switched to the topic of Lü Liuliang: "And take Lü Liuliang, a true worthy from the late Ming dynasty: born under the Ming, nourished on Ming food and water, naturally he owed his loyalties to the Ming. It would be proper to give him an honorary official title, to encourage all our countrymen to be scholars, and to attain learning like his." The contrast with another figure who had now become so prominent a spokesman for the Manchu camp was clear enough to Huang: "Compare [Lü] with Zeng Jing. The master [Lü's] arguments seek to clarify all vanities, and in discussing this dynasty's clothing and caps, he thinks it better to follow the procedures of former times, rather than to cover our heads in foreign caps, and dress ourselves in foreign clothes."

These words were outrageous, commented the governor-general of the southwest provinces in his report to the emperor. Even though an extended search of Huang's home revealed no other treasonous writings, and under torture Huang revealed no other plots—and stated that he had never met Nian Gengyao in person—yet his outspokenness in such a volatile frontier region, and his effrontery in discussing national politics while only the meanest of commoners, clearly merited the death penalty.

Execution should be carried out as soon as possible. In a brief notation at the end of the report, the emperor endorses the decision to execute Huang.

Other echoes of the Zeng Jing case continue to resonate in different parts of China: in Sichuan, the disgruntled former servants of one official report that their master has hidden away works by Lü Liuliang, and they show the authorities a batch of writings by their employer that they believe to be treasonous. The province of Jiangsu, so full of accomplished scholars, proves fertile ground for similar accusations against prominent families: stored mounds of wood blocks of their various collected works are painstakingly checked, and all their relatives and friends minutely questioned. Yet no incident, perhaps, so catches the strange level where treason and delusion meet as one that occurs early on a summer day in 1735, in a small town in Guangxi province, when a man in rags pushes his way into the official residence of the local garrison commander.

Like any other peddler or porter in the area, the man carries a bamboo pole across his shoulders, from which two large baskets are suspended. Challenged by the guards to identify himself, the intruder declares that he is on special assignment, having had secret communications with the current emperor's ninth and tenth brothers. In interrogations spread over the next several days, the stranger gives various different names, sometimes claiming to be a native of Shandong, at others that he is from Hunan. But he is consistent in stating that his age is fifty-two, and that as a special agent he is pretending to be a wanderer living from hand to mouth—an odd similarity between this man and the fake Wang Shu. This similarity must seem even stronger to the emperor as he reads that the peddler, to bolster his claims, shows his questioners a single-page commission he is carrying, in which his assignment is clearly spelled out. The commission is dated September 3, 1734, the place of issue is given as Beijing, and the issuing authorities are listed as being the personnel in three different ministries—those of punishments, war, and civil administration. These ministries authorize the bearer to make full enquiries concerning two of the emperor's brothers, the ninth and the fourteenth. By "imperial command," the bearer is further authorized to take fourteen copies of the *Awakening from Delusion* and to distribute them among the local civilian and military officials, with a view to gauging the officials' sincerity and loyalty to the throne. Those found derelict in honesty or duty are to be impeached by the senior provincial officials, and also to be harshly beaten. These cases will in turn be reported back to the Ministry of Punishments. By a further imperial patent, the bearer is also instructed to conduct a special investigation in the province of Guangxi into the activities of the emperor's fourteenth brother, Yinti. By virtue of the imperial office, said bearer has accordingly been named "imperial high commissioner from the capital" and has been granted an honorific poem in praise of his sincerity and virtue and a seal of attestation from a village elder.

In forwarding this curious document to the emperor in late July 1735 and summarizing the interrogations he has conducted, the ranking military officer of Guangxi province writes that he does not feel the interloper is mad, despite his bursting into the office, his constant changes of name and native place, his references to the imperial brothers, and his false claims to special commissioner's rank. "There must be something else going on here," he feels, and as a result of that intuition he is checking with the Guangxi governor-general and governor to see whether they have come across any similar cases or plots involving single-page affidavits of this kind. The emperor's appended comment shows that he is not as worried as the general, but is unwilling to drop the matter altogether: "The man is probably crazy," he writes. "And yet you had better check this out carefully."

The emperor has never issued an official pronouncement concerning Zeng Jing's role in tracking down the fake Wang Shu, though stories about that strange and lonely figure may well have drifted from southern Hunan across the border into northern Guangxi. But even without any direct link, this peddler, whoever he is, seems somehow to be embarked on a similar path. These wanderers, with their carefully orchestrated tales, have the strength and ability to construct a universe of doubt in which everything can turn into something else, and a crazy man in rags, claiming his two empty baskets are filled with copies of the *Awakening from Delusion,* can come to occupy the attention of the most powerful people in the land.

If the officials in Guangxi ever do check into the case of the man with the baskets more deeply, Emperor Yongzheng never gets to read their findings. For two months after writing his brief notation, and two months short of his fifty-seventh birthday, stricken beyond all recall by a sudden two-day illness, he is dead.

Fifteen

Retribution

The new emperor, Qianlong, is just twenty-four when he ascends the throne. Like his father before him, he is the fourth in age among his royal brothers, but none of the others dispute his right to the succession, as so many did in the case of his father. This time there is no doubt about which son the father favors most, though no public announcement has ever been made: Emperor Yongzheng has secretly written out his fourth son's name years before and kept it sealed in a casket in the Forbidden City throne hall, with orders that it be opened only on the eve of his death. The senior ministers follow this procedure, opening the box on October 7 when the emperor is obviously fading fast. The next day, when Emperor Yongzheng dies, the fourth son begins his rule, taking the name Qianlong. Despite all this elaborate procedural secrecy, few at court are surprised by the choice. Most have understood for years that Qianlong is the one being groomed and educated for power.

During the first six weeks of his reign, Emperor Qianlong is absorbed with the rituals of mourning his father and making the essential moves to ensure that the transition of power is smooth. For stability, he keeps his father's key ministers in their previous positions, both in Beijing and in the provinces. On the first occasions when he feels it necessary to alter some of his father's major policies, he acts cautiously, as is proper for someone just beginning to feel his way. But on November 21, 1735, he changes the pattern, announcing a major reappraisal: he simply cannot believe, he tells the court, that it was really his late father's intention to punish all the descendants of his treasonous brothers—especially the eighth and the ninth—so harshly that for all future time they should be permanently disgraced and treated like the most humble of commoners. The ranking princes within the imperial family, along with all the senior ministers, should examine this problem and report back to the emperor on how best to proceed. On this question the discussion should be absolutely open and all levels of view should be heard, however long the process might take.

That same November day, the emperor raises another matter with his ministers. This time, he does not request advice:

"An edict. Even if the treacherous and immoral actions of Zeng Jing were to be treated as the most grave of crimes under the law, that still would not suffice to cover the full extent of his guilt. My late imperial father had a breadth of judgment similar to that of Heaven, and was even more bountiful in his capacity for forgiveness; and so although Zeng Jing's guilt was certainly no less than that of Lü Liuliang, in the case of Lü Liuliang my father applied the law clearly and firmly, whereas with Zeng Jing he chose not to follow the law but to move beyond it. My father's reasoning was that Lü Liuliang's slanders were directed at our imperial ancestors, whereas Zeng Jing's were directed only at his own imperial person. Now it is I who have the responsibility for ruling the country, so I intend to follow the example set by my father in the case of Lü Liuliang, and apply it clearly and firmly to Zeng Jing. By executing this worst of all traitors, I will assuage the sense of outrage felt by my ministers and my people."

The order to arrest Zeng Jing is to be sent at once to the senior officials in Hunan, the emperor continues, along with an arrest order for Zhang Xi. After their arrest, the two men are to be brought under strict guard to Beijing. This matter must be treated as the highest priority, and absolutely no leaks about it will be tolerated. The various relatives and dependents of both Zeng Jing and Zhang Xi are also to be rounded up, and held under close guard by the local officials in whose jurisdictions they are living, pending receipt of a further edict on how to dispose of them all. Qianlong remands the entire matter to the Ministry of Punishments for immediate action.

A copy of the edict is dispatched to Hunan by military courier, where Governor Zhongbao receives it in his Changsha office at noon on December 10. Though the governor has not been sending in any reports on Zeng Jing's doings, he knows exactly where the former conspirator can be found—in quarters attached to those of his current supervisor, the prefect of Changsha. Zhongbao at once orders the Hunan judicial commissioner to meet up with the prefect, and to arrest Zeng Jing; they do so, and immediately afterward begin to search through his rooms, impounding all documents—books, manuscripts, random jottings—that they find there.

As it was back in 1728, so now too, speed is essential to prevent any of Zeng's relatives or the members of the Zhang family from hearing that the case has been reopened. So on the same December day when Zeng is arrested, Governor Zhongbao names the members of two other arrest groups: one, under the command of the magistrate residing in Changsha, is to proceed at once to Anren county to arrest Zhang Xi and bring him back under guard to Changsha. (They also instruct the local Anren authorities there to round up all Zhang Xi's family members and imprison them.) The other squad, under the leadership of a military officer in the Changsha garrison, travels farther south, to Yongxing county. There they coordinate the arrests of all the surviving members of Zeng Jing's family.

There are no leaks and no mistakes, and everything goes smoothly as planned. The various family members are held in the county prisons nearest to their homes, while Zhang Xi is brought swiftly back to Changsha. On December 29, Governor Zhongbao can report to his new emperor, only nineteen days after the orders had been received, the two conspirators, trussed and closely guarded, have left Changsha and begun the long journey to Beijing. Governor Zhongbao has already taken the precaution of writing ahead to the officials through whose jurisdictions the two prisoners and their escort will be passing, alerting them to be ready with an extra complement of guards for each stage of the prisoners' journey. Along with the prisoners, the governor sends the various manuscripts he has found in Zeng Jing's possession: some of them might well turn out to be treasonous. It has long been his own personal opinion, Governor Zhongbao tells the emperor, that Zeng and Zhang were guilty of crimes that cried out for the death penalty. Only the late emperor's remarkable compassion had saved them from receiving such a punishment long ago.

While the officials in Hunan are thus doing his bidding, the emperor is preparing for the prisoners' arrival in Beijing. Since he has remanded the case to the Ministry of Punishments, he wants someone he trusts absolutely at the helm there. Accordingly, on November 22, only one day after sending out the edict ordering the arrest of Zeng Jing and Zhang Xi, the emperor makes one of his first significant changes of personnel: he transfers the president of the Ministry of Public Works, a fifty-year-old career official from a wealthy Hangzhou family named Xu Ben, to be president of the Ministry of Punishments; and at the same time the current president of Punishments is shifted over to be president of Public Works. One week later, to underscore the deep faith that the new emperor has in him, Xu Ben is named a member of the Grand Council, as the small inner circle of the emperor's most trusted senior advisers is now coming to be known.

Xu Ben has been a model official: a *jinshi* degree recipient in 1718 and a research scholar in the Hanlin Academy, he has held major posts in at least five different provinces as well as in a range of Beijing ministries. At an early stage of his career, Xu Ben served for several years under the powerful Manchu governor-general Ortai, and is considered a member of Ortai's inner circle. Ortai, in his turn, once Yongzheng's closest confidant, is now a key adviser to Emperor Qianlong, and one of the most powerful grand councilors. Thus, just as Ortai is perfectly placed to push through Qianlong's cherished policies, so Xu Ben is admirably positioned to implement the policies desired by either man.

No matter whether it is Ortai or Emperor Qianlong himself who has engineered Xu Ben's transfer, the reason for it becomes immediately clear. In a carefully worded petition to the emperor, using his new title of Punishments minister, Xu Ben addresses the crucial problem of which everyone at court and in the provinces must surely be aware: now that the arrest order for Zeng Jing has gone out, what is to be done with those hundreds of thousands of copies of the *Awakening from Delusion*, that book so full of gossip and slander against the ruling house that nevertheless bears the imprimatur of the late emperor himself?

Starting with a brief historical preamble on the book's composition, Xu Ben recalls how the previous emperor ordered his own edicts and questions to Zeng Jing combined with Zeng Jing's responses and confessions, to form the text of the book in question. Xu points out also the thoroughness with which the *Awakening* has been distributed across the entire country, so that it could be used at the bimonthly readings of the emperor's exhortations, as well as being passed down for discussion in the community compact groups at the village level. The late emperor's objective in doing this, Xu Ben declares, was "to use the traitors' snarling and barking" as a way to "arouse the world and waken the people." Though so many of the words in the *Awakening from Delusion* were treacherous, they helped to inform the people at large of the constant struggle between virtue and its opposite. Thus, the people, even those from the farthest and most backward areas, "were moved to revere that inner goodness that comes from love and loyalty, and to a fuller personal understanding of the meaning of morality."

But that was some time ago, continues Xu. Even those who at that time were the most stupid and deluded have by now been enlightened. The former emperor is dead, leaving behind the memory of his love and goodness, something that would never be forgotten. So "what is now the purpose," asks Xu, "of continuing to circulate these slanderous and destructive words against our ruler-father, and reciting them again and again every month? Truly, this is something neither the officials nor the people can bear to listen to anymore." There is one basic solution, concludes Xu: "I respectfully request the emperor to end the practice of discussing the *Awakening from Delusion* at the beginning and midpoint of every month."

In a brief edict to the senior officials of the country, issued on December 2, Emperor Qianlong responds: "As requested by Ministry President Xu Ben, all reading and discussion of the *Awakening from Delusion* shall cease. All copies of the original book that have been distributed shall be collected by the senior provincial officials, and returned to the Ministry of Rituals. At a later day I will issue another edict on this." The implication is clear: after the copies have been returned to the Ministry of Rituals, all of them will be destroyed. On December 12, his crucial duty done and any potential opposition now stilled, Xu Ben steps down from the Grand Council and returns to his full-time post in the Ministry of Punishments. Thus, even before Zeng Jing is brought into Beijing by his guards, the book he helped to compile under imperial auspices has itself become a forbidden text, one that can only be stored away in secret; keeping a private copy of the *Awakening from Delusion* has now become an act subject to all the same perils that had attended the keeping of Lü Liuliang's most anti-Manchu writings.

Zeng Jing and Zhang Xi are brought into Beijing around the twentieth of January, 1736. It is the second time they have made this particular journey, and faced the prospect of death. But in 1729, though jailed, Zeng Jing at least was given space and light, ink and a writing brush, for Hangyilu and his staff were coming by at intervals with fresh questions from the emperor, and piles of documents for him to read. But now no one comes calling, and nobody cares what he thinks.

Strangely, one voice survives to break through the shroud of silence that hangs around the Beijing prison where Zeng Jing is now immured. It is that of Fang Bao, oldest of the scholars called in by Emperor Yongzheng to join the task force in its rebuttal of the works of Lü Liuliang. It was in Fang Bao's house that the Che brothers met their future tutor, Sun, in happier days before Zhang Xi's visit plunged their lives into chaos. Fang spent much of the years 1712 and 1713 in the Ministry of Punishments Beijing cells, charged with being an accessory in another literary treason case, expecting death at any day. Only by the blindest chance was he released, and hence able some years later to write a record of his experiences. There were four cell blocks in the main prison, Fang remembered, each laid out on a similar pattern. At the center of each block was a long room where the jailers lived, with windows for light at one end and openings for ventilation at the other. But the cells grouped around the jailers' room had neither light nor air; fifty or more prisoners were crammed into each windowless chamber, chained together in rows every night from dusk till dawn, behind a bolted door. At night that door was never opened, and each morning the dead were removed by the jailers, leaving a little more room for the others until new prisoners came in to take the dead ones' places. An easing of conditions came only if one had influential relatives, with money, who were willing to come by the prison to plead one's cause with the guards and buy the right to have their imprisoned family members unshackled and put in the so-called custody sheds nearby, where the conditions were somewhat more humane.

But neither Zeng Jing nor Zhang Xi has to endure such conditions long. The reappraisal of their case is swift and secretive, and is over in less than a week. On January 31, 1736, Emperor Qianlong himself announces the verdict, presenting it in the form of an edict. His words are curt and cold: "Zeng Jing and Zhang Xi are seditious, rebellious, treacherous, lawless. On the grounds that their slanders were aimed only at his own person, my late imperial father, with a sagacity akin to that of Heaven, chose to spare them from death. Furthermore, he expressly ordered that his own sons and grandsons must not, at any time in the future, reopen the case and punish them with death or dismemberment. But though the late emperor, in his own day, chose to be so lenient, I at this present day find it impossible to be so compassionate. Though the two ways that we have each chosen to handle this case appear to be so different, yet he and I have the same view of natural principles and of human emotions. Besides which, in their anger and their resentment, the hundreds of millions of our people, whether officials or commoners, all want to see justice and punishments promptly and correctly applied according to the standards of today. How can I stand against the feelings my people have about the nature of the common good and of evil? Let Zeng Jing and Zhang Xi, in accordance with the law, be executed by being sliced to death." According to the laws applicable in such treason cases, the families of Zeng Jing and Zhang Xi would soon be following them in death, save for those still under sixteen, and perhaps some of the womenfolk, who would be sent to a life of slavery and exile with the armies in the north. And such of their property as remained was forfeit to the state.

For Zeng Jing and Zhang Xi, after such an edict, there can only be the waiting for the end. But even in cases where the death penalty was applied, Fang Bao recalled, money played its part: "Whenever the death sentence is about to be carried out, the executioner waits outside the door and lets his confederates enter the cell to ask for money or property. In the case of the rich they ask the relatives, for the poor they simply ask the condemned man himself." The families of prisoners about to be beheaded could pay to receive the head back, so it could be buried with the body. The families of those sentenced to death by strangulation could pay for the first twist of the rope to be the last. Even in the worst death of all, money could speak, as Fang had seen for himself: "If slicing is the penalty, they say: 'If you satisfy me, I will stab you to the heart. Otherwise, even after your four limbs have been sliced away, your heart will still be beating.'"

This time for Zeng and Zhang there are no last appeals, no sudden clemencies. And nobody raises a voice in protest as the two men die, though one man raises his in glee. It is the student Qi, arrested years before when he believed the emperor's words, and tried to reach Yongzheng with his written protest at the pardoning of Zeng Jing and the posthumous degradations imposed on Lü Liuliang. Qi is still in his Hangzhou prison cell when friends bring him the news of Zeng Jing's execution: "Oh, what a truly wonderful thing!" he writes in his diary. "And yet, I still bitterly regret that Lü and his family cannot be brought back to life."

And so it seemed as if the case was over. Later in 1736 the new emperor ordered Xu Ben to serve concurrently as president of the Ministry of Rituals, and surely that appointment was made so that the man who had first suggested the recall of the *Awakening from Delusion* could oversee the book's destruction. But despite all that careful planning, some copies of the now-banned imperial text escaped the meshes of the law. Some scholars believed in the power of the text as a historical source and hid it away at home, as so many others had hidden dangerous things across the years. One copy was kept by the emperor's staff, in the inner archives of the imperial household, as a reference for the future. Some copies made their way by surreptitious means to Japan, where the shoguns were eager for any item that would given them insight into the workings of the Chinese government. Some were stockpiled by bold booksellers, confident that one day the book would appreciate in value, either as a curiosity or as a source of information about the vanished past. Some parts of the book were doubtless lodged in people's memories, from all those monthly readings, and passed on by them to their children, as an example of how an emperor of old had tried to clear the record and purify his name. And some aspects of the story were simply transformed into the way people wanted them to be: in the most enduring of these retellings, it was one of Lü Liuliang's granddaughters who brought about Emperor Yongzheng's sudden death. Driven by the search for vengeance, and herself an adept in the magic arts of combat, she beguiled the sensual ruler into admitting her to his bedchamber, only to sever his head with a flash of her flying knife.

Thus it can be said that both emperors got it wrong. One emperor thought that by airing all the negative facts against himself, he could purge the record of the noxious rumors, and because of his honesty posterity would revere his name. But his people remembered the rumors and forgot the disclaimers. The second emperor thought that by destroying the book he would lay his father's ghosts to rest. But his people thought that the reason he wanted to destroy the book was because so much of what it contained was true.

And because of the book, the stories it generated and the leads it provided, the other figures all came crowding: the fake Wang Shu in his purple jacket and black felt hat, the geomancer Chen and the Daoist by the bridge, Secretary Tang with his blinding rage, the exiled eunuchs on their way to the south, the merchants traveling on their river boat, the medicine peddler who had heard too much, four strong men in military garb, a man in rags with two large baskets suspended from his shoulder pole—and so many others known and unknown. Emperor Yongzheng's attempt to patch his reputation was no match for such a multitude, nor could his earnest son banish the chattering host.

So much to-do because a small-time teacher had a schoolhouse on the Anren road; and because a man he called his messenger ran across another road, far away, with a letter in his hand.

A Note on the Sources

Interest in the intertwined cases of Zeng Jing (Tseng Ching) and Lü Liu-liang developed near the end of the Qing dynasty (c. 1899), when Chinese reformists living in exile in Japan came across copies of Zeng Jing's *Awakening from Delusion* (*Dayi juemi lu*), which was still banned within China. The text, a trove of highly explicit criticism of the Manchu rulers of the Qing—albeit from more than one hundred and fifty years before—offered an excellent opportunity to embarrass the current dynastic leaders. In the 1920s, a decade after the dynasty had collapsed, researchers at the Qing Archives kept in the Forbidden City—now renamed the Imperial Palace Museum—found a number of reports to the emperor Yongzheng dated in the 1720s and 1730s that added invaluable detail on Zeng Jing's attempted plot, his arrest, and the subsequent interrogations of Zeng himself and many of his followers. An unpunctuated and unedited version of these materials appeared in sequential issues of the Imperial Palace Museum publication *Wenxian congbian* and were subsequently slightly expanded and rearranged into a single sequence, which was published by the same museum in the collectanea on Qing dynasty literary suppression cases, the *Qingdai wenziyu dang* (cited in the Notes as *QDWZYD*). A facsimile reprint of the entire *Dayi juemi lu* was published in Taipei in 1966, and a punctuated version, with the addition of a punctuated version of the backup documents from the earlier Imperial Palace Museum collectanea, with transcriptions into colloquial Chinese, was published in Beijing in 1999, following a popular TV series on Emperor Yongzheng.

The Zeng Jing case was introduced in some detail to English-speaking readers by L. C. Goodrich in 1935 in his pioneering work *The Literary Inquisition of Ch'ien-lung*, pp. 84–87, after Goodrich had acquired a copy of the *Awakening from Delusion* in Beijing (then called Peiping). A decade later, Fang Chao-ying made a masterful summary of the current state of knowledge on the case in his brief biography "Tseng Ching" in Arthur W. Hummel, ed., *Eminent Chinese of the Ch'ing Period* (cited in the Notes as *ECCP*), pp. 747–749. By far the most important subsequent study of Lü Liuliang and Zeng Jing was that by Thomas S. Fisher in his 1974 Princeton University Ph.D. dissertation, "Lü Liu-liang (1629–83) and the Tseng Ching Case (1728–33)," revised sections of which were subsequently published in English and Chinese. Careful discussions of aspects of the case also appeared in Huang Pei, *Autocracy at Work* (1974), pp. 215–220; Pierre-Henri Durand, *Lettrés et pouvoirs* (1992), pp. 374–383; Silas H. L. Wu, "History and Legend" (1998); F. W. Mote, *Imperial China, 900–1800* (1999), pp. 898–900; and Pamela Kyle Crossley, *A Translucent Mirror: History and Identity in Qing Imperial Ideology* (1999), pp. 253–259.

An immense amount of documentary sources with which to supplement the earlier published materials on Zeng Jing and the case as a whole have appeared in recent years. I have drawn most heavily on two of these, both photo-offset reproductions of the original incoming provincial reports to Emperor Yongzheng, with his handwritten comments. One is the multivolume series, published by the Palace Museum in Taipei between 1977 and 1980, entitled *Gongzhong dang Yongzhengchao zouzhe* (Secret palace memorials of the Yongzheng reign), cited in the Notes as T followed by the volume number and page; the other is the series of materials drawn from the Beijing Imperial Palace Museum collections, published in

1991 under the title *Yongzhengchao hanwen zhupi zouzhe huibian* (A compilation of the Chinese-language reports and imperial endorsements from Yongzheng's reign), cited in the Notes as B. The Beijing collection in fact includes most of the documents from the Taipei collection, but these reproductions of the reproductions are often so blurred that they are virtually impossible to decipher. Accordingly, the documents held in Taipei will be cited from the Taipei volumes.

In 1993, another valuable set of imperial documents was published by the Number One Archive of the Beijing Imperial Palace Museum, namely, the daily court diary of Emperor Yongzheng's reign, entitled *Yongzhengchao Qijuzhu ce* (abbreviated in the Notes as *Qijuzhu*). Though the sections of the diary from mid-1730 onward are lost (except for sections for 1734), the extant portions cover all the crucial early years of the Zeng Jing case. In particular, using these diaries one can track every single one of the major edicts that make up the bulk of the *Awakening from Delusion* and establish a firm chronology for the sequence of imperial actions. (This had been impossible using the *Dayi juemi lu* alone, since almost all the key documents in that compilation had the dates cut from them.) One significant aspect of these Imperial Palace Museum sources is that we no longer have to rely on the heavily censored texts such as the Veritable Records (*Qing shilu*) or the official compilation of Yongzheng period reports and rescripts known as the *Zhupi yuzhi* for the background material. Instead, we can see the originals.

A Note on Conventions

Chinese dates in the Qing dynasty were given in the form of the reign-year of the current emperor, followed by the lunar month and day; in the text, I have converted these to the Western Gregorian calendar, unless the lunar date was important to the story. Chinese distances were designated in *li*, equivalent to one third of a mile; I have converted all these to the Western equivalent. Chinese names are cited in the way they were at the time, with the family name (usually monosyllabic) followed by the given name of either one or two syllables. Manchu names are presented in the form of one single but multisyllable name, reflecting the usage during the Qing dynasty.

Notes

———

Prologue

2 Delivering the letter: The original text of General Yue Zhongqi's secret report on the incident, dated Yongzheng 6/9/28 (October 30, 1728), is in B13/555-558 (i.e., Beijing collection of the compilation of the secret Chinese-language reports from Yongzheng's reign, vol. 13, pp. 555–558), and transcribed in *QDWZYD*, pp. 1–4. A fair copy is included in T11/432–436 (i.e., the Taipei collection of secret palace memorials of the Yongzheng reign). The movements of the messenger Zhang Xi (Zhang Zhuo) and his cousin can be charted via their later interrogations (see notes for Chapter 4 below). A precise account of the letter's delivery to Yue is in Fisher (1974), pp. 215–216. On the reception in the suburbs that morning, see T11/441–442, report of Shise, also dated 6/9/28. Detailed street layouts of Xi'an at the time are in *Chang'an xianzhi* (1812), *juan* 3, p. 2; walls and drum tower, ibid., *juan* 10, p. 2.

2 The general's name: Various other translations are possible for the name by which the conspirators addressed General Yue: Fang Chao-ying in "Tseng Ching,"

p. 748, renders it "Heaven's Official and Generalissimo"; Fisher (1974), p. 216, has "Commander-in-Chief who carries the Heavenly Orders."

Chapter 1: The General

5 General Yue: His biography is in *ECCP,* pp. 957–959, and a good summary is in Fisher (1974), pp. 215–217. Yue's extensive land and property holdings are listed in *Wenxian congbian,* reprint, pp. 232–233. His son Yue Jun at this time was acting governor of Shandong. Though Bartlett does not focus on the Zeng Jing case, an illuminating account of Yue's relationship with Yongzheng is given in Bartlett, *Monarchs and Ministers,* pp. 56–64.

6 The hero Yue Fei: A detailed analysis is in Kaplan, "Yueh Fei"; a briefer survey, in Helmut Wilhelm, "From Myth to Myth." Yue Zhongqi quotes a passage from the treasonous letter linking him to Yue Fei in B13/555, report of Yongzheng 6/9/28. F. W. Mote, in *Imperial China,* pp. 898 and 1049 n.23, expresses skepticism that General Yue was really Yue Fei's descendant.

6 Zeng Jing's treasonous letter: The original letter has not survived, and these and the following passages are drawn either from Emperor Yongzheng's rebuttal edict on the treasonous letter issued on 6/11/11 (December 11, 1728, discussed in notes for Chapter 2 below), and presented as item two in the *Dayi juemi lu* (hereafter cited as *DYJML*), or from the references to the letter in Yongzheng's and Hangyilu's questions to Zeng in 1729.

7 On the virtuous minister: *DYJML,* 1/60b (i.e., *juan* 1, p. 60b), and 1/61a, where the phrase "*shishen,*" "losing moral character," is a pun for a woman losing her virginity.

7 On barbarian rulers: *DYJML,* 1/39a; 1/44b–45.

7 On portents: No light, *DYJML,* 1/44a; Confucian temple burns, 2/64a; rivers dried, 1/45a and 3/1a; five stars, 1/46b.

7 Comments on society: *DYJML,* 1/58b.

8 Comments on self: *DYJML,* 1/69b–70a.

8 Empty past: *DYJML,* 1/49a and 1/56b.

8 Master of the Eastern Sea: *DYJML,* 1/66b.

8 On Emperor Yongzheng: Charges highlighted in *DYJML,* 1/15–36; summation, 1/56b.

8 Yue in Chengdu, 1727: B10/20 and 10/24, reports by Yue and Huang dated Yongzheng 5/6/19, referring back to the events of 5/6/17.

9 Yue's self-blame: B10/44–45, dated Yongzheng 5/6/22. A revised version of the same report is in B10/45–48.

9 Emperor's public edict in response: *Qing shilu,* 59/3–4 (i.e., *juan* 59, pp. 3–4), dated Yongzheng 5/7/3 (August 19, 1727).

9 Emperor's confidential comments: B10/218–219; interlinear comments to report of 5/7/13.

10 Dr. Liu's visit: B10/218, B10/317.

10 Investigator's report on Chengdu case: T8/631–635, dated Yongzheng 5/8/6.

11 Xi'an Manchu city and training grounds: Wu Bolun, *Xi'an lishi shulue*, 1979 edition, pp. 275–276, and map, p. 272; 1984 expanded edition, pp. 300–304, and map, p. 292.

11 Tea and the first interrogation: Yue's own report, B13/555–556, and *QDWZYD* pp. 1–2, in which Yue tells Yongzheng he put on a "fair-weather face" ("*ai-yan*"). Fisher (1974), pp. 217–222, gives the most detailed account of these meetings available in English. Shise's separate report, discussing his own role as eavesdropper, is in T10/441–442.

13 Governor Xilin and torture: B13/556; *QDWZYD*, pp. 1b–2.

13 October 29 interrogation, discussion of Zou Lu and Nian Gengyao: B13/556–557; *QDWZYD*, pp. 2–3; Fisher (1974), pp. 218–219. The "six provinces" were Huguang (made up of Hubei and Hunan), Jiangxi, Guangxi, Guangdong, Yunnan, and Guizhou.

15 October 30 dispatch of first report: B13/558, *QDWZYD*, p. 3.

16 The courier system: Full details are in the Qing statutes (*Daqing Huidian shili*), *juan* 1042; reprint, pp. 17494–17501. A careful analysis and description of the Qing transmission system is also given in Fairbank and Teng, "On the Transmission of Ch'ing Documents"; see ibid., pp. 14–17, on the officially calculated distances, and p. 30 for standard times. Two fascinating studies that show the Qing system of reports and interrogations during each of the following two reigns are Kuhn, *Soul Stealers*, and Naquin, *Millenarian Rebellion*.

17 Li Yuan and the messenger Zhang: B13/571, report dated Yongzheng 6/9/30; *QDWZYD*, p. 4. The *Chang'an xianzhi, juan* 8, p. 14, gives his name as Li Yuansheng, and the date of his appointment as 1727. The ruse is discussed in Fisher (1974), p. 220.

18 The oath: B13/571; *QDWZYD*, pp. 4. There is no surviving record of the exact words of the oath sworn by Yue.

18 The first six conspirators' names: General Yue appended the names and addresses to his report of 6/9/30: see B13/572. The list does not appear in *QDWZYD* or other sources.

19 Yue and Zhang, November 1 discussions: See B13/587–589, dated 6/10/2, which also appends this second list of seven names; *QDWZYD*, pp. 4b–6 (without the list); Fisher (1974), pp. 220–222.

Chapter 2: The Emperor

23 Reports at the palace: See the detailed studies by Fairbank and Teng, "Transmission" and "Types and Uses"; Wu, *Communication and Imperial Control;* and Bartlett, *Monarchs and Ministers.* There were also significant numbers of Manchu-language imperial reports and notations: see Bartlett, *Monarchs and Ministers,*

p. 130. Yang Qiqiao, *Yongzhengdi,* gives a detailed analysis of how the official Qing-published collections of these documents often dramatically altered both the reports and rescripts that it presented.

24 Batches of reports: This can be clearly demonstrated by the table of contents to the Beijing and Taipei collections of secret palace reports (*Gongzhong dang Yongzhengchao zouzhe* and *Yongzhengchao hanwen zhupi zouzhe huibian*).

25 Emperor Yongzheng's character: The best brief summary is by Fang Chaoying in *ECCP,* pp. 915–920; Yongzheng's development of the communications system is carefully explored by Bartlett, *Monarchs and Ministers.* Broader biographical studies are Huang, *Autocracy at Work,* and Feng, *Yongzheng zhuan.* The struggles between Yongzheng and his brothers are graphically described by Silas Wu in *Passage to Power.* The other charges are itemized in the *Dayi juemi lu* itself.

25 Brothers' deaths: see *ECCP* under "Yin-jeng," "Yin-ssu," and "Yin-t'ang," and Anonymous, "Yinsi, Yintang an." The exact meanings of the brothers' insulting name changes are discussed in Shen Yuan, "'Aqina,' 'Saisihei' kaoshi" (including the highly original idea that 'Aqina' might refer to fish frozen to death in the ice), and Wang Zhonghan, "On Acina and Sishe." I follow Wang here.

25 Imperial residences and journeys: For a succinct summary of these, see Rawski, *Last Emperors,* pp. 31–36.

25 The Manchu race: A detailed and subtle discussion of the Manchus' views of race/ethnicity/identity is in Pamela Crossley, *The Translucent Mirror;* Lü Liuliang's perspective is explored in Fisher (1974), Chapter 5, "Ethnic Thought." Also see Chapter 10 below on Zeng Jing and the *Awakening from Delusion.*

26 Yongzheng and portents: Vivid details from original sources are marshaled in Silas Wu, "History and Legend," and in Chen Hsi-yuan, "Propitious Omens."

26 Zhejiang province: The first morality supervisor was appointed in 1726. The link between the appointment of this new official and Yongzheng's suspicion of various Zhejiang scholars is discussed in Fisher (1974), pp. 275–276. On the Tang dynasty precedents for the office, see Chapter 14 below.

27 Yongzheng's first response to Yue: His running script comments are in B13/558; transcription in *QDWZYD,* pp. 3–4. Fisher (1974), p. 219, gives a brief summary of the response. Bartlett, *Monarchs and Ministers,* pp. 61–63, gives lengthy translations of some of Yongzheng's warmest responses to Yue on other occasions.

28 Shise's report: B13/567–568, dated Yongzheng 6/9/28.

29 Renegade Chinese and Miao: *Qing shilu,* 74/9b–11, 74/14b–15. On contacts with Japan, see Silas Wu, "History and Legend"; for Java and Luzon, see *Qing shilu* 74/2b. For Yongzheng's dislike of Catholic missionaries see especially Fu, *Documentary Chronicle,* vol. 1, pp. 154–156.

29 Yongzheng's second response to Yue: Running script B13/571, transcribed *QDWZYD,* p. 4.

30 Nian Gengyao: *ECCP*, pp. 587–590. For Nian and Yue, see Anonymous, "Yue Zhongqi zouzhe," pp. 435–436. On the illness and death of Nian's sister, see *Qing shilu*, 38/13b, 38/17.

31 Wang Jingqi's Casual Notes: *ECCP*, pp. 812–813. Wang Jingqi, *Xizheng suibi* (*Casual Notes of My Journey to the West*): famine and casualties, 28a; hardships, 15; "rouged bandits," 16–17; officials' case studies, 26, 46b, 49b; Zhang Pengge, 43.

33 Yongzheng's response to Wang: *Qing shilu*, 39/7, 39/13b, 39/21b–22. The facsimile of the emperor's furious personal comment is given on p. 18 of the illustrations section of the *Zhanggu congbian*, 1964 reprint. Xu Zengzhong, "Zeng Jing fan Qing an," pp. 166–168, pays particular attention to the Wang case as contributing to Yongzheng's hatred of scholars from the Zhejiang region.

33 Yongzheng on six names: B13/572.

33 Procedural exception: In the early Manchu secret report system, reports were returned to their senders, and no files were kept. Bartlett, *Monarchs and Ministers*, pp. 226 and 369 n.114, shows how such copying became more common in 1729 and 1730. Copying Yue's report in 1728 thus anticipated a slightly later development.

34 Yue's response to the emperor's comments: B13/687–688, report of 6/10/17 to edict received 6/10/16; *QDWZYD*, p. 7.

34 Yue's third report and list of seven names: B13/587–589, dated 6/10/2; *QDWZYD*, pp. 4b–6, without the names. A summary of the Yinian uprising is given in Silas Wu, "Passage to Power," pp. 107–108, 111, 213.

35 *Capital Gazette*: Variously "*jingbao*," "*dichao*," or "*tangbao*." A useful discussion of the system and the variety of cheap copies available later in the dynasty is in Britton, *Chinese Periodical Press*, pp. 7–15, and plates 1–8. See also Fairbank and Teng, "Transmission," p. 36 n.32, and "Types and Uses," pp. 61–62; and Bartlett, *Monarchs and Ministers*, pp. 44, 56, 158, and 304 n.10.

36 Court letters: Silas Wu, *Communication*, pp. 102–105; Bartlett, *Monarchs and Ministers*, pp. 103–112.

36 November 11 court letter: Li Wei report on court letter and Colonel Tian, B13/808; and see the facsimile of this court letter in B13/813. General Hailan's report is transcribed in *QDWZYD*, p. 9. For Fan Shiyi on his own court letter, see T11/756–757 (also reproduced in B13/924). Distances and normative times for these three courier routes are given in Fairbank and Teng, "Transmission," pp. 13–15. The reports of the principals give the days of receipt: November 23 for Fan, November 24 for Li Wei, November 28 for Hailan. It is clear that in 1728 all those involved in the case traveled more swiftly than the rules stipulated.

38 Emperor receives treasonous letter: Yue Zhongqi sent it on 6/10/17, and thus the arrival date in Beijing would have been on or around 6/10/27 (November 28).

38 Response to treasonous letter: Though omitted from the *Qing shilu* and the *Donghua lu*, the entire document is preserved in the Court Diaries (*Yongzheng-*

chao Qijuzhu ce of Yongzheng's reign; cited hereafter as *Qijuzhu*), under the date Yongzheng 6/11/11 (December 11, 1728), where it fills pp. 2392–2413 of the Beijing Palace Museum 1993 edition. Because of the date of issue, contemporary officials called it the "6/11 edict." This document subsequently became the second item in the *DYJML*, 1/14–52b (i.e., *juan* 1, pp. 14–52b), and that is the version cited here. Feng Erkang, "Zeng Jing toushu an," discusses how Zeng Jing's letter was seized on by Yongzheng as a way to fight back at his opponents.

38 Conscience triply clear: *DYJML*, 1/15.

38 On Kangxi's death: Ibid., 1/15b–17.

39 Vicious brothers: Ibid., 1/21–28.

39 Palace women: Ibid., 1/17–20b.

39 Avarice: Ibid., 1/29b–30b.

39 Drinking: Ibid., 1/32b–33. For an earlier (1727) accusation of his heavy drinking, see *Qing shilu*, 44/35.

39 Dislike of sex: *DYJML*, 1/33.

39 Betrayals and Nian: Ibid., 1/33b–34.

40 Brothers' eunuchs: Ibid., 1/37–38.

40 Manchus at conquest: Ibid., 1/40–45b.

40 Confucian temple fire: Ibid., 1/46.

40 Zeng Jing, Zha, and Wang: Ibid., 1/48b–49.

40 All now known: Ibid., 1/51.

41 Concluding reflections: Ibid., 1/51b–52b.

41 Edict issued: the exact date and those summoned to attend are in *Qijuzhu*, pp. 2391–2392. The emperor was apparently not there in person. The business for the rest of that day, recorded in ibid., p. 2413, fits exactly (albeit in extended form) with that in the *Qing shilu*, 75/9b, for the same day, though the edict itself is not included in the Veritable Records, presumably on the orders of Yongzheng's successor, Qianlong.

Chapter 3: The Messenger's Trail

43 Fan receives message: T11/756 specifies receipt by Fan Shiyi on Yongzheng 6/10/22 (November 23, 1728).

43 Banner system: A richly detailed discussion of the formation of the Chinese banners is in Crossley, *Translucent Mirror* (see especially pp. 44–49, and 90–99). As she explains there, the conventionally used racial distinctions between the "Chinese" banners and those labeled as Manchu and Mongol are in fact a later-eighteenth-century construct, and thus are inadequate to explain what the early Manchus saw as "Nikan" identity; for this reason, instead of "Chinese bannermen," Crossley uses the term "Chinese-martial bannermen." For simplicity's sake, however, I still use the term "Chinese bannermen" here.

44 Fan's biography: *ECCP,* p. 229; *Qingshi gao,* p. 9357; *Qingshi liezhuan,* 15/22b. Fan Shiyi was a grandson of the celebrated collaborator Fan Wencheng.

44 Fan's plan: Fan's own detailed report to Yongzheng, including all his interrogations of the suspects, is in T11/756–761 (also reproduced in B13/924–929), dated Yongzheng 6/11/11. Additional detail on Fang Bao (Fang Pao) is in *ECCP,* pp. 235–237.

49 Yongzheng's response to Fan: T11/761 (B13/929).

49 Li Wei's biography: *ECCP,* pp. 720–721; *Qingshi gao,* p. 1033; *Qingshi liezhuan,* 13/37a. The reports by Li Wei to Yongzheng are made the subject of special study by Yang Qiqiao, *Yongzhengdi,* pp. 127–143. The horoscope incident is mentioned in B9/316–317, dated Yongzheng 5/3/24 (April 15, 1727). For Yongzheng's discussion with general Yue of another official's horoscope, see Bartlett, *Monarchs and Ministers,* p. 62.

50 Li Wei and Zha Siting case: *ECCP* 22 (Cha Ssu-t'ing); *Qing shilu,* 48/25–27, 50/18b–19b, and 57/6–7; Meng Sen, *Qingchu san dayian kaoshi.* B8/314–317 has Li Wei's account of his search of Zha's home. Yongzheng's sentence on Zha is in *Qing shilu,* 57/7. A fine analysis of the relationship between the Zha Siting case and a similar case in 1755, including the ethnic issues, is given in Chu Ping-tzu, "Factionalism in the Bureaucratic Monarchy."

52 Public morality post instituted: *Qing shilu* 49/2, 49/6, October and November, 1726.

52 Zhang Xi's list of literary works: *QDWZYD,* p. 5.

52 Li Wei's plan: Li's detailed report, including his transcript of the interrogations, is in B13/808–813, dated Yongzheng 6/11/3 (December 3, 1728). A summary of Li Wei's Zhejiang investigation is in Fisher (1974), pp. 237–241. Li Wei's fellow interrogator was the swiftly rising official Gao Bin, at this time serving as Zhejiang financial commissioner; for Gao's career, see *ECCP,* pp. 412–413 (under "Kao Pin").

53 The Lü family arrest and testimony: B13/808–811. On Lü Liuliang's poetry anthologizer Zhang Lixiang see *ECCP,* 45–46 (under "Chang Li-hsiang"); on Lü's son Lü Baozhong see *ECCP,* 552 ("Lü Pao-chung"). Lü Liuliang originally founded this bookshop in Nanjing during 1673, and his son Lü Baozhong helped him run it: see Fisher (1974), p. 123.

57 Yan's testimony: B13/809.

58 Shen's testimony: B13/809.

59 Li Wei's reflections: B13/812.

59 Li Wei sends suspects to Beijing: B14/22–24, dated Yongzheng 6/11/22, where Li Wei states he sent off the prisoners on 6/11/6 (December 6, 1728). In a report of 6/12/11, in B14/195, Li Wei states that Colonel Huang returned to Hangzhou on Yongzheng 6/12/9.

60 Boat trip and gifts: B14/22–23 and 25. Li Wei sent two reports on this, both dated 6/11/22.

Chapter 4: In Hunan

61 Hailan's arrival: Exact times are given in B32/659–660 (*QDWZYD*, p. 9), undated report of approx 6/10/28, dispatched under the names of Hailan and Governor Wang Guodong. Hailan's only initial information on the locations of the suspects would have been from the two attachments to Yue Zhongqi's initial reports: see B13/572 for Zeng Jing, and B13/589 for the Zhangs and the location of Pengtang.

62 Hunan descriptions: Distances, *Yongxing xianzhi* (1883), *juan* 4, p. 2, shows the Yongxing county town was 70 to 80 *li* (one li equals one third of a mile) from the Anren and Ling borders, and Changsha was 560 *li* by land and 1,110 *li* by water. For mountains and maps, ibid., 2/8–15; the 20 wards are listed in ibid., 4/7–27; Wu Sangui, ibid., 25/3. For the Yongxing troops available, see ibid., 14/5, on the initial 1681 appointing of a sublieutenant (*bazong*); ibid., 23/1b, shows the fifty soldiers scattered in groups of two to four. Ibid., 35/22, shows that an officer named Hu Qigui was the sublieutenant between 1725 and 1730.

63 The Hunan plan: Undated reports from Hailan and Wang Guodong, B32/659–660 and B31/354 (*QDWZYD*, pp. 9–10b). The worries over unrest are spelled out in B31/354. (Fisher [1974], p. 224, gives a rather different chronology.) For the Miao groups in the area see *Yongxing xianzhi* (1883), 24/1. The terms for the many levels of local military personnel are nicely marshaled in Brunnert and Hagelstrom, *Political Organization,* items 749–753.

64 Magistrate Dai: *Yongxing xianzhi* (1883), 35/8, shows that his full name was Dai Wenmuo, he was a *juren* from Jining in Shandong, and took office in 1728. The same source says he won special merit for his handling of the Zeng Jing case, for which he later won promotion to a board position. For conflicting dates of his *juren* degree (1711 and 1716) and a brief biography, including his successful cases, see *Jining zhilizhou zhi, juan* 7, p. 50, and *juan* 8, part 3, p. 14.

65 The Hunan arrests: Undated report by Hailan and Wang Guodong, B32/660–663 (*QDWZYD*, pp. 11–13b); and B14/132–133 (*QDWZYD*, pp. 15b–16b), report of the Huguang governor-general Maizhu, dated Yongzheng 6/12/6 (January 5, 1729). Maizhu, from the Manchu Bordered Blue Banner, became a grand secretary in 1736. His biography is in *Qingshi gao, liejuan* 76, reprint, p. 10253.

66 Zeng Jing's first interrogation: B32/661–662 (*QDWZYD*, p. 12), in the undated report sent under the names of Hailan and Governor Wang Guodong. Fisher (1974), pp. 226–229, gives a detailed analysis of this and the other interrogations of Zeng Jing.

66 Teacher Liu: Interrogation, B32/173 (*QDWZYD*, p. 14), undated report by Hangyilu, Hailan, and Wang; Fisher (1974), p. 229. On "teacher Liu," full name Liu Zhiheng, who served as the Yongxing county education supervisor from 1713 to 1723, see *Yongxing xianzhi* (1883), 35/12b and 38/4b. Liu wrote at least two books, one on "the investigation of things" (*Gewu ji*), and one on philosophical principles (*Woji tu*).

67 Scholar Qiao: B32/660 (*QDWZYD*, p. 11), undated report by Hailan and Wang; Fisher (1974), p. 225.

69 Zhang family's testimony: B32/660–661 (*QDWZYD* pp. 11b–12), undated report by Hailan and Wang; Fisher (1974), p. 226.

71 Search of Zhang home: B32/662 (*QDWZYD*, p. 12b).

71 Emperor sends news to Yue: B14/145 (*QDWZYD*, p. 17), rescript to Yue report of 6/12/7. A fair copy of the same document is in T12/1.

72 Assignment of Hangyilu: Emperor's criticism of Governor Wang, and Wang's reply, B31/353 (*QDWZYD*, pp. 10b–11). Hangyilu's biography is in *Qingshi gao*, p. 10287.

72 Zeng Jing second interrogation: B32/172–173 (*QDWZYD*, p. 14), undated report by Hangyilu, Hailan, and Wang Guodong, including their decision to have Zeng Jing write down his confession.

73 Zeng's first written confession: The original text seems to be lost. The version of the confession presented here is drawn from the relevant passages in the *Awakening from Delusion* (*Dayi juemi lu*), where the emperor often refers back to this first confession "written in Hunan." (Zeng Jing repeated some of this material in his later Beijing-written confessions.) On Zeng's birthdate and upbringing, *DYJML*, 1/75b, 3/16b, 2/44b. On Chen Meiding, ibid., 2/33a. On Chenzhou examinations and introduction to Lü's works, ibid., 1/67b, 1/73b, 3/14b, 2/28b. On death of Kangxi, ibid., 1/55b. On migration to the west and Changsha portents, ibid., 2/2–3. On people passing his door, ibid., 3/14b.

78 Materials sent to Yongzheng in January 1729: B32/174 (*QDWZYD*, p. 15b).

78 Yue and Zhang Xi: B13/938–940 (*QDWZYD*, pp. 7b–9), dated Yongzheng 6/11/14 (December 14, 1728). For the comments on Yongzheng's drinking see B13/940, citing General Lu Chenyang as reported in the *Capital Gazette*. A biography of General Lu (with whom Yue had served in both Sichuan and Shaanxi) is in *Qingshi gao*, p. 10420.

80 Rumors of Yue's treason: These were spread by a Daoist named Li Buqi, who had reason to hate General Yue. The reports by Yue himself, and by the Xi'an garrison general, Cangseri, are in B14/61 and 63, both dated 6/11/27. Yongzheng's full commentary on the incident, and defense of Yue, is recorded in the Court Diaries, *Qijuzhu*, p. 2466, under the date 6/12/10.

80 January 1729 court letter: Cited in B32/178 (*QDWZYD*, p. 18b), undated report by Hangyilu, Hailan, and Wang.

80 Zeng Jing's third interrogation and first reference to Wang Shu: B32/178–179 (*QDWZYD*, p. 19), as reported by Hangyilu, Hailan, and Wang Guodong; Fisher (1974), p. 231. Zeng Jing recalled the exact date of Wang Shu's visit as being Yongzheng 1/4/27 (May 31, 1723). The *jinshi* examination lists show that the real Wang Shu obtained his degree in 1712, having ranked number 32 in class 2, and was posted to the Hanlin Academy.

82 Conspirators transferred to Changsha: The arrival dates of February 19 and 26 (7/1/22 and 7/1/29) are given in *QDWZYD*, p. 19. Yue Zhongqi reported that Zhang Xi left Xi'an on 6/12/20: T12/186–187, dated 7/1/13.

82 Journey to Beijing: All the details of the prisoners' transfer and Yongzheng's comment are in B32/179 (*QDWZYD*, pp. 19b–20), undated report by Hangyilu, Hailan, and Wang Guodong. Their departure date from Changsha is given as Yongzheng 7/3/10.

Chapter 5: The Phoenix Song

83 Lü's life and thought: The key source in English is Thomas Fisher's 1974 Ph.D. thesis, "Lü Liu-liang and the Tseng Ching case." See especially his Chapter 5, on Lü's "ethnic thought." Since that time there have been numerous essays in Chinese and Japanese: especially useful here has been Shao Dongfang, "Qing Shizong 'Dayi juemi lu'" (1999). Lü Baozhong's memoir of his father, Lü Liuliang, is printed as an appendix to Lü Liuliang's *Lü Wancun wenji*, vol. 2, pp. 1–15. De Bary and Lufrano, *Sources,* pp. 18–25, gives a sketch of Lü's overall thought, with extended citations.

84 Lü's anti-Manchu writings: A careful and learned analysis is presented in Fisher (1974), based on wide reading in the available sources by Lü. Though many of Lü's literary and philosophical works have survived (see Chapter 12 on Yongzheng's decision not to destroy them), some of Lü's diary entries have survived only because of the passages cited by Yongzheng. These appear in the Court Diaries under the date of 7/6/21 (*Qijuzhu*, pp. 2889–2898), which was later incorporated in the *Awakening from Delusion (Dayi juemi lu)*, pp. 4/1–4/17b. (The versions cited in the *Qing shilu* are much abbreviated.) Given the extraordinary frankness of these passages, it is hard to doubt that the emperor was citing original material.

84 Lü's friend Shen: *DYJML*, 4/4.

84 Lü on Chinese sycophants: Ibid., 4/4–5; the poem was "Ode on the Pacification of Pingliang" (in Gansu province).

85 Lü on the candy-man: Ibid., 4/3b; the passage is discussed in Fisher (1974), pp. 134–135.

85 Recluse in mountains: *DYJML*, 4/2a, and ibid., 2/33a, as cited by Zeng Jing.

85 Death of Ming fugitives: Ibid., 4/6b; a briefer version is in *Qing shilu*,

81/28b, and affirms this passage was in Lü's personal diary. A moving biography of this last Ming claimant, Chu Yu-lang, and his Christian family, is given in *ECCP*, 193–195.

86 Lü on Wu Sangui: *DYJML*, 4/5.

86 Lü on Kangxi: Ibid., 4/11b–12. The painter was Gu Yuncheng.

86 Lü's Portents: Ibid., 4/10.

87 The phoenix: Ibid., 4/10b–11a. Lü mentioned that the birds appeared in Shanxian, Henan.

87 "Song of the Pines": Lü Liuliang, *Dongzhuang shicun*, "Zhenla ninghan ji," pp. 3b–4b. A detailed analysis of the poem is given in Fisher (1974), pp. 197 and 368 n.51.

88 "Songs of the Rivers and Mountains": Lü Liuliang, *Dongzhuang shicun*, "Changchang ji," pp. 10b–12. For an understanding of this difficult poem, with its complex interwoven commentaries, I am particularly indebted to Fisher (1974), pp. 197–200, 368 n.52, quotation p. 199. For two recent analyses of such memorialization and Ming loyalism, see Jonathan Hay, "Ming Palace and Tomb," and Tobie Meyer-Fong, "Making a Place for Meaning."

89 Zeng Jing on barbarians: Cited in *DYJML*, 2/13b; 2/10; 2/15.

89 Zeng and Ming transition: Zeng's word here translated as "thugs" was the Hunanese colloquial phrase "*guanggun*," as the emperor noted sarcastically: see *DYJML*, 2/5b–7 and 2/8b. For a Qing discussion of the slang used in Yongxing county see *Yongxing xianzhi* (1883), *juan* 18, pp. 6–7.

89 Manchus as robbers to be killed: *DYJML*, 2/11b–12; 2/21b; 2/27.

90 Yan Hongkui: The original edict is in *Qijuzhu*, pp. 2866–2870, dated 7/6/14, subsequently printed in *DYJML*, 4/24–29.

90 Yan on clothing: *DYJML*, 4/26. The special hat was the "*liuhe yitong*," and Yan acknowledged Gu Yanwu's *Rizhilu* as one of his sources on the hat's history.

90 Yan and Rehe floods: *DYJML*, 4/24b–25.

91 Bloodstained figure: Ibid., 4/25.

91 Stellar conjunctions: Ibid., 4/25b.

91 Yan and anomalies of nature: Ibid., 4/26.

91 Yan and Zhang Xi's visit: Yongzheng comments specifically on this diary entry in Ibid., 4/30. The emperor also later issued his own briefer attack on Yan's student Shen: see *Qijuzhu*, pp. 2874–2876, dated 7/6/15. This was not included in *DYJML*, but a shorter version is in *Qing shilu*, 82/13b–16 (*QDWZYD*, p. 25).

91 Ortai on favorable portents: B14/149–151, Ortai's report dated Yongzheng 6/12/8 (January 7, 1729). The incident was thoroughly covered in the Veritable Records—see *Qing shilu*, 77/4b–5, 6–7b, 12, and 78/5 and 13b. An excellent analysis of the event is in Chen Hsi-yuan, "Propitious Omens," pp. 77–84. The relevance of the sightings to the Zeng Jing case is discussed in ibid., 85–92.

93 The Fujian male children's case: T12/790–792, report of Fujian governor

Gao Qizhuo, dated Yongzheng 7/4/3 (April 30, 1729). Reports on the case from other officials are in T13/120–121 and B15/825–826. The emperor discusses the case in *DYJML*, 3/45b.

94 The Manchu princes' Chinese tutors: Yongzheng and Nian, *ECCP*, 587–589; third prince and Chen, *ECCP*, 93–94; twelfth prince and Jin Hong, *QDWZYD*, p. 28; eighth prince and Ch'in Tao-jan, *ECCP*, 167, and Anonymous, "Yinsi Yintang an," pp. 4b–5; ninth prince and He Cho, *ECCP*, 284; fourteenth prince and Ts'ai Huai-hsi, *ECCP*, 931. For a discussion of the role of Manchu and other companions in Qing princes' lives, see Rawski, *The Last Emperors*, Chapter 5, "Palace Servants," especially pp. 173–174 on "banner servants" and "companions."

95 The real Wang Shu: His biographies can be found in *Qingshi gao*, p. 13887, and *Qingshi liezhuan*, 71/33b–34b.

95 Yue's comment: B13/940, in his report of 6/11/14 (*QDWZYD*, p. 9).

95 Yongzheng's comment to Ortai: B13/915; cited in Chen, "Propitious Omens," p. 82.

Chapter 6: Talking Back

97 Hunan and Wang Shu: See the discussion in Chapter 4 above.

97 December 11 report: see the discussion in Chapter 2 above. The full text is in *Qijuzhu*, pp. 2392–2413, dated 6/11/11. The *Capital Gazette* summary of the edict is mentioned by the Guangxi governor, Jin Hong, in his report dated 7/6/4, T13/325, where he notes that it concentrated on the delivery of the treasonous letter to Yue.

98 Draft to Ortai: T12/876–877, Ortai's report dated Yongzheng 7/4/15 (May 12, 1729). Ortai calls this version a "draft" (*chalu*) and offers a partial summary of the document's contents, which clearly identify it as the edict of 6/11/11. He also mentions that the version he saw had fifty-two pages. This might merely be due to the scribes' writing more words to the page than the court diarists. It could also have been a cut version. The full 6/11/11 version transcribed by the diarists Dai Han and Kaitai is the one that became the second item in the *Awakening from Delusion (DYJML)*, where it comprises leaves 14–52b of the first *juan*. Some years later, Dai Han still referred to this as the "6/11 edict" (see Anonymous, "Fan Shijie chengci an," p. 1b). Also see Chen Hsi-yuan, "Propitious Omens," p. 80, for a reference to this same document.

98 April 21 mass copying: The details of this, along with the distribution and reprinting plans, were recorded by the Guangxi governor, Jin Hong, in T13/324, and by Tian Wenjing, the Henan governor and acting director of irrigation and flood control, in B15/344. Both of them mention the emperor's edict of 7/3/24 (April 21, 1729) as being the key moment in going public with the document, and both ordered their financial commissioners (*buzheng shi*) to supervise the distribution process in their regions. For the Ming dynasty precedents for such documentary distribution in the early Ming, see the discussion in Anita Andrew, "Zhu Yuanzhang and the 'Great Warnings,'" especially Chapters 2 and 4.

99 Ortai's response: T12/876–877, dated 7/4/15.

101 Zeng's new June confession: This is summarized in the court letter sent out by Prince Yi, B15/825–826 (*QDWZYD*, pp. 25b–26), received 7/6/18 by Guangxi's governor Jin Hong; and a longer version received by Hunan's governor Wang Guodong on 7/6/10 (July 5, 1729), in B31/387–389 (*QDWZYD*, p. 28). Allowing for a courier time of fifteen days from Beijing to Changsha would place the date of the composition of the court letters at approximately June 20.

103 Critique of Yan Hongkui: The edict is given in *Qijuzhu* pp. 2866–2870, dated 7/6/14 (July 9, 1729); this version also appears (without the date) in *DYJML*, 4/24–30b. A much abbreviated version appears in *Qing shilu*, 82/11–13 (*QDWZYD*, pp. 23b–24b), where the date is given as 7/6/13 (July 8). The Rehe flood story is discussed in *QDWZYD*, p. 24; ibid., p. 23b, mocks Yan's "Ming" stance; ibid., p. 24b, casts Yan as a lick-spittler. A summary of the critique is in Fisher (1974), p. 245.

104 Critique of Yan's student Shen: The full text is in *Qijuzhu*, pp. 2874–2876, under the date 7/6/15 (July 10). The *Qing shilu*, 82/13b–16 (and *QDWZYD*, p. 25) have the same date. See also Fisher (1974), p. 246.

104 Attack on Lü Liuliang: Here there is a major disparity in recorded dates. The court diary (*Qijuzhu*, pp. 2889–2898) gives the whole lengthy attack under the date 7/6/21 (July 16, 1729). The much abbreviated version in the *Qing shilu*, 81/26–33 is dated 7/5/21 (June 17), and that date is copied in *QDWZYD*, pp. 20–23b. The full court diary version is the one used in the *DYJML*, 4/1–17, where the date is dropped. I follow the date used in the court diary. A detailed summary of the emperor's critique of Lü Liuliang is given in Fisher (1974), pp. 242–245, and 465–467, Appendix RR; in his essay "Qingdai wenzi pohai" Fisher gives full background for his argument that Yongzheng was distorting the intellectual record here, so as to scapegoat Lü Liuliang, for his own personal and political reasons.

105 On Lü and Zeng: See *QDWZYD*, p. 22.

105 On Zha and Wang: Ibid., p. 22b.

105 Lü's earlier life and loyalism: Ibid., p. 21. Fisher (1974), pp. 45–46, argues that Lü made a deliberate decision not to attend the examination. For an absorbing account of Lü's various business interests in publishing, compilations, and art sales, see Fisher, ibid., 31–35, 38–39, 94–96, 105–106.

107 Emperor comes late to Lü's work: *QDWZYD*, p. 23.

107 Requests advice on penalties: Ibid., p. 23b.

108 Guangxi governor reports on eunuchs: See Jin Hong in B15/825–826, B16/240–241, and B16/464–465 (*QDWZYD*, pp. 26–28). Yongzheng's praise of Jin

Hong is in the rescript appended to B16/465 (*QDWZYD*, p. 28). For these reports on the eunuchs, see also Fisher (1974), pp. 233–234. The investigation was sharpened by the meticulous new Hunan governor, Zhao Hongen: see T14/869–870, dated Yongzheng 7/11/7.

109 Yongzheng's follow-up edicts: These are cited in *DYJML*, 3/34 and 3/36, perhaps drawn in part from material sent along with Zhao Hongen's report dated 7/11/7 in T14/869–870.

109 Governor Wang arrests and interrogations: B31/387–389 (*QDWZYD*, pp. 28–30), undated response to questions received 7/6/10. For Dr. Chen, see B31/387; licentiate He, ibid., 387–388; geomancer Chen and the poem, ibid., 388. A fine account of these summer interrogation findings is in Fisher (1974), pp. 234–237. Yongzheng was briefly more generous to Wang in this period: Wang reports the receipt of a gift of lichees, along with a thoughtful evaluation of his financial reports, on Yongzheng 7/Run7/18 (September 10, 1729). See B31/391 (*QDWZYD*, p. 30b).

111 Yongzheng's furious reply: The first was in the form of a rescript on Wang's initial report on the geomancer, B31/389 (*QDWZYD*, p. 30); a second and far longer one, even angrier in tone, was sent as a court letter, reaching Wang on Yongzheng 7/9/6 (October 27, 1729): see B31/394–395 (*QDWZYD*, pp. 35–36).

112 New public morality supervisor: This was Li Hui, who reached Changsha on 7/5/20 (June 16, 1729), T25/870. For his and Governor Wang's undated follow-up reports, see B31/389–390, B31/391–392, B31/394–396 (*QDWZYD*, pp. 30b–31, and 35–37). Geomancer Chen on the four military men is in B31/395; on the old Daoist and the poem, B31/396. See also Fisher (1974), pp. 235–237.

113 On Wang Zhuo: Undated, unsigned memorandum in T25/671, from Ministry of Punishments, stating that Hangyilu will take Wang Zhuo to confront Zeng Jing; and T25/864, undated report from Wang Guodong stating that Wang Zhuo has been arrested and sent under guard to Beijing on August 27 (1729).

114 The real Wang Shu: The double-checking was done by Governor-general Yinjishan: see his report of Yongzheng 8/2/3, in B17/851–852 (*QDWZYD*, pp. 39–40). On the portrait, see T16/526–527 and B19/909-910. Also see Chapter 11.

Chapter 7: Summer Lessons

116 Emperor's new program: Announced in edict to Grand Secretariat, dated Yongzheng 7/6/2 (June 27, 1729), specifying Hangyilu and Hailan as the main interrogators and the reading of Yue as the initial focus. See *DYJML*, 3/13–14, for the edict and the date. The edict indicates Zeng had "already" (*congqian*) been shown some of Yue's reports, presumably as a test of this new strategy.

116 Zeng's mother and son released: Ibid., 3/17a.

116 Zeng's reply on Yue: Ibid., 3/14b–17b. In several cases, Zeng's responses to

his Beijing interrogators were neatly transcribed, and the fair copies kept at the court. For this one, see B30/957–962.

118 Provincial reports: Yongzheng specified that "several hundred" be perused by Zeng. See his brief edict, undated, in *DYJML*, 3/24a.

119 Zeng's response on provincial reports: *DYJML*, 3/24–27. Fair copy, B30/963–967. For Yongzheng's disciplined work habits, see Silas Wu, *Communication and Control.*

120 The legal cases: Hangyilu, introducing this assignment, mentions that the cases all date from the eleventh day, fourth lunar month, of the current year or after—i.e., after May 8, 1729. *DYJML*, 3/5. The court diary for that and many other dates shows how thoroughly Yongzheng and his senior officials did indeed review troublesome cases.

123 Zeng on the cases: *DYJML*, 3/6b–8. He handled each one sequentially, following up on the brief synopses offered by Hangyilu. His reflections on rumor and random gossip came at the end of his response, ibid., 3/10.

124 Bans on cattle slaughter and gambling: *Qing shilu*, 82/22b, dated 7/6/23 (July 18, 1729).

124 Minting of coins: Emperor's analysis, *DYJML*, 2/41b–44. On the shifting metallic ratios in Qing and earlier coinage, and the reasons for them, see Richard von Glahn, *Fountain of Fortune,* especially pp. 147, 208–209.

125 Zeng's reply: *DYJML*, 2/44b–45b. His remarks on the "community compact" (*xiangyue*) are in ibid., 2/46a. For the fair copy, see B30/951–957.

126 Economic dialogue: On Hunan hardships, *DYJML*, 3/1–3. On grain and silver transfers, ibid., 3/3b–4b. On the worst sufferers, ibid., 1/60. There is no evidence in the Yongxing gazetteer that this was a bad time for Zeng Jing's own home region; indeed, 1724 is listed there as a particularly prosperous year. See *Yongxing xianzhi* (1883), *juan* 53, p. 3.

126 The Lu Shengnan case: Main edict, *Qing shilu*, 83/1b–15, dated Yongzheng 7/7/3 (July 28, 1729). Manchu and Mongol models, ibid., 83/2b; parallels to Lü Liuliang and Zeng Jing cases, ibid., 83/5; differences in upbringing from Zeng, ibid., 83/14b.

127 Death sentence for Lu Shengnan: Decided on, 83/19b–20; carried out, ibid., 89/30b–31 (February 9, 1730).

128 November 2 edict: *Qijuzhu*, pp. 3128–3134, dated Yongzheng 7/9/12, and *DYJML*, 1/1–13 (without the date). An abbreviated version is in *QDWZYD*, pp. 31–35, and in *Qing shilu*, 86/8a–18. For the opening quotations from the "Shujing" (classic of documents), see Legge, "The Shoo King," Part 5, book 17, Chapter 4, p. 490, and *Qing shilu*, 86/8–9; bad influence of Lü Liuliang and Yan on Zeng's thinking, *Qing shilu*, 86/9b; on irrelevance of distinctions based on geographical origin, ibid., 86/9b–11b; new types of recluses, ibid., 86/12; horrors and maiming of civil conflict, ibid., 86/13; invokers of the Ming, ibid., 86/13b–14; Confucius on the "Yi and Di having their rulers" (from *Analects* 3:5), ibid., 86/14b; for the peroration and wide distribution of this edict to the countryside, ibid., 86/18. The *Donghua lu,* 15/41b, under the date of 7/9/12, correctly identifies this edict with the *DYJML,* though the publication only came several months later.

130 November 19 edict: Cited as the preamble to their final report by the senior officials, and clearly dated 7/9/29 (November 19, 1729), in B16/852. See also *Qijuzhu,* pp. 3166–3167.

131 November 26 report: B16/852–855 (with the appended name list in ibid., 855–860), dated 7/10/6. The *Qijuzhu,* p. 3180, gives an abbreviated version of this report as a preamble to the edict of 7/10/7 (November 27), and a fuller version as the preamble to the edict of 7/10/8 (ibid., p. 3186). The entire version is in the *DYJML,* 3/28–31b, although there the date is dropped.

Chapter 8: The Pardon

133 Yongzheng's November 27 edict: I accept as definitive the version of this edict entered in the Court Diaries (*Qijuzhu,* pp. 3180–3181), and dated Yongzheng 7/10/7 (November 27, 1729); this matches the version printed in *QDWZYD,* pp. 38b–39, from a manuscript copy at Peking University. These both contain the passage on Wu Sangui (referred to there by the name of his 1673 uprising, the "Sanfan"). That reference is dropped, and other changes made, in the version printed in the Veritable Records (*Qing shilu,* 87/4b–6), also transcribed in *QDWZYD,* pp. 37b–38. These variant versions are dated 7/10/6 (November 26).

134 Li Fu's presence: Mentioned in all three versions, above. Li Fu's remarkably contentious career is described in *ECCP,* 455–457, and in *Qingshi gao,* pp. 10321–10325. His role at the death of Yintang is elaborated on in Anonymous, "Yinsi Yintang an."

134 Wang Suzheng's anger: B17/680, dated Yongzheng 8/1/13 (March 1, 1730), referring back to an imperial rebuke of 7/11/24 (January 12, 1730) concerning a still earlier incident.

135 Subprefect Zhu: Zhu Zhenji, case reported by the Guangdong financial commissioner, Wang Shijun, T14/390, dated 7/9/15. (His follow-up report on Zhu's death sentence in B19/281 is dated 8/10/11.) According to a reprise on the whole Zhu case by the Guangdong governor-general, Hao Yulin (T17/395-397, dated 8/12/20), Zhu was initially only beaten, since that was the precedent set by Governor-general Li Wei in the Zhang Changyan case.

135 Subdirector Zhang: Zhang Changyan case, reported by the acting Zhejiang financial commissioner, Cheng Yuanzhang, undated, B33/142, datable on internal evidence to Yongzheng seventh year, tenth month (i.e., late November or early December 1729). On Zhang's beating see previous note.

135 Yongzheng's November 28 edict: this is entered in the court diary on that

date, 7/10/8 (*Qijuzhu,* pp. 3186–3196), and is printed in *DYJML,* 3/31b–49b. The emperor cites both Guangxi's governor Jin Hong and Hunan's governor Zhao Hongen as his sources on the eunuchs. Zhao was only appointed Hunan governor in Yongzheng 7/9/2 (October 23, 1729), and his earliest extant report on the exiles is dated 7/11/7 (December 26, 1729), see B17/167. He had however sent a joint report on some other matters with Huguang's governor-general Maizhu on 7/9/19 (see B16/650), and perhaps a now lost report of theirs dealt with eunuchs.

136 Contents of the November 28 edict: On the case's strangeness, *DYJML,* 3/31b–32; Lü's influence on Zeng, ibid., 3/33; eunuchs on the road and story of "fourteen" to "four," ibid., 3/34b; on Yinti in west and his troops, ibid., 3/37–41; other Hunan rumors, ibid., 3/42b–43b; Zeng Jing helps lead Yongzheng to truth, ibid., 3/45b; pardon for Zeng makes sense, ibid., 3/47a; crime and change, ibid., 3/47b; Zeng's confessions, ibid., 3/48; emperor's family never to change the verdict to spare Zeng, ibid., 3/49b; punishments for Lü and others, ibid., 3/49b.

139 The two follow-up edicts: See *Qijuzhu,* pp. 3209–3214 (dated 7/10/12), and 3216–3218 (dated 7/10/13); both were printed (undated) in *DYJML,* 3/50–59b and 3/60–64b. On emperor and tenth brother's eunuch, see ibid., 3/61; Yongzheng weeps as he writes, ibid., 3/62b and 3/64b.

140 Prince Yi's final petition: The Court Diaries date this to 7/10/15 (see *Qijuzhu,* pp. 3224–3225). The version in *DYJML,* 3/64b–67b, undated, includes a long preamble not in the Court Diaries, and adds the name of Prince Yi (which is also not in the Diaries).

141 The petition rejected: This text is identical in the Court Diaries (*Qijuzhu,* p. 3225) and the *DYJML,* 3/67b–68. The *Donghua lu* (15/47) gives the whole or part of many of these texts, but confusingly dates them all 7/10/8.

141 Zhuge Jisheng: Though the original document seems not to have survived, it can be fully reconstructed from Tang Sungao's critique of Zhuge Jisheng, as discussed and forwarded to Yongzheng by the Huguang censor, Tang Jizu, B17/925–931, dated 8/2/13; and by Governor-general Maizhu, B17/671–672, dated 8/1/10.

142 Praise for four Canton scholars: *Qing shilu,* 89/14b.

143 Confucian temple portents: Discussed in *Qing shilu,* 89/22–24. Yue Jun's promotion was announced next day, ibid., 89/24.

143 Zeng Jing quizzed on Confucian portents: *DYJML,* 3/64–66b.

144 *My Return to the Good*: Zeng Jing's "Guiren shuo," included in *DYJML,* 4/31b–45.

145 Date of the *Awakening:* In his question to Zeng Jing, Yongzheng specifically mentions that the restoration supervisor Liu Bao reported that the auspicious portents were sighted on 7/11/26 (January 14, 1730). The Court Diaries state that Yongzheng discussed this report and gave his own response on January 31, 1730 (7/12/13): see *Qijuzhu,* pp. 3354–3356. As far as I can ascertain, this is the latest date for an incident specifically referred to in the *Awakening from Delusion,* and strongly suggests that final editing of the book began during February. On the wood blocks and distribution, see the discussion in Chapter 10.

145 Never met face-to-face: See the emperor's second interlinear comment in Li Wei's report of 8/3/10 (T15/842), that "it seemed inappropriate for me ever to see Zeng Jing face-to-face" (*"dan Zeng Jing zhen weibian jianmian"*).

145 Parting gifts for Zeng: As reported by Zeng Jing in his memorandum of 8/6/2 to the Hunan governor, B18/1014, and shown to his friends back in Yong-xing.

145 Date Zeng Jing departs: See the first note in Chapter 9 for this mid-February date.

Chapter 9: The Solitary Bell

147 Zeng leaves Beijing: In his report dated 8/2/3 (March 21, 1730), B17/851–852 (*QDWZYD,* pp. 39–40), Yinjishan stated that he met Zeng Jing and Hangyilu "on the Huaian road." According to another of his reports of the same date, in B17/848, it was on 8/1/11 (February 27, 1730) that he left Qingjiang to return to Suzhou. Thus he must have met up with Zeng Jing "on the Huaian road" in the last two days of February. This would place Zeng Jing's departure from Beijing in the third week of February, 1730. On 8/1/23 (March 11), Zeng Jing was in Hangzhou with Governor-general Li Wei: see Li Wei's report of 8/2/8 in B17/894–895, *QDWZYD,* p. 40.

147 Hangyilu: His assignment to escort Zeng Jing is recorded by both Yinjishan and Li Wei, see note above.

149 Yinjishan's report: Dated 8/2/3, B17/851–852 (*QDWZYD,* pp. 39–40). Yinjishan dutifully reported the dream, as described to him by Hangyilu.

149 Li Wei on Zeng Jing: T15/842, report of 8/3/10, supplementing report of 8/2/8.

150 Zeng leaves Hangzhou: Li Wei report of 8/2/8 (*QDWZYD,* p. 40b), and Zeng Jing memorandum of 8/6/2 cited above.

150 Maizhu on Tang Sungao: B17/671–672 (dated 8/1/10, February 26, 1730), citing reports from the magistrate who employed Tang. A biography of Maizhu is in *Qingshi gao,* p. 10523. He was named a grand secretary in 1735. An analysis of the Tang case is given in Wang Fansen, "Cong Zeng Jing an," pp. 10–11.

151 Secretary Tang's manuscript: Though the copy of Tang's manuscript forwarded by Maizhu has not survived, another copy of the same document reached the hands of a circuit censor in western Hunan, who forwarded it to the emperor. See Tang Jizu, B17/928–931, enclosure with report of 8/2/13 (March 31, 1730). It is that copy that is cited here.

151 As "solitary bell": B17/928; emperor misled over Lü Liuliang, ibid., p. 929;

contempt for Zhuge's argument, ibid., 929; wrongful emphasis on Lü's personal writings, ibid., 930; horror of demands for Lü's debasement, ibid., 930; Tang's wish to confront Zhuge in Beijing, ibid., 930; Tang Sungao as lone heroic voice, ibid., 931.

155 Secretary Tang's historical references: For Zhong Shanfu, see Watson, *Tso-chuan*, p. 77, and Arthur Waley and Joseph Allen, *Book of Songs*, p. 276. On Wei Zheng's fame as a courageous remonstrator, see Howard Wechsler, *Mirror to the Son of Heaven.*

156 Emperor on killing Tang: The emperor's tough words appear in B17/672, as the rescript to Maizhu's report of 8/1/10. The emperor wrote this so swiftly that it is hard to decipher all the characters, but the main instructions are unambiguous.

157 Maizhu on Tang's death: B18/188, an eight-line report, dated 8/3/17 (May 3, 1730).

157 Censor Tang's report: By mid-April at the latest, Yongzheng would have received Tang Jizu's report of March 31, enclosing the second full copy of Tang Sungao's manifesto (see B17/928–931, enclosure with report dated 8/2/13). The emperor's follow-up comment appears in a rescript to Maizhu's report dated 8/3/17 (May 3, 1730), B18/188. Tang was from Jiangdu, Yangzhou, and a *jinshi* of 1721. His biography is in *Qingshi gao*, p. 10434.

Chapter 10: Coauthors

159 April 4 completion: The exact date on which the finishing of the blocks was announced at court is given as Yongzheng 8/2/17 (April 4, 1730) in the report of the Fujian area commander Chu Youde; see *Ming Ch'ing Tang-an*, vol. A44, document 83, p. 5, Section 1, lower left panel. The same date can be found in other reports of receipt of the *DYJML*, printed in the same source.

159 Size of the book: The total of 509 pages reflects a Western mode of calculation. Chinese books were printed in double leaves, folded over at the center, thus the Chinese count is 255 double leaves, divided as follows: Section 1, 76 double leaves; Section 2, 66 double leaves; Section 3, 68 double leaves; Section 4, 45 double leaves.

159 Foreword to the *Awakening:* For the original of this November 2 edict, printed in *DYJML*, 1/1–13, see the Court Diaries, *Qijuzhu*, pp. 3128–3134, under the date of 7/9/12. A shorter version of this edict appears in the Veritable Records, *Qing shilu*, 86/8–18. This shorter version is the one transcribed in QDWZYD, pp. 31–35. (As in virtually every case, the date is dropped in the *DYJML* version.) For a high valuation of the argumentation to be found in this edict, see Fisher (1974), pp. 270–271: "Rarely in Chinese history has there been a more cogent statement of culturalism as an ideology than Yung-cheng's opening edict of the *Ta-I chueh-mi lu.*" See ibid., pp. 271–275, for Fisher's detailed summation of Yongzheng's arguments on race and rulership. A more recent analysis is Shao Dongfang, "Qing Shi-zong Dayi juemi lu," especially Part 2, on the distinctions between "*hua*" and "*yi.*" See also Crossley, *Translucent Mirror,* pp. 255–258. Crossley sees two "voices" at work in these discussions: one "philosophical," and one representing the early Manchu khanates; Grand Secretary Zhu Shi, whom she believes to be "the primary writer on behalf of the Yongzheng emperor" (p. 257), was an expert in both traditions; he also edited the Veritable Records of both Kangxi's and Yongzheng's reigns. See his biography in *ECCP,* pp. 188–189 ("Chu Shih").

160 Second part of Section 1: *DYJML,* 1/14–53b; this was the eighty-three-page rebuttal of Zeng Jing's letter, first issued in 6/11/11 (December 11, 1728), in the Court Diaries (*Qijuzhu*), pp. 2392–2413. In the *DYJML* it fills seventy-seven pages.

160 Zeng's responses to Yongzheng: These fill *DYJML,* 1/53–2/66. Many of these responses are discussed in Chapter 7.

161 Zeng's responses to Hangyilu: *DYJML,* 3/1–27.

161 Machinations at court: These match up with the original Court Diaries (*Qijuzhu,* abbreviated here as *QJZ*) as follows: *DYJML,* 3/28–31b is *QJZ* pp. 3180–3181; *DYJML* 3/31b–49b is *QJZ* pp. 3186–3196; *DYJML* 3/50–59b is *QJZ* pp. 3209–3214; *DYJML* 3/60–64b is *QJZ* pp. 3216–3218; *DYJML* 3/64b–68 is *QJZ* pp. 3224–3225.

161 On Lü and Yan: *DYJML,* 4/1–17b and 4/24–30b. These are also in the *Qijuzhu:* see pp. 2866–2870 for Yan Hongkui, dated 7/6/14; pp. 2889–2898 for Lü Liuliang, dated 7/6/21.

162 *Return to the Good*: "Guiren shuo." *DYJML,* 4/31b–45. Emperor's introduction, ibid., 4/31. Zeng's name, "Jing," appears at the top of the third column from the end of the essay.

163 "Glibness": the Chinese term is "*ning.*" See Legge, "Confucian Analects," Book 11, Chapter 24, Sections 1–4, p. 246. Also in *DYJML,* 1/12b.

163 Autobiographical passages: We can sometimes see how these draw on Zeng's own earlier writings, on his three oral Hunan confessions, and on his written Hunan confession, though this is not always possible. Fair copies of many of the Beijing confessions later incorporated in the *DYJML* are preserved in B30/924–974, but are all undated.

163 Zeng's in-laws the Chens: *DYJML,* 2/29 and 2/33.

165 Zeng and the present age: Lü Liuliang as source, *DYJML,* 2/11; individual virtue, ibid., 1/53, 1/54b–55, 1/55b–56; inequalities, ibid., 1/58b–60. Zeng also pointed out how the examination system had grown corrupted by careerism and superficiality, ibid., 2/17b–20.

165 "Well-field" land system: "*Jingtian,*" *DYJML,* 1/73b–74b; and Sichuan migration, ibid., 2/2–3. For an evaluation of these institutions by Huang Zongxi, once a close friend of Lü Liuliang, see Wm. Theodore de Bary, *Waiting for the Dawn,* pp. 43–48, 128–138.

165 Decentralization: *"Fengjian," DYJML,* 2/24b, responding to Yongzheng's comments in ibid., 2/21b–24. See also de Bary, *Waiting for the Dawn,* pp. 125–127, and Fisher (1974), pp. 164–169.

166 Community covenants: The *"xiangyue." DYJML,* 2/39b–42b. For careful analyses of the history and reality of such compacts see Monika Ubelhor, "Community Compact"; Robert Hymes, "Lu Chiu-yuan, Academies," pp. 440–451; Kandice Hauf, "The Community Covenant." The passages quoted from Zeng Jing are in *DYJML,* 2/39b–40, on the *"lantian"* and Zhu Xi models; and ibid., 2/40–41, for current implementation. (My special thanks to Shee-yi Liu for help with these passages.) Zeng's discussions on them are preserved also in B30/949–951.

168 Guan Zhong on race: The debate is in *DYJML,* 2/10b–11b. The key classical passages on Guan Zhong can all be found in Legge, "Confucian Analects," pp. 162–163 (Book 3, Chapter 22, Sections 1–3); p. 278 (Book 14, Chapter 10, Section 3); pp. 281–282 (Book 14, Chapter 17, Sections 1–2); and p. 282 (Book 14, Chapter 18, Sections 1–3) on the hair and clothes. The Guan Zhong debate between Yongzheng and Zeng Jing has intrigued many scholars: see Fisher (1974), pp. 189–196; Crossley, pp. 248–253; and the general discussions in Wang Fansen, "Cong Zeng Jing an"; and Shao Dongfang, "Qing Shizong."

171 "Doctrine of the mean" argument: *DYJML,* 2/13b–14; Legge, "Doctrine of the Mean," Chapter 1, Section 5, p. 385.

171 The sixty-first hexagram: "inner trust" (*zhongfu*). The discussion is in *DYJML,* 2/13b–15. For analyses of this hexagram and the commentaries on it, see Richard Wilhelm, *The I Ching,* pp. 235–239 and 698–703; and Richard Lynn, *Classic of Changes,* pp. 523–529. For the two seventh- and twelfth-century commentaries cited here, see Lynn, *Classic of Changes,* p. 528 n.4.

173 Blocks ready: We do not know when the carving began, but the completion date of Yongzheng 8/2/17 (April 4, 1730) is given in several documents preserved in the *Ming-Ch'inq Tang-an:* see, for example, A44–68 (third leaf); A44–83 (third leaf). (I am especially grateful to Professor Liu Cheng-yun, of the Academia Sinica, Taipei, for these and other references.) The same documents show that detailed distribution plans were ready by 8/2/23 (April 10, 1730). *Ming-Ch'ing Tang-an,* A44–83 (pp. 5–2 and 5–3), gives the full roster of officials to whom the *Awakening* was to be sent.

174 First recipients: Area Garrison Commander Yue Hanqi, of the Yuezhou region in Shandong, *Ming-Ch'ing Tang-an,* A43–99, received 8/3/11, reported 8/5/1; General Yue, *QDWZYD,* p. 40b, received 8/3/19, reported 8/3/26; Guangdong's commander Li Weiyang, *Ming-Ch'ing Tang-an,* A43–112, received 8/4/19, reported 8/5/8; Hunan's governor Zhao Hongen, B18/792, receipt date illegible, reported 8/5/26; damaged Hunan copies, computer reference to unpublished Academia Sinica file, #091947, dated 8/5/21.

174 Foreword on compulsory study: These are the closing sentences of the foreword, *DYJML*, 1/13. The same sentences were in the original November 2 edict (*Qijuzhu*, p. 3134), though there they lacked the same force, given the absence at that time of any distribution mechanism. There are echoes here of the founding Ming emperor's distribution of certain transcripts to every school in the 1390s. Those texts were made the basis for special exams in the Ming (193,400 students were reported to have taken such exams in 1397), and the Ming ruler used familiarity with the books as a determinant of loyalty to the dynasty. The books were even used as travel passes for those from the countryside informing on their fellows. See Anita Andrew, "Zhu Yuanzhang and the 'Great Warnings,'" especially pp. 155–156, 164, 210.

175 Taiwan copies: B19/336, received 8/10/18, reported 8/10/24.

Chapter 11: The Source

177 Zeng Jing's return: The instructions Hangyilu relayed to them from the emperor are quoted by the Hunan governor, Zhao Hongen, and Morality Supervisor Li Hui in their joint report of 8/2/4 (March 22, 1730), T15/635. In T16/134, report of 8/4/3, Governor Zhao states that Zeng reached Changsha on 8/2/25 (April 12, 1730).

178 Zeng and mother's funeral: The exact dates are given by Zeng Jing in the memorandum he wrote for Governor Zhao and Li Hui on Yongzheng 8/6/2 (July 16, 1730), preserved in B18/1014–1015.

178 Zeng's hunt for the fake Wang Shu: This account follows Zeng Jing's own in B18/1014–1015 (see previous note), which also gives all the dates (in lunar calendar form), transposed here into their Western equivalents. The survival of this document, perhaps the most remarkable one in the whole record of the case, is due to Governor Zhao Hongen of Hunan, who enclosed it along with his own report of 8/7/15 (August 28, 1730), B18/1013–1014.

181 Five bits of paper: These also have survived, since Governor Zhao sent them to the emperor along with Zeng's memorandum; they can be seen in B18/1018–1019.

182 Zeng returns to Changsha: Again, the dates are given by Zeng Jing himself, in a memo written to the morality supervisor: see B30/435, dated "sixth month," with an appended notation that it was received at the official's office on 8/6/13 (July 27, 1730). The journey from Yongxing to Changsha took Zeng ten days.

183 Governor Zhao's first report: B18/1013–1014, dated 8/7/15 (August 28, 1730).

183 Death of Prince Yi: *Qing shilu*, 94/2b–14b. On Prince Yi's political and economic roles, see the detailed account in Beatrice Bartlett, *Monarchs and Ministers*, pp. 71–79.

183 Yongzheng's comments: In a court letter to governor Zhao forwarded by Grand Secretary Marsai, B19/61–62, dated 8/8/19 (September 30, 1730). Zhao received the court letter on 8/9/16 (October 27, 1730); see B19/906–908.

183 Finding the fake Wang Shu: All the follow-up interrogations by Governor Zhao and his colleagues are summarized in a massive report by Zhao, dated 9/1/28 (March 6, 1731), B19/908–919.

183 Calligrapher Zeng Shengren: B19/908–909.

185 The priest's tale: B19/909.

186 The local scholars: B19/909–911.

186 Zeng Jing rechecked: B19/911.

186 At Daling Mountain: B19/911.

187 The coffin: B19/912.

188 The attendant, Luo: B19/915–917. Yongzheng 2/2/2 was equivalent to February 25, 1724. The fake Wang Shu died on 2/3/20 (April 13, 1724), according to Governor Zhao, B19/907. The moment of the fake Wang Shu's death is recounted by Luo in B19/917.

Chapter 12: Sounds of Discord

191 Drowning Zeng Jing: Governor Zhao saw the placard on 8/8/11 and reported it to the emperor on 8/8/19 (September 3, 1730); see B19/207–208 (*QDWZYD*, p. 44).

192 One thousand ounces of silver: Marsai's court letter quoted and acknowledged by Governor Zhao in his report of 8/10/28 (December 7, 1730), T17/127 (also B19/363). Zhao mentioned that the "local funds" from which the money would be drawn were the recently instituted "*yanglian*," or "nourish honesty," moneys collected from local taxes. On the origins of the "*yanglian*" reforms see Madeleine Zelin, *The Magistrate's Tael*, pp. 95–100. Zeng's own letter of thanks, dated simply "eighth year, ninth month," is in T17/128–129. Zhao and Li Hui had noted Zeng's excessive language in their report of 8/6/20 (August 3, 1730), B30/433–434. For the restrictions of Zeng's movements see Zhao and Li, T18/287, dated 9/5/27 (also B20/623).

193 General Yue's report on the *Awakening*: Received 8/3/19, report dated 8/3/26 (May 12, 1730), B18/266–268 (*QDWZYD*, pp. 40b–42).

194 Zhang Xi's version: *DYJML*, 3/17b–18b. The phrase rendered "a fine fellow indeed" is "*hao Hanzi.*" For Qu Dajun's life, see *ECCP* 201–203 ("Ch'ü Ta-chun"). In the initial reports on Qu there was some muddle over the characters for his alternate name, Qu Wenshan, as the Guangdong governor pointed out: B19/281–283. See also Wang Fansen, "Cong Zeng Jing an," 13–14.

196 Yue's response: See especially B18/268, for Yue's plaints and the emperor's belief he has exaggerated the matter. The subsequent slide in Yue's career is charted in *ECCP* 958 and in Yue's biography in *Qingshi gao*, p. 10372.

196 Qu Minghong: Report by the acting Guangdong governor, Futai, B19/315–317, dated 8/19/19; *ECCP*, p. 202; a later report from Governor-general Shi Yulin is in B19/382.

197 Chen Quan case: As reported by Li Wei, B18/874–875 (*QDWZYD*, pp. 42–43), dated 8/6/6 (July 20, 1730).

198 Xu Jun's fate: Report by Governor Yinjishan of Jiangsu, B18/829, dated 8/6/13 (July 27, 1730). Xu was executed later that year, *Qing shilu*, 99/2. For the examination brilliance of the Xu family, see *ECCP*, pp. 310–312, under "Hsü Ch'ien-hsueh."

199 "Lü family orphan": See Li Wei's report of 8/7/25 (September 7, 1730, B18/1071–1072) on the members of the Lü family he has tracked down. The emperor's anxious question on the "orphan" is in B18/1072. In that same report, Li Wei mentions that he and the emperor talked about this problem together the previous year, when Li Wei had an imperial audience in Beijing.

200 Yongzheng seeks those with special powers: A fine account of this quest is in Silas H. L. Wu, "History and Legend," pp. 1233–1238, from which these examples are drawn. The Veritable Records also have numerous accounts of unusual promotions (or disgrace) for those claiming special healing powers, bunched between late 1730 and early 1731: see, for example, *Qing shilu*, pp. 98/14b–16b, 99/20, 102/13.

201 January 1731 judgment: *Qing shilu*, 101/7 (*QDWZYD*, p. 45), dated 8/12/19 (January 16, 1731).

201 Emperor consults with students: *Qing shilu*, 101/8 (*QDWZYD*, p. 45). Not until Yongzheng 10/12/12 (January 27, 1733) did the emperor bring this process of consultation to a close. Fisher (1974), pp. 388–389 n.111, notes that he has seen a Hubei report dated June 5, 1731, giving the results of the students' responses in that province. But see also the case of Qi Zhouhua discussed in the next note.

202 The muzzling of Qi: For Qi Zhouhua, see especially the analysis in Wang Fansen, "Cong Zeng Jing an," pp. 14–16, and his analysis there of Qi's account of his experiences. See also *ECCP*, pp. 123–125 ("Ch'i Chou-hua"). For Li Wei and Wang Guodong in the ministry, see *Qingshi* tables, pp. 2620–2621.

204 The Shanxi placard: The graphic account, including the poem and the text, is in a report by Governor Gioro Shilin of Shanxi, dated Yongzheng 9/2/10, T17/614–615 (also B19/1003). The singing sound of the double-edged sword is an image drawn from a Han dynasty history, while the bristling hair under the cap is a central motif in Sima Qian's famous depiction of the unsuccessful assassin Jing Ke.

205 Emperor's comment: T17/615.

206 Shanxi case solved: Report by the Shanxi judicial commissioner, Song Yun, dated 9/2/25 (April 1, 1731), B20/27–28.

206 Fan in Fujian: The reports of the Fujian officials investigating the Fan Shijie case, dated Yongzheng 8/11/– and 9/6/13, are bunched together in B20/715–723. Fan's own essay, written in September 1730, is printed in its entirety in *Wenxian congbian*, vol. 7, pp. 3–5b, under the title "Fan Shijie yuancheng" (Fan Shijie's original draft essay). On the Fan case in general, see Wang Fansen, "Cong Zeng Jing an," p. 12.

207 Four military men: That the hunt continued steadily can be seen in reports from Guangdong, such as Governor Futai's of 8/3/17 (T15/910–912), and General Miao Hong's of 8/4/28 (T16/335–336).

Chapter 13: Spreading the Word

209 Task forces for the west and northwest: See *Qing shilu*, 104/14b–15, dated Yongzheng 9/3/20.

210 Yue criticized: For the progression of Yongzheng's comments see *Qing shilu*, 99/3b (8/10/5) for audience; 99/3b–4 (8/10/6) on Muslims; 100/13b–14b (8/11/17) on Yanan area redistricting; 101/3 (8/12/8) on Yue's unsung return; 103/4b (9/2/7) Hangyilu summoned back to Beijing; 103/16b–18 (9/2/20) on Yongzheng's sixteen-point critique. A careful analysis of the correspondence between Yongzheng and Yue in 1728–1730 about the western campaigns, including the emperor's writing of long and affectionate personal letters to Yue that are "informal, rambling, and spontaneous," is given in Bartlett, *Monarchs and Ministers*, pp. 56–63 (quotation, p. 60). That relationship later soured. A central theme of her book is the interconnection between the complex logistics of these campaigns, with the need for secrecy, and the development of what later became the Grand Council.

210 Balancing act: Postearthquake reassurances, *Qing shilu*, 97/12 (8/8/20); recall of Shaanxi troops from Tibet, ibid., 103/8 (9/2/12).

211 Supplies and procurement: Ibid., 103/18–19 (9/2/22).

211 Task force members: Ibid., 104/14b–15 (9/3/20).

212 Task force leaders: Ibid., 105/13 (9/4/8). On Shi Yizhi, see *ECCP*, 650–651 ("Shih I-chih"). Zheng Chanbao appears in *Qingshi*, pp. 1497 and 1510.

212 Two scholars: Sun Renlong and Setungge, both listed in the *jinshi* tables for 1730. (Neither one's name appears in the main Qing biographical listings.)

213 Yongzheng's rationale: *Qing shilu*, 105/5b–13; ibid., 7–8, on Galdan and Zungars; ibid., 11b, on Shaanxi taxes; ibid., 12, on eighth and fourteenth brothers, Nian Gengyao, and their cultic followers.

214 Special audience: The key source for this is a later report from one of the task force leaders, Zheng Chanbao, B22/37 (fair copy in T19/560), dated 10/3/19, which states that this audience was held on Yongzheng 9/5/4 (i.e., June 8, 1731). In B20/889 (fair copy in T18/535), dated 9/7/11, Zheng specifically mentions the lectures on the *Awakening from Delusion*. More information on the same audience, and the emperor's decision to include Zhang Xi in the group, is given by another task force leader, Shi Yizhi, in his report of 10/2/3, B21/796–797 (fair copy T19/395–396). In that report, Shi also mentions the retainer secretly instructed to monitor Zhang Xi.

214 Division of the territory: Zheng Chanbao report of 9/7/11 (August 13, 1731), B20/888–889.

215 Isolated regions: Zheng Chanbao report of 9/9/24 (B21/241–242), mentions arrival at Yanan on 9/6/12 (July 15, 1731) and readings of the *Awakening from Delusion* to "not less than several thousand people."

215 Zheng's Gansu report: B21/237–239, dated 9/9/24 (fair copy, T18/847–848), mentions an October 22 assemblage of "not less than ten thousand" to hear the edicts and the *Awakening* read.

216 Jiuquan report: T19/111–112, dated 9/11/5 (December 3, 1731), report from acting Shaanxi governor-general, Chalanga. The report is cosigned by two censorial officials (Erge and Kong Yupu) who were also present. (During the Qing, this border town was also named Suzhou [using the character "*su*" of Gansu province.]) This report by Chalanga is the only one to name any of the accompanying *jinshi* scholars.

216 Return to Lanzhou: Zheng Chanbao report, B21/690–691, dated 10/1/18 (February 13, 1732). In this report, Zeng also mentions the Jiuquan meetings, the *Awakening*, Chalanga, and the audiences even farther west.

216 Orders for task force leaders: These instructions are repeated by Zheng Chanbao in his report of 10/3/19, B22/37.

217 Zhang Xi's contrition: As reported by Shi Yizhi, T19/395–396, dated 10/2/3 (March 10, 1732). The emperor's comment is written at the end of the same report, and was relayed to the Hunan governor, Zhao Hongen. Zhao repeated the emperor's words in his own report, T19/841 (see next note).

218 Zhang's return: Governor Zhao reported that Zhang reached Changsha on May 7, 1732, and summarized the details of Zhang's return to Anren county. See T19/841, report by Zhao dated Yongzheng 10/Fifth intercalary month/7 (June 28, 1732).

218 Refutation of Lü Liuliang's writings: The opening statement by the editor-in-chief, Zhu Shi, to the *Bo Lü Liuliang*, vol. 1, second prefatory section, p. 1, says that Gu floated his suggestion on Yongzheng 9/3/25 (May 1, 1731). The *jinshi* tables show Gu Chengtian had placed eleventh in the second class of the 1730 *jinshi* examination, and had at once been appointed to the Hanlin Academy. See also *Qingshi,* p. 1315, Section 4. For the story of Gu's good fortune, see Fisher (1974), pp. 248 and 388 n.110.

219 The rebuttal group: Besides Gu, the others were Wu Longying, eleventh in second class, *jinshi* examination of 1724, admitted to the Hanlin Academy; Cao Yishi (a renowned poet, whose four daughters were also fine poets, see *ECCP*, 545, "Ts'ao I-shih"), eighty-fifth in second class, 1730, admitted to the Hanlin Academy; and the famous scholar Fang Bao, *ECCP*, 235 ("Fang Pao"). The nominal editor-in-chief was Grand Secretary Zhu Shi (*ECCP*, pp. 188–189), who was also a tutor to Yongzheng's favorite son, the future Emperor Qianlong: on the close relationship between the two, see Kahn, *Monarchy,* pp. 159–163. A fascinating sardonic poem by Lü Liuliang, titled "The Real Chin-shih," is discussed in Fisher (1974), pp. 206–211. Fisher, ibid., pp. 253–255, concludes that despite its editors' qualifications, the *Bo Lü Liuliang* is intellectually unimpressive.

221 Rebuttal draft: The rebuttal volumes can be read alongside the original volumes of Lü Liuliang's own commentaries on the Four Books, *Lü Wancun xiansheng sishu jiangyi,* which moved methodically through each of the books, taking selected sentences in sequence. (Some of the passages explored in Lü's original were ignored by the rebuttal group.) The Guan Zhong passage appears in the rebuttal volume of *Analects,* Section 2, pp. 34b–35b; the Mencius passages on the *"jingtian"* and *"fengjian"* systems appear in the rebuttal volume under Book of Mencius, Section 1, pp. 3b–5, and section 2a, pp. 22b–24, respectively. On the critical process as a whole, see Fisher (1974), pp. 253–255. Samples of Lü's commentaries on the Four Books, including his remarks on the "well-field" system and overcentralization of government, are given in de Bary and Lufrano, *Sources,* pp. 19–25.

222 Yongzheng's comments: The decision to publish was announced on Yongzheng 9/12/16 (January 13, 1732). See the prefatory edict to the *Bo Lü Liuliang* volumes, vol. 1, p. 1.

223 Variant texts of the *Awakening:* This was the conclusion of officials in Fujian investigating Fan Shijie's strange remarks about Yongzheng's third brother; see Wang Fansen, "Cong Zeng Jing an," p. 12.

223 First recipient: Li Jiangong, Shandong military commander, Yuezhou region; see his report in B24/897–898, dated Yongzheng 11/8/6 (September 13, 1733).

224 Zeng's home leave: Governor Zhao and Li Hui jointly relayed Zeng's request, on Yongzheng 9/5/27, see T18/287 (*QDWZYD,* pp. 50b–51). The emperor's permission reached them on 9/7/20 (August 22, 1731).

225 Yongxing houses: Such Qing homes (some have the date of construction incised on stone slabs, set into the wall near their entrance doors) can still be both seen and visited in Yongxing, on the Anren road (author's personal visit, autumn 1999). According to the *Yongxing xianzhi* (1883), *juan* 53, p. 3, 1732 was an unusually prosperous year in Yongxing itself.

225 Zhang Xi's return home: As stated by Governor Zhao, in his report of 10/intercalary 5/7, T19/841, Zhang was sent home to Anren in the early summer of 1732. (Anren and Yongxing are double-cropping regions, so the second rice harvest comes in late September.)

225 Zeng's return to Changsha: The date of 10/8/22 (October 10, 1732) was confirmed by Governor Zhao and Li Hui in their joint report of 10/9/7 (October 25, 1732), B23/258 (*QDWZYD,* pp. 50b–51). In accordance with Chinese calendrical procedure, the year 1732 had an extra "intercalary fifth month," designed to reconcile the lunar calendar to the solar sequence; thus Zeng Jing's home leave was in fact thirteen months, rather than twelve, as would have been true in any noninter-calary year.

Chapter 14: Transformations

228 Lü Liuliang guilty: *Qing shilu*, 126/8–9 (*QDWZYD*, p. 51), dated 10/12/12. Fisher (1974), p. 388 n.111, mentions that at least one such provincial opinion survey (that for Hubei) is still extant. The case of Qi Zhouhua (see Chapter 12) shows that there was some firm dissent, but that it may well have been concealed from the emperor. For the surprising resilience of the Lü clan in exile, see Waley-Cohen, *Exile in Mid-Qing China*, pp. 59, 223–225.

228 Yan Hongkui posthumously sentenced: *Qing shilu*, 126/14–15b (*QDWZYD*, pp. 51b–52), dated 10/12/17 (February 1, 1733).

228 Zeng's leisure: B23/258 (*QDWZYD*, p. 51) shows the emperor's laconic comment "Noted" (*"lan"*).

229 Li Hui's troubles: These are spelled out in a report by Governor Zhao Hongen, B23/257, dated 10/9/7 (October 25, 1732).

230 Public morality supervisors: For the genesis of the system set up by Yongzheng, see *Qing shilu*, 49/2 and 6–7b. Wang Guodong's career as governor of Hunan has been seen here through the lens of the Zeng Jing case; for a more detailed biography, see *Qingshi gao*, pp. 10296–10297. Wang's thanks for the presents appear in T25/800, 815. For dismissal of Wang's Zhejiang successor, Cai Shishan, see *Qing shilu*, 100/5. For the career of the Fujian morality supervisor, Liu Shishu, see *Qingshi gao*, pp. 10294–10295. For Li Hui's biography, see ibid., 10295–10296.

231 Dismissal of Li Hui: *Qing shilu*, 133/3b (dated 11/7/3); and *Qingshi*, p. 125.

231 Governor Zhao on Zeng Jing: B24/842 (dated 11/7/24, September 2, 1733).

232 Zhao's mother's death: Zhao's moving account of her is in B25/739–740, dated 11/10/2 (November 8, 1733).

232 Mourning rituals: A particularly bleak example had been Yongzheng's attempt to curtail Li Wei's mourning for his mother, which led to an impassioned protest by Li himself (see Li's report of 7/7/15 in T13/606–608, also in B15/767–769). The editor-in-chief of the Lü Liuliang rebuttal project, Zhu Shi, had also been placed under intense pressure by the imperial curbs on mourning implemented by Yongzheng's father, Kangxi: see the fine analysis by Norman Kutcher, *Mourning in Late Imperial China*, pp. 97–101, 137–138.

233 Zhongbao takes over: Comments by Yongzheng and Zhao Hongen, B25/744 (dated 12/1/2). Zhongbao's own early reports, B25/653 (dated 11/12/18) and B25/748 (dated 12/1/17). Zhongbao was from the Manchu Bordered Yellow Banner; his biography is in *Qingshi*, pp. 5391–5392. For a sample of his early reports, see B25/747–751.

234 A Hunan general: Yang Kai, report of 12/13/–, in B26/92. His base, Zhenganzhen, was in the Fenghuang region.

234 Acting governor of Hubei: Wu Yingfen, report of 13/intercalary 4/17, in B28/249.

234 Li Wei's case of 1734: Report of 12/7/20, T23/306–307 (and B26/702–703).

235 Fortune-teller Huang: Joint report by Governor-general Yinjishan (recently transferred to the southwest from Jiangsu) and the Yunnan governor, Zhang Zhongsui, dated 12/10/10, in B27/107. The incident had occurred on 12/9/4 (September 30, 1734).

237 Sichuan case: Reports by Huang Tinggui, 10/4/29 (B22/227–230) and 10/11/24 (B23/657).

237 Jiangsu cases: See the case of Shen Lun, checked by the new governor-general, Zhao Hongen, B27/424 (dated 12/12/9).

237 The Guangxi peddler: Report by the Guangxi garrison general, Huo Sheng (enclosing a copy of the peddler's "commission"), dated 13/6/8 (T24/791–793, also B28/567–568).

238 Yongzheng's death: The brief official statements on his death are in *Qing shilu*, 159/19b–20, and in the first *juan* of the new emperor, Qianlong's, Veritable Records, pp. 6b–7. The cause of death is not specified.

Chapter 15: Retribution

239 Qianlong's accession: See Kahn, *Monarchy*, pp. 239–243, on succession procedures; ibid., pp. 115–143, gives a detailed analysis of Qianglong's education and preparation to rule. For a brief summary of his reign, see *ECCP*, pp. 369–373 ("Hung-li"). Qianlong lived until 1799.

240 Yongzheng's brothers: *Qing shilu*, Qianlong 4/28. A response from the senior officials is preserved in B30/901–903.

240 First edict on Zeng Jing: *Qing shilu*, Qianlong 4/29 (*QDWZYD*, p. 52b), dated Yongzheng 13/10/8. (Imperial tradition mandated that the reign year remain unchanged until the end of the calendar year in which the previous emperor died.)

241 Zhongbao acts: See his report of Yongzheng 13/11/18 (December 31, 1735), in B30/900–901.

242 Xu Ben: His transfer to the Ministry of Punishments is in *Qing shilu*, Qianlong 4/35, dated Yongzheng 13/10/9 (November 22, 1735). His appointment into the recently formed Grand Council is mentioned in ibid., Qianlong 5/8b, dated Yongzheng 13/10/6 (November 29, 1735). Biographies of Xu Ben are in *Qingshi gao*, p. 10455, and *Qingshi liezhuan*, 16/10. See also *ECCP*, p. 602 ("Hsü Pen"), identifying him as a member of Governor-general Ortai's clique. For some of the intricacies of Xu's career at this time, see Bartlett, *Monarchs and Ministers*, pp. 143, 148, 160, and 341 n.16.

242 Xu Ben's petition: His petition, alas undated, is in T26/834–835 (also B32/511). Since he identifies himself as the Ministry of Punishments president, it must have been written on or after November 22, the date of his appointment.

243 Qianlong's December 2 edict: *Qing shilu,* Qianlong 5/17, dated Yongzheng 13/10/19.

244 Xu Ben steps down from Grand Council: Though this is not mentioned in the veritable records, the *Qingshi,* p. 2487, specifies it was on Yongzheng 13/10/29 (December 12, 1735).

244 Fang Bao on the prison: For a translation of his graphic account, see Cheng Pei-kai and Michael Lestz, *A Documentary Collection,* pp. 55–56. On Fang Bao's background, see *ECCP,* pp. 235–237 ("Fang Pao").

245 Qianlong's verdict: *Qing shilu,* Qianlong 9/10b–11 (*QDWZYD,* p. 52b), dated Yongzheng 13/12/19.

245 Death penalty: Fang Bao's grim assessment is in Cheng and Lestz, *Documentary Collection,* p. 57.

246 Qi's glee: Wang Fansen, "Cong Zeng Jing an," p. 15, citing Qi Zhouhua's diary. For Qi's later years, see *ECCP,* pp. 123–125 ("Ch'i Chou-hua").

246 Xu Ben in Ministry of Rituals: His appointment is listed in *Qingshi gao,* p. 10456.

246 Survival of *Awakening:* See the discussion in Wu, "History and Legend," pp. 1245–1248 for Japan, and pp. 1223–1224 for the story of Lü Liuliang's granddaughter. Records of the state's seizures of illegal books during Qianlong's reign show how copies of the *Awakening* continued to be stashed away; see for example, the inventories of bookshops, in *Wenxian congbian,* reprint, pp. 195 (mentioning twenty copies), 201 (a single copy), 219 (ten copies).

247 The Anren road: For a fascinating discussion of what she calls "the culture of the road into town," see Macauley, *Social Power and Legal Culture,* pp. 121–125.

Bibliography

Andrew, Anita Marie. "Zhu Yuanzhang and the 'Great Warnings' (Yuzhi da gao): Autocracy and Rural Reform in the Early Ming." Ph.D. thesis, University of Minnesota, 1991.

Anonymous. "Fan Shijie chengci an" (The petition by Fan Shijie). *Wenxian congbian*, vol. 7. Beijing: Palace Museum, n.d. Reprint, Taipei: 1964, pp. 68–72.

Anonymous. "Yinsi, Yintang, an" (The cases of Yinsi and Yintang). *Wenxian congbian*, vol. 1, pp. 1–12; vol. 2, pp. 13–25; vol. 3, pp. 26–35. Beijing: Palace Museum, n.d. Reprint, Taipei: 1964, pp. 1–18.

Anonymous. "Yue Zhongqi zouzhe" (The reports to the palace by Yue Zhongqi). *Wenxian congbian.* Beijing: Palace Museum, n.d. Reprint, Taipei: 1964, pp. 432–436.

Anonymous. "Zhang Zhuo toushu an" (The case of the letter delivered by Zhang Zhuo). *Wenxian congbian*, vol. 1. Beijing: Palace Museum, n.d. Reprint, Taipei: 1964, pp. 22–35.

Anonymous. "Zeng Jing qiantu Zhang Zhuo toushu an" (The case of how

Zeng Jing sent his follower Zhang Zhuo to deliver a letter). First published in *Qingdai wenziyu dang* (Collectanea of literary inquisition cases in the Qing Dynasty). Peiping: Peiping Palace Museum, 1931–1934. Reprint, Shanghai: 1986.

Awakening from Delusion: See *Dayi juemi lu.*

B, followed by volume and page numbers (e.g., B10/20): See *Yongzhengchao hanwen zhupi zouzhe huibian.*

Bartlett, Beatrice S. *Monarchs and Ministers: The Grand Council in Mid-Ch'ing China, 1723–1820.* Berkeley: University of California Press, 1991.

Britton, Roswell S. *The Chinese Periodical Press, 1800–1912.* Shanghai: 1933.

Brunnert, H. S., and V. V. Hagelstrom. *Present Day Political Organization of China.* Translated by A. Beltchenko and E. E. Moran. Rev. ed. Beijing: 1911.

Chang'an xianzhi (The gazetteer of Chang'an/Xi'an). 36 *juan.* 1812. Reprint, Taipei: 1967.

Chen Hsi-yuan. "Propitious Omens and the Crisis of Political Authority: A Case Study of the Frequent Reports of Auspicious Clouds During the Yongzheng Reign." *Papers on Chinese History* (Harvard University), vol. 3 (Spring 1994): 77–94.

Cheng Pei-kai and Michael Lestz. *The Search for Modern China: A Documentary Collection.* New York: Norton, 1999.

Chu Ping-tzu. "Factionalism in the Bureaucratic Monarchy: A Study of a Literary Case." *Papers on Chinese History* (Harvard University), vol. 1 (Spring 1992): 74–90.

Crossley, Pamela Kyle. *A Translucent Mirror: History and Identity in Qing Imperial Ideology.* Berkeley: University of California Press, 1999.

Daqing huidian shili (Statutes and precedents of the Qing dynasty). 19 vols. 1894. Reprint, Taipei: 1963.

Dayi juemi lu (A record of how true virtue led to an awakening from delusion). Compiled on orders of Emperor Yongzheng, 1730. 4 *juan.* Reprint, Taipei: Wenhai Chubanshe Reprint Series, no. 36, 1966. (Cited in Notes as *DYJML.*)

Dayi juemi lu. Edited and rendered into vernacular Chinese by Zhang Wanjun et al. Beijing: Zhongguo Chengshi Chubanshe, 1999.

de Bary, Wm. Theodore, trans. *Waiting for the Dawn: A Plan for the Prince—Huang Tsung-hsi's 'Ming-i-tai-fang lu.'* New York: Columbia University Press, 1993.

de Bary, Wm. Theodore, and Richard Lufrano, comps. *Sources of Chinese Tradition.* 2nd ed. Vol. 2. New York: Columbia University Press, 2000.

Donghua lu (Documentary history of the Qing dynasty). Edited by Wang Xianqian. 88 vols., n.p., 1899.

Durand, Pierre-Henri. *Lettrés et pouvoirs: un procès littéraire dans la Chine impériale* (Scholars and power: A literary trial in imperial China). Paris: 1992.

DYJML (e.g., *DYJML,* 1/60b): See *Dayi juemi lu,* 1730 edition and 1966 reprint.

ECCP: See Arthur W. Hummel, ed., *Eminent Chinese of the Ch'ing Period (1644–1912).*

Fairbank, J. K., and S. Y. Teng. "On the Transmission of Ch'ing Documents." 1939. Reprinted in *Ch'ing Administration: Three Studies.* Cambridge, Mass.: Harvard-Yenching Institute, 1960, pp. 1–35.

———. "On the Types and Uses of Ch'ing Documents." 1940. Reprinted in *Ch'ing Administration: Three Studies.* Cambridge, Mass.: Harvard-Yenching Institute, 1960, pp. 36–106.

Fang Chao-ying. "Tseng Ching." In Arthur W. Hummel, ed., *Eminent Chinese of the Ch'ing Period (1644–1912).* 2 vols. Washington, D.C.: Government Printing Office, 1943, pp. 747–749.

Feng Erkang. *Yongzheng zhuan* (Biography of Yongzheng). Beijing: 1985.

———. "Zeng Jing toushu an yu Lü Liuliang wenzi yu shulun" (Discussion of the relationship between the Zeng Jing case and the literary inquisition against Lü Liuliang). *Nankai xuebao* 5 (1982): 41–46; *Nankai xuebao* 6 (1982): 28.

Fisher (1974): See Thomas Stephen Fisher, "Lü Liu-liang (1629–83) and the Tseng Ching Case (1728–33)."

Fisher, Thomas Stephen. "Lü Liu-liang (1629–83) and the Tseng Ching Case (1728–33)." Ph.D. thesis, Princeton University, 1974.

Fisher, T. S. "Accommodation and Loyalism: The Life of Lü Liu-liang (1629–1683)." *Papers on Far Eastern History* (Canberra, Australia) 15, 16, 18 (March 1977, September 1977, September 1978).

Fisher, Tom S. "New Light on the Accession of the Yung-cheng Emperor." *Papers on Far Eastern History* (Canberra, Australia) 17 (March 1978).

[Fisher, T. S.] Fei Sitang. "Qingdaide wenzi pohai he 'Zhizao yiji' de moshi" (The relationship between the distortion of words in the Qing and the model of "Manufactured Deviance"). In Bao Shouyi, ed. *Qingshi guoji xueshu taolunhui lunwenji* (Collected proceedings of the international conference on Qing history). Liaoning: 1986, pp. 531–553.

Fu Lo-shu. *A Documentary Chronicle of Sino-Western Relations 1644–1820.* 2 vols. Tucson: University of Arizona Press, 1966.

Gongzhong dang Yongzhengchao zouzhe (Secret palace memorials of the Yongzheng reign). 32 vols. Taipei: Palace Museum, 1977–80. (Cited in the Notes as T, followed by volume and page numbers.)

Goodrich, Luther Carrington. *The Literary Inquisition of Ch'ien-lung.* Baltimore: Waverly Press, 1935.

Hauf, Kandice. "The Community Covenant in Sixteenth Century Ji'an Prefecture, Jiangxi." *Late Imperial China* 17, 2 (December 1996): 1–50.

Hay, Jonathan. "Ming Palace and Tomb in Early Qing Jiangning: Dynastic Memory and the Openness of History." *Late Imperial China* 20, 1 (June 1999): 1–48.

Huang Pei. *Autocracy at Work: A Study of the Yung-cheng Period, 1723–1735.* Bloomington: University of Indiana Press, 1974.

Hummel, Arthur W., ed. *Eminent Chinese of the Ch'ing Period (1644–1912).* 2 vols. Washington D.C.: Government Printing Office, 1943. (Cited in the Notes as *ECCP.*)

Hymes, Robert. "Lu Chiu-yuan, Academies, and the Problem of the Local Community." In W. T. de Bary and John W. Chaffee, eds., *Neo-Confucian Education: The Formative Stage.* Berkeley: University of California Press, 1989, 432–456.

Jining zhilizhou zhi (Gazetteer of Jining district). 11 *juan.* 1859. Reprint, Taipei: Xuesheng shuju, 1968.

Kahn, Harold L. *Monarchy in the Emperor's Eyes: Image and Reality in the Ch'ien-lung Reign.* Cambridge, Mass.: Harvard University Press, 1971.

Kaplan, Edward Harold. "Yueh Fei and the Founding of the Southern Sung." Ph.D. thesis, University of Iowa, 1970.

Kuhn, Philip A. *Soul Stealers: The Chinese Sorcery Scare of 1768.* Cambridge, Mass.: Harvard University Press, 1990.

Kutcher, Norman. *Mourning in Late Imperial China: Filial Piety and the State.* Cambridge, UK: Cambridge University Press, 1999.

Legge, James, trans. "Confucian Analects." In *The Chinese Classics.* 7 vols. Reprint, Taipei: 1963; vol. 1, pp. 137–354.

———. "The Doctrine of the Mean." In *The Chinese Classics.* 7 vols. Reprint, Taipei: 1963; vol. 1, pp. 382–434.

———. "The Shoo King, or the Book of Historical Documents." In *The Chinese Classics.* 7 vols. Reprint, Taipei: 1963, vol. 3, pt. 1, pp. 1–630.

Lü Liuliang. *Dongzhuang shicun* (Collected poems of Lü Liuliang). 1911. Fengyulou congshu ed., second collection.

———. *Lü Wancun wenji* (Collected literary works of Lü Liuliang). Reprint, Taipei: 1973.

———. *Lü Wancun xiansheng sishu jiangyi* (Mr. Lü Liuliang's commentaries on the Four Books). Edited by Chen Cong. Reprint, Taipei: 1978.

———. *Lü Wancun xiansheng sishu yulu* (Mr. Lü Liuliang's discussions of the Four Books). Edited by Zhou Zaiyan. Reprint, Taipei: 1978.

Lynn, Richard John, trans. *The Classic of Changes: A New Translation of the I Ching as Interpreted by Wang Bi.* New York: Columbia University Press, 1994.

Macauley, Melissa. *Social Power and Legal Culture: Litigation Masters in Late Imperial China.* Stanford: Stanford University Press, 1998.

Meng Sen. *Qingchu san dayian kaoshi* (An examination of the sources on three major early Qing controversial cases). 1934. Reprint, Taipei: 1966.

Meyer-Fong, Tobie. "Making a Place for Meaning in Early Qing Yangzhou." *Late Imperial China* 20, 1 (June 1999): 49–84.

Ming-Ch'ing Tang-an (Sources on Ming and Qing history). Edited by Chang Wei-jen. Taipei: Academia Sinica, 1986.

Mote, F. W. *Imperial China, 900–1800.* Cambridge, Mass.: Harvard University Press, 1999.

Naquin, Susan. *Millenarian Rebellion in China: The Eight Trigrams Uprising of 1813.* New Haven: Yale University Press, 1976.

QDWZYD: See *Qingdai wenziyu dang.*

Qingdai wenziyu dang (Collectanea of literary inquisition cases in the Qing dynasty). Peiping: Palace Museum, 1931–1934. Reprint, Shanghai: 1986.

Qijuzhu: See *Yongzhengchao Qijuzhu ce.*

Qingshi (History of the Qing dynasty). 8 vols. Taipei: Guofang Yanjiu Yuan, 1961.

Qingshi gao (Draft history of the Qing dynasty). Compiled by Zhao Ersun. 529 *juan.* Beijing: 1927. Reprint, Beijing: 1977.

Qingshi liezhuan (Biographies of Qing dynasty figures). 10 vols. Shanghai: 1928. Reprint, Taipei: 1962.

Qing shilu: Daqing shizong xianhuangdi shilu (Veritable Records of the Yongzheng reign). Edited by Ortai et al. Mukden: 1937.

Rawski, Evelyn S. *The Last Emperors: A Social History of Qing Imperial Institutions.* Berkeley: University of California Press, 1998.

Schneewind, Sarah. "Competing Institutions: Community Schools and 'Improper Shrines' in Sixteenth-Century China." *Late Imperial China* 20, 1 (June 1999): 85–106.

Shao Dongfang. "Qing Shizong 'Dayi juemi lu' zhongyao guannian zhi tantao" (An examination of the key concepts in Yongzheng's 'Dayi juemi lu'). *Hanxue yanjiu* 17, 2 (1999): 61–89.

Shen Yuan. "'Aqina,' 'Saisihei' kaoshi" (A study of the names Acina and Sesshe). *Qingshi yanjiu* 25 (1991): 90–96.

T, followed by volume and page numbers (e.g., T12/876–877): See *Gongzhong dang Yongzhengchao zouzhe.*

Ubelhor, Monika. "The Community Compact (*Hsiang-yueh*) of the Sung and Its Educational Significance." In W. T. de Bary and John W. Chaffee, eds., *Neo-Confucian Education: The Formative Stage.* Berkeley: University of California Press, 1989, pp. 371–387.

von Glahn, Richard. *Fountain of Fortune: Money and Monetary Policy in China, 1000–1700.* Berkeley: University of California Press, 1996.

Waley, Arthur, trans., and Joseph R. Allen, ed. *The Book of Songs.* New York: Grove Press, 1996.

Waley-Cohen, Joanna. *Exile in Mid-Qing China: Banishment to Xinjiang, 1758–1820.* New Haven: Yale University Press, 1991.

Wang Fansen. "Cong Zeng Jing an kan shibashiji qianqide shehui xintai" (The usefulness of the Zeng Jing case in studying the emotional life of early-eighteenth-century society). *Dalu zazhi* 85, 4 (1992): 1–22.

Wang Jingqi. *Xizheng suibi* (Casual notes of my journey to the West). *Zhanggu congbian.* Reprint, Taipei: 1964, pp. 114–142.

Wang Zhonghan. "On Acina and Sishe." *Saksaha: A Review of Manchu Studies,* no. 3 (Spring 1998): 31–35.

Watson, Burton, trans. *The Tso chuan: Selections from China's Oldest Narrative History.* New York: Columbia University Press, 1989.

Wechsler, Howard J. *Mirror to the Son of Heaven: Wei Cheng at the Court of T'ang T'ai-tsung.* New Haven: Yale Univeristy Press, 1974.

Wenxian congbian (Collected Source Materials). 43 vols. Peiping: Palace Museum, 1930–37. Reprint, 2 vols. Taipei: 1964.

Wilhelm, Hellmut. "From Myth to Myth: The Case of Yueh Fei's Biography." In Arthur F. Wright and Denis Twitchett, eds., *Confucian Personalities.* Stanford: Stanford University Press, 1962, pp. 146–161.

Wilhelm, Richard. *The I Ching or Book of Changes.* Translated by Cary F. Baynes. Princeton: Bollingen Foundation, Princeton University Press, 1967.

Wu Bolun. *Xi'an lishi shulue* (Historical materials on the city of Xi'an). Xi'an: Shaanxi Renmin Chubanshe, 1979; expanded edition, 1984.

Wu, Silas Hsiu-liang. *Communication and Imperial Control in China: Evolution of the Palace Memorial System, 1693–1735.* Cambridge, Mass.: Harvard University Press, 1970.

———. *Passage to Power: K'ang-hsi and His Heir Apparent, 1661–1722.* Cambridge, Mass.: Harvard University Press, 1979.

Wu, Silas H. L. "History and Legend: *Yung-cheng Chien-hsia* Novels." In *Tradition and Metamorphosis in Modern Chinese History: Essays in Honor of Professor Kwang-ching Liu's Seventy-fifth Birthday.* Taipei: Institute of Modern History, Academia Sinica, 1998.

Xu Zengzhong. "Zeng Jing fan Qing an yu Qingshizong Yinzhen tongzhi quanguode dazheng fangji" (On the relationship between the Zeng Jing anti-Qing case and Yongzheng's absolutist tendencies in government). *Qingshi luncong* 5 (1984): 158–178.

Yang Qiqiao. *Yongzhengdi ji qi mizhe zhidu yanjiu* (A study of the secret report system of emperor Yongzheng). Hong Kong: 1981

Yongxing xianzhi (Gazetteer of Yongxing county]. 55 *juan* in 10 vols. 1883. Reprint, Taipei: Xuesheng Shuju, 1975.

Yongxing xianzhi (Gazetteer of Yongxing county). Beijing: 1994.

Yongzhengchao hanwen zhupi zouzhe huibian (A compilation of the Chinese-language reports and imperial endorsements from Yongzheng's reign). Published for the Beijing Number One Archive. 40 vols. Jiangsu: 1991. (Cited in the Notes as B, followed by volume and page numbers.)

Yongzhengchao Qijuzhu ce (Court Diaries of the Yongzheng reign). 5 vols. Beijing: Palace Museum, Number One Archive, 1993.

Zelin, Madeleine. *The Magistrate's Tael: Rationalizing Fiscal Reform in Eighteenth-Century China.* Berkeley: University of California Press, 1984.

Zhanggu congbian (Collected Historical Source Materials). 10 vols. Peiping: Palace Museum, 1928–29. Reprint, Taipei: 1964.

Zhu Shi et al., eds. *Bo Lü Liuliang sishu jiangyi* (A refutation of Lü Liuliang's commentaries on the Four Books). 1733. Reprint, Taipei: 1978.

Zi, Etienne. "Pratique des examens littéraires en Chine." *Variétés sinologiques,* no. 5 (Shanghai, 1894). Reprint, Taipei: 1971.

———. "Pratique des examens militaires en Chine." *Variétés sinologiques,* no. 9 (Shanghai, 1896). Reprint, Taipei: 1971.

Index